Dan van der Vat was born in Holland and educated in England. A former foreign correspondent of *The Times*, he is now foreign leader-writer of *The Guardian*. After three books about the First World War at sea, he has turned to the Second for his next voyage into naval history.

D1639205

By the same author

The Grand Scuttle
The Last Corsair

DAN VAN DER VAT

The Ship That Changed The World

The Escape of the *Goeben* to the Dardanelles in 1914

GRAFTON BOOKS

A Division of the Collins Publishing Group

LONDON GLASGOW
TORONTO SYDNEY AUCKLAND

Grafton Books
A Division of the Collins Publishing Group
8 Grafton Street, London W1X 3LA

Published by Grafton Books 1986

First published in Great Britain by
Hodder and Stoughton Ltd 1985

Copyright © Dan van der Vat 1985

ISBN 0-586-06929-1

Printed and bound in Great Britain by
Collins, Glasgow

Set in Times

All rights reserved. No part of this publication may
be reproduced, stored in a retrieval system, or
transmitted, in any form, or by any means, electronic,
mechanical, photocopying, recording or otherwise,
without the prior permission of the publishers.

This book is sold subject to the condition that it
shall not, by way of trade or otherwise, be lent,
re-sold, hired out or otherwise circulated
without the publisher's prior consent in any
form of binding or cover other than that in
which it is published and without a similar
condition including this condition being imposed
on the subsequent purchaser.

For my wife

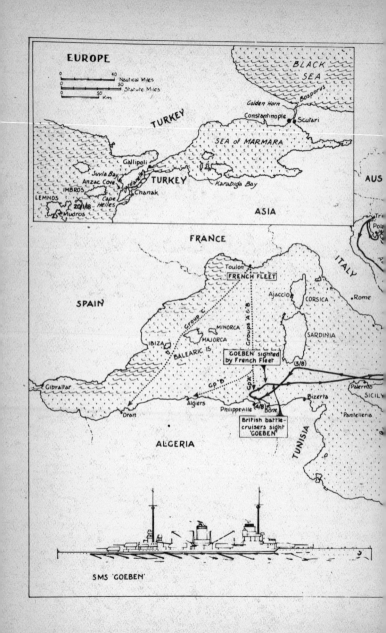

EUROPE

0 40 Nautical Miles
0 50
0 50 Statute Miles
   Km

BLACK SEA

TURKEY

Golden Horn Bosporus

Constantinople Scutari

SEA of MARMARA

Gallipoli

Suvla Bay
Anzac Cove
IMBROS Chanak
LEMNOS Cape Helles Karabiga Bay
Mudros 20/11/18

TURKEY

ASIA

AUS

FRANCE

Toulon

FRENCH FLEET

Ajaccio CORSICA Rome

ITALY

Tri
Pola

SPAIN

Groups A 6 B

Group C

MINORCA
MAJORCA
IBIZA
BALEARIC IS.

GOEBEN sighted by French Fleet

SARDINIA

3/8

Gp. b
Gp. a

Palermo SICILY

Gibraltar

Algiers
Philippeville
4/8 Bône

British battle-cruisers sight 'GOEBEN'

Bizerta

Pantelleria

Oran

ALGERIA

TUNISIA

SMS 'GOEBEN'

COURSE OF SMS 'GOEBEN'
29 July – 10 August 1914

300 Nautical Miles
300 Statute Miles
400 Km

RUSSIA

AZOV SEA

Odessa
CRIMEA
Novorossiysk
Sevastopol
Feodosia
29/10/14
BLACK SEA

HUNGARY

RUMANIA

SERBIA

BOSNIA

HERZEGOVINA
MONTENEGRO

BULGARIA

Bosporus

Edirne
Constantinople
Scutari
Dardanelles
SEA of MARMARA
ANATOLIA

Salonika
Karabiga Bay
(10/8)
Chanak
Tenedos
TURKEY

Durazzo
Brindisi
Otranto
CS Maria di Leuca
(1/8)

ALBANIA
TROUBRIDGE

Fano I.
Corfu
GREECE

LEMNOS
IMBROS

AEGEAN SEA

Smyrna

(8/8)

Dheilousa I.

LEVKAS
CEPHALONIA
PELOPONNESE
ZANTE
Sapienza

(6/8)

(8/8)
Dodecanese
Scarpa

IONIAN SEA

Where TROUBRIDGE
could have met
'GOEBEN'

(7/8) C Malapan
C Malea

HMS 'GLOUCESTER'
& SMS 'BRESLAU'

CRETE

CYPRUS

MEDITERRANEAN SEA

Alexandria
Suez Canal

CYRENAICA

EGYPT

A ship, like a shell, is merely a weapon to be expended profitably.

B. H. Liddell Hart, *History of the First World War*

All delays are dangerous in war.

John Dryden, *Tyrannic Love*

Contents

Illustrations

Acknowledgments

The principal sources for this third foray into the naval history of the First World War are once again the collections of documents kept by the West German Federal Military Archive (Bundesarchiv-Militärarchiv) in Freiburg-im-Breisgau and by the Public Record Office in Kew, Richmond, Surrey. I should like to express my thanks to the staff of these institutions, particularly to the ever-patient Frau Müller in Freiburg.

Until recently the records of courts-martial were not normally released to the public until seventy-five years later, a rule which the British government has happily modified – but not in time for the research and writing of this book. Fortunately Mr E. W. R. Lumby of the Navy Records Society was given a special dispensation which enabled him to include in full the record of the court of inquiry, and of the court-martial of Admiral Ernest Troubridge, in his *Policy and Operations in the Mediterranean 1912–14*, published by the Society in 1970. I therefore owe a special debt of gratitude to Dr N. A. M. Rodger of the Public Record Office in his capacity as Honorary Secretary of the Society for allowing me to draw upon Mr Lumby's book. As is the case with all the other sources I have used, I am solely responsible for any analysis, deductions, conclusions and interpretations derived from it for the purposes of this book, and for any error arising therefrom. There is however no fiction or 'faction' in this book: the facts to which I have done my best to be true render both superfluous.

The literary sources to which I have referred are

described in a Note at the end of this volume. My thanks are due to the following for permission to use copyright material: Messrs Cassell Ltd (*History of the First World War* by B. H. Liddell Hart); Constable and Co (*August 1914* by Barbara Tuchman); Hamlyn Group Ltd (*The World Crisis* by Winston S. Churchill); Hutchinson Ltd (*Two Lone Ships, Goeben and Breslau* by Georg Kopp, translated by Arthur Chambers); Oxford University Press (*From the Dreadnought to Scapa Flow* by Arthur J. Marder); the Rt Hon. Lord Tweedsmuir (*Greenmantle* by John Buchan).

I am no less grateful to Ion Trewin and Christine Medcalf of Hodder and Stoughton for unfailing encouragement and hospitality; to John Trotter and Alice Gay for their help in Paris; to the library staff of the British Museum and of the Borough of Richmond upon Thames at Twickenham for tracing obscure books; and to all those relatives, friends and colleagues who have provided support by their interest.

Introduction
Sevastopol, Dawn, 29 October 1914

At dawn on 29 October 1914, the great guns guarding the Russian imperial naval base at Sevastopol opened fire in earnest for the first time in sixty years. An immense cannonade from more than 300 artillery pieces flashed and boomed in the light haze of an autumn Thursday which changed the great European conflict already in progress for three months into the First World War. The crashing uproar of the uneven but intense barrage made the city tremble as an acrid cloud of smoke built up over the old stone fortifications. The target was a group of three grey shapes, one very much larger than the other two, which lay on the fringe of visibility about four miles offshore. They were soon obscured in a forest of splashes, but within a minute incoming heavy shells, each weighing more than one third of a tonne, added a terrible new note to the infernal cacophony. Passing close overhead with a roar like an express train at full speed, the huge projectiles exploded on impact with an effect the defenders could not fail to notice even amid their own deafening detonations. As the Russian gun teams sweated and swore round the breeches of their cannon, their officers were engaged in the hopeless task of trying to spot the fall of shot through rangefinders, field glasses and telescopes. The very intensity of the barrage nullified their attempts but, considering that Sevastopol had not come under attack from the sea since the Crimean War in 1854, the Russian shooting was very good. The three ships they were firing at were seen to be moving backwards and forwards at speed in an effort to spoil the aim

of the gunlayers. Before the pillars of water thrown up by
the shore artillery enveloped the ships, those with the
most powerful telescopes in Sevastopol would have made
out the fleck of red flying over each of the intruders – the
flag of the Ottoman Empire of Turkey, which had not
been seen on the waters of the Black Sea for the thirty-
six years since 1878, when Turkey and Russia had last
been at war. The dominant ship of the three could easily
be identified as a battlecruiser of the most modern type,
equipped with five turrets, each with a pair of long guns.
They fired a total of forty-seven rounds of 11-inch (28-
centimetre) shell interspersed with a dozen shots from the
lighter, secondary armament of 5.9-inch (15-centimetre)
guns, before the capital ship and her diminutive destroyer
escorts turned away. In Sevastopol one or two fires were
burning and a number of buildings and installations had
sustained a degree of damage, but the unaccountably idle
ships of the Russian Black Sea Fleet in the harbour, the
bulk of the Tsar's naval forces in the area, had not been
hit. As naval bombardments went in the days of the 'all-
big-gun' ship, it had not been much, and certainly no
match for the earth-shaking defensive barrage from the
shore which had begun the exchange. The forts had
opened fire at 6.30 A.M., less than a quarter of an hour
after first light began to reveal the presence of the enemy.
At 6.45 the battlecruiser ceased fire and ten minutes later
the coastal artillery was also silent. Had the watchers on
the shore been able to make out the name painted on the
stern and the side of the big ship, they would have read
the words, *Sultan Yavuz Selim*, a name which did not
appear in any nautical reference book. Nor, according to
the current *Jane's Fighting Ships*, holy writ in such matters, did the notoriously neglected and decrepit Turkish
Navy possess a ship of such firepower, size and speed, to

say nothing of its modernity and cost. But all was not as it seemed.

At first light that morning the Turkish torpedo-gunboat *Berk* appeared off Novorossiysk, a smaller port on the north-east coast of the Black Sea and east of the Crimean peninsula on which Sevastopol stands, to deliver a warning that the town's oil tanks, corn silos and ships in harbour would be subjected to bombardment four hours later. This gesture, made under a white flag, was intended to enable the authorities to evacuate the undefended port area and thus reduce casualties. At 10.50 A.M., the slender, low-lying shape of an up-to-date, four-funnelled light cruiser duly arrived offshore. She too flew the Ottoman ensign at her foretop and she bore, inscribed in fresh paint, the name *Midilli*, another soubriquet unlisted in *Jane's*. But she was no apparition. She fired salvo after salvo of 4.1-inch (10-centimetre) shells from her main armament, a total of 308 rounds. Soon many of the fifty oil storage tanks were blazing fiercely and a broad stream of burning fuel began to flow like high-speed lava down the hill into the town, where thousands of people ran for their lives. In the harbour fourteen steamers were sunk or damaged. The only response from on shore was a ragged fusillade of impotent rifle fire from well out of range. For the rest of the day the scene of the attack was marked by a gigantic pall of black smoke.

Elsewhere in the Black Sea that fateful morning, other smaller and older units of the Turkish fleet also went into action. The cruiser *Hamidieh* bombarded Feodosia on the eastern coast of the Crimea after delivering a warning of her intentions. To the north-west of the Crimea the port of Odessa came under fire from a pair of minuscule torpedoboat-destroyers, the *Mouavenet* and the *Gairet*, each of just 160 tons displacement. It was because they had begun shelling somewhat ahead of time that the guns of Sevastopol had been ready to open fire as soon as the three ships sent there became visible after dawn. Excited wireless messages in uncoded Russian had gone out from Odessa to all ports and ships and were intercepted by the raiders. During the exchange of heavy gunfire at Sevastopol, in which the attacking battlecruiser sustained two hits from 10-inch shells which punctured her after-funnel without exploding, local telegraphists could be heard signalling repeatedly and in plain language, 'War has begun . . . war has begun . . .' The big ship's main wireless aerial was also destroyed, one of her untrustworthy boilers and a searchlight knocked out, and a boiler-room was damaged by shrapnel.

As the *Sultan Yavuz Selim* headed west from Sevastopol, bound for the Bosporus, the narrow channel which leads out of the Black Sea to Constantinople, she sighted the SS *Prut*, a Russian steamer converted into a mine-layer. The great warship signalled: 'Stop. Lower boats.' After the crew had abandoned ship the *Prut* was sent to the bottom by gunfire from the secondary armament. She had been carrying 700 mines and a cargo of coal. But, although her entire crew had been given ample time to take to the boats, one man adamantly and flamboyantly refused to join them, despite repeated warnings. Aboard the battlecruiser sailors stared in astonishment as the solitary figure, soon identified by his attire as a Russian Orthodox Church chaplain, took up station by the flag at the stern of the steamer. In his left hand he carried a bible or prayerbook and with his right he repeatedly made the sign of the cross in the Orthodox manner (from right shoulder to left)as the 5.9-inch shells struck home. And there he stayed defiantly as the blazing steamer sank by the stern, taking the fanatical priest to his voluntary grave.

Also on the way back from Sevastopol, the battlecruiser

was subjected to a recklessly brave attack by three modern Russian torpedoboat-destroyers. This she was able to fend off without difficulty at long range, severely damaging the leading ship before the Russians thought better of their daring and withdrew, driven off by 131 rounds of 5.9-inch shell. When the Russian collier SS *Ida*, carrying a full load to Sevastopol, was encountered, she was seized by a prize crew and diverted to Constantinople. One of the two escorting destroyers, the *Samsun*, took aboard the captain of the *Prut*, two other officers and seventy-two members of her crew as prisoners of war. The rest were allowed to get away in their lifeboats.

As the *Sultan Yavuz Selim*, flying the flag of a rear-admiral, sailed west, her symbolic but also historic mission accomplished, the other ships of the Turkish fleet engaged in the attacks on the Russian coast reported in with the catalogue of their achievements. The *Midilli* wirelessed that she had been able, before shelling Novorossiysk, to lay mines in the Kerch Channel east of the Crimean peninsula, leading from the Black Sea to the Sea of Azov. These were soon to claim unsuspecting victims in the shape of two Russian steamships. The two destroyers with the battlecruiser sowed the approaches to Sevastopol with mines as they withdrew. The *Hamidieh* reported sinking two captured steamers after allowing their crews to abandon ship. At Odessa the bold little destroyer *Gairet* had gone close enough inshore to sink a Russian gunboat at her moorings in a dashing torpedo attack. The last report came from a ship with the decidedly un-Turkish name of *Nilufer*. She was able to reveal that after completing her assigned task of helping to lay mines between Odessa and Sevastopol without being detected, she had encountered the steamer *Tsar Alexander* of the Russian Volunteer Fleet, taken off the passengers and crew and sunk it with her light guns. The *Nilufer* was in fact a merchantman converted into an auxiliary cruiser, her name meaning 'Bank of the Nile' – in German.

For although all the ships engaged in the coordinated series of operations against the Russians in the Black Sea that day flew the red ensign of the Ottoman Empire, the flag officer aboard the *Sultan Yavuz Selim*, who was in charge in his new-found capacity as Commander-in-Chief of the Turkish fleet, was the German Rear-Admiral Wilhelm Souchon. Under his feet on the admiral's bridge was one of the finest ships in the world at the time, pride of the German shipbuilder's art, designed by the great naval architect Professor Kretsschner and built by Blohm & Voss at Hamburg, armed and armoured by Krupp of Essen. For all that they wore the fez as part of their uniform, the bulk of the crew spoke only German and persisted in referring to their ship as the *Goeben*. The other modern ship in the attacking force, the *Midilli*, was no more Turkish than the flagship and was still called the *Breslau* by her no less German crew. And although these two splendid ships had been formally handed over to the Turkish Minister of Marine at a ceremony off Constantinople in the middle of August 1914, just two weeks after the Great War began, they were still on the books of the German Imperial Navy as constituting its Mediterranean Division of which Admiral Souchon remained the chief.

For nearly twelve weeks prior to the onslaught on the Russian coast, Souchon had fought a frustrating battle with the Turkish authorities, seeking clearance to take his fine ships to war against Germany's enemy, Russia, with whom she was locked in massive combat on her eastern front in Europe. In the end it was only by effectively taking the law into his own hands with the secret connivance of the pro-German element in the Turkish government that Souchon was able to strike his deadly blow against Russia by forcing Turkey into the war on Germany's side. Four days after the series of raids on October 29, his mission was fully accomplished when Russia responded by declaring war on Turkey. Russia's allies, Britain and France, followed suit on November 5. The consequences soon became a catastrophe for Russia, for much of the Middle East, for Britain and France, Australia and New Zealand and not least for Turkey herself. In the considered opinion of General Erich Ludendorff, the architect of so many of Germany's ultimately fruitless but devastating victories on land, Souchon's initiative and the ensuing entry of Turkey into the war enabled the Reich of Kaiser Wilhelm II to last two years longer than would otherwise have been possible against increasingly unfavourable odds. And for that diabolical extension of the bloodiest conflict in all history until then, millions of men of a dozen nations paid with their lives, bringing down four empires in the process.

Turkey had in fact signed a secret alliance with Germany at the outset of the war, but had persistently sidestepped putting it into practice. Her army, despite the best efforts of a generous stiffening of German officers under the able General Otto Liman von Sanders, was far from ready. To be able to profit from the diplomatic masterstroke of the secret treaty, Germany had to find and send to Turkey a military force capable of immediate action against Russia. All she had within reach were the two ships of the naval Mediterranean Division. On the outbreak of hostilities they were, therefore, ordered to sail right out of the Mediterranean to Constantinople. Souchon's was a forlorn hope, faced as he was with the bulk of the French Navy and the British Mediterranean Fleet. By all the odds stacked against him, which included severe mechanical troubles aboard his flagship, he should never have reached the Dardanelles. But, thanks largely to a tragedy of errors by his enemies afloat, he did. What follows is an account of those errors and their consequences.

PART ONE
The Prelude

War is the province of chance. In no other sphere of human activity must such a margin be left for this intruder. It increases the uncertainty of every circumstance and deranges the course of events.

Karl von Clausewitz,
War, Politics and Power

He told me just how and why and when Turkey had left the rails. I heard about her grievances over our seizure of her ironclads, of the mischief the coming of the *Goeben* had wrought, of Enver and his precious Committee and the way they had got a cinch on the old Turk.

. . . a battlecruiser with her boilers burst.

John Buchan, *Greenmantle* (1916)

1

Germany woos and wins Turkey

On the second day of August 1914, the Imperial German Ambassador of Constantinople and the Grand Vizier of Turkey signed a treaty of alliance on behalf of their governments. The pact was aimed at Russia, the most important enemy of both the signatories, the upstart Prussian Empire in the west and the moribund Ottoman Empire to the south-east. Now the Russian bear, itself the largest land empire in all history and already lumbering into action against the Germans at its throat, was soon to find another enemy gnawing at its underbelly. The treaty was the greatest (some would say the only) triumph of German diplomacy in the period leading up to the opening of general hostilities in the war which was to shape the twentieth century. It was also to ensure that the international conflict soon to become known simply as 'the Great War' truly earned its epithet (to say nothing of its later title of the First *World* War). Unlike most German diplomatic moves since the dismissal of Bismarck in 1890, when the erratic and autocratic Kaiser Wilhelm II effectively took charge of foreign policy, the Turkish coup had been thoroughly prepared, persistently pursued and concluded with panache. Before the treaty the principal German influence in Turkey had been, appropriately enough, military. Hundreds of German officers had moved in on the invitation of the 'Young Turks' (who seized power in a coup in 1909) to modernize, reorganize and train the enfeebled and neglected Turkish Army from its general staff downwards. But theirs was a colossal task and, despite the rapid progress already achieved, it was far from complete when the war began. The Turks were nowhere near ready for battle.

In accordance with the interests of both sides the treaty was to remain secret for the time being. Meanwhile Turkey announced to the world that its stance in the imminent conflict would be one of 'armed neutrality' and that it was ordering a general mobilization to support that posture. But for the Germans, seeking to establish a death-grip on Russia, the alliance with the much derided 'sick man of Europe' remained a profoundly important breakthrough. Yet, because of the military unpreparedness of Turkey, it was not enough. The army was in no condition to undertake a move against southern Russia, and the rotting navy, not even seen in the Black Sea for nearly forty years, was in even worse case. To be in a position to exploit their new-found and immensely significant stranglehold on the Turkish-controlled Straits between the Mediterranean and the Black Sea and thus close the door on Russia, the Germans needed an immediate infusion of modern and mobile military force – not only to be able to move against Russia but also to keep the ever wavering, always intriguing Turks in line. Only one solution was available: the Mediterranean Division of the Imperial German Navy, commanded by Rear-Admiral Wilhelm Souchon and consisting of just two modern warships. But one of these was SMS *Goeben*, Souchon's formidable flagship and the fastest major man-of-war in the Mediterranean, a battlecruiser with ten 11-inch guns. She was accompanied by the elegant light cruiser SMS *Breslau*. On the afternoon of August 3, therefore, the powerful wireless transmitter at Nauen, east of Berlin, began sending repeatedly a coded message from the German Admiralty to the flag officer commanding the Mediterranean Division, telegram number 51: *Alliance concluded with Turkey*. Goeben, Breslau *proceed immediately to Constantinople*. The order reached Souchon in the early hours of the 4th. In the words of Winston Churchill, then in London as First Lord of the Admiralty, its execution and the consequences which flowed from it meant 'for the peoples of the East and Middle East more slaughter, more misery and more ruin than has ever before been borne within the compass of a ship.' The dispatch of the *Goeben* was no less fateful than the German decision to send Lenin to Russia in a sealed train in 1917. The train completed what the battlecruiser began: the demolition of imperial Russia. The ship turned the German war on Russia into a siege which eventually gave the relentless man in the private carriage his opportunity to change history.

If Germany's successful wooing of Turkey before the war was the Kaiser's greatest diplomatic victory against the Triple Entente of Russia, France and Great Britain, it must also be seen as a monumental blunder on their part. While it was hardly likely that Russia alone, the traditional enemy, could hope to lull Turkish suspicions sufficiently to obtain a guarantee of neutrality, the French and above all the British had enormous residual influence in Constantinople which, judiciously exercised, could have blocked German ambitions there. To understand why the Germans won it is necessary to trace the origins of the political situation in Turkey as it stood in 1914.

The decline of the Ottoman Empire began in the latter part of the sixteenth century, when its expansion was halted by rival powers and its own exhaustion after a century of wars. Its last major onslaught on the West fizzled out after the abortive siege of Vienna in 1683, whereupon the decline accelerated, to the advantage of the Austrian and Russian empires. The survival thereafter of Turkey as an important power depended on internal inertia and the rivalry of external powers, anxious to ensure that its territory should not fall of a piece into the 'wrong' hands. This 'eastern question' was a major preoccupation of European diplomacy from the latter part of the eighteenth century onwards. During the nineteenth, great swathes of territory in North Africa and the Middle East were lost to the British and the French, although the Sultans retained nominal suzerainty, and nationalism in the Balkans brought further losses to add to the eighteenth-century encroachments of the Austrians and the Russians. The aspirations of their Slav cousins in the Balkans, and their own for access from the Black Sea to the Mediterranean, led the Russians to invade Turkey's Danubian provinces (today's Bulgaria and Rumania) in 1851 and to destroy the Turkish fleet in the Black Sea in 1853. As in 1770, Russia was poised to take control of the heart of the Ottoman Empire; as ever, the other leading powers would not allow the overripe fruit to fall. Austria intervened in the Balkans, and Britain and France declared war on Russia in 1854. The appalling display of all-round incompetence which became known as the Crimean War followed, the Russians losing by default in 1856. Savage Turkish repression of Slav revolts in the Balkans led to another Russian invasion in 1877, but the rival powers once again thwarted Russia at the Congress of Berlin in 1878. She was obliged to withdraw as the disputed territory in the Balkans came under Austrian or returned to Turkish control. Serbia, Montenegro and Rumania became independent.

As Britain's post-Crimean disgust with Turkey grew (Lord Salisbury's dictum that in siding with Turkey Britain had backed 'the wrong horse' summed up the prevailing attitude), Germany's interest also grew. From 1875 onwards, Bismarck pursued a policy of dividing Ottoman territory in the Balkans between Russia and Austria-Hungary with Germany acting as mediator. It was in Germany's strategic interest in the event of war with Russia to acquire a dominating influence over the Turks, whose territory could be used to sever Russian access to the Mediterranean through the Dardanelles. But German influence was first exercised half a century earlier, when Sultan Mahmud II sought foreign help in reforming the army after crushing the Janissaries, until then the elite military caste, in 1826. Only Prussia, the rising military power in Europe, responded with a military mission, establishing a connection which has lasted, despite many vicissitudes, to modern times and the uneasy presence in West Germany of a Turkish community of 1.7 million. Resolutely ignoring the cruelty and corruption of the absolute rule of Sultan Abdul Hamid II, 'the Damned' (1876–1909), Germany poured in financial aid, including money for railway construction (Wilhelm II had conceived the ambition of building a Berlin–Baghdad railway). The Kaiser himself made a state visit in 1898, during which he supported the Turkish pretension to be the natural leader of Islam.

The vacuum created by Britain's dwindling interest in keeping up its role as Turkey's traditional protector because of the Ottoman Empire's position astride the route to India was soon and eagerly filled by Germany. Anglo-German discussions in 1895 on the future of the Ottoman Empire foundered in misunderstandings and the rather different calculations of both countries on existing and potential alliances with the other major powers. The alliance concluded in 1894 between France, Britain's traditional enemy, and Russia, which was Turkey's, led the British Cabinet to conclude that a naval attack on Constantinople as a means of forcing the Sultan to abandon the Armenian massacres was much too risky. The

alternative, since no other power supported Britain on
this, was to do nothing. Comforted by their control of
Egypt and Cyprus as protection for the imperial seaway
in the eastern Mediterranean, the British chose the latter
course. The survival of the Ottoman Empire thereupon
devolved upon the Germans, whose declining ally,
Austria-Hungary, needed it as a check on its Russian
rival in the Balkans. Such was the position as the twentieth century began: after the Kaiser's visit the Germans
not only started work on the railway from Constantinople
to Baghdad but also on a new port at Haidar Pasha on
the Asian shore of the Bosporus. Gone were the days
when the Germans, as under Bismarck, eschewed com-
mitments in Turkey itself for fear of annoying the Russians. Germany, not Britain, was now the main obstacle to
Russian ambition in the Near and Middle East; at the
same time and at a stroke it became identified by the
British as a threat to the route to India at least as
worrying as Russia. Much of the groundwork was thus
laid for the eventual Anglo-Russian agreement of 1907,
which completed the Triple Entente that was to take the
field against the Central Powers (Germany and Austria-
Hungary) in 1914. The Anglo-French Entente Cordiale
had already been concluded in 1904.

The shifts in Turkey's geopolitical role in the rivalry
among the other powers were complemented by
upheavals within the ramshackle Ottoman Empire against
the inept tyranny of Abdul Hamid. The first decade of
the new century brought the rise to power of the Committee for Union and Progress (CUP), who soon became
known as the 'Young Turks'. This reformist group of
youthful, privileged intellectuals and officers wanted to
modernize and liberalize the empire as a last chance of
holding it together. Its main strength derived from its
ultimately dominant influence in the army officer corps,

and its chance came in 1908. The quasi-democratic constitution promulgated by Abdul Hamid on his accession in
1876 had been suspended soon afterwards on the grounds,
as he claimed, that the population was too ignorant to be
ready for it, and the new Chamber of Deputies was sent
home. Under the threat of revolt by the CUP and its
supporters, the Sultan proclaimed the constitution anew
in July 1908 and announced a general election which the
CUP won overwhelmingly. The new Chamber was
opened on December 17. By that time the empire had
lurched a few more steps towards disintegration: Bulgaria
had declared itself completely independent in October (it
had been an autonomous principality since 1878), Austria
annexed Bosnia and Herzegovina which it had been
administering, and Crete broke away to join Greece,
which had won its independence some ninety years earlier. The Sultan's Arab subjects were also getting restless.
The end of despotism did not bring unity: three tendencies
existed among the politically aware, the 'Pan-Turkish',
which wanted to bring all the Turks in Asia under one
flag; the 'Pan-Islamic', which claimed the leadership of
all Muslims for Turkey; and the 'Ottomanist', which
believed that modernization would save the empire by
giving it greater cohesion. In February 1909 the CUP
used its parliamentary majority to oust the old guard
in government by unseating the Grand Vizier (Prime
Minister), Kemal Pasha, and formed a government of its
own. In March self-serving Islamic agitators fomented a
popular revolt in Constantinople, supported by disaf-
fected troops of the First Army Corps and demanding a
return to Islamic government. The rebellion was quickly
and brutally put down by the Third Army Corps based in
Salonika, and sixty were hanged. Suspected, probably
unjustly, of complicity, Abdul Hamid II was deposed and
banished to Salonika. He was succeeded by his younger

brother Rashid, who took the name Mehmet V. He was to be the last Sultan; he was also the first to limit himself to a constitutional role. The CUP, however, proceeded to subvert the constitution by using the revolt as a pretext for suppressing opposition parties as it shifted away from Ottomanism to Turkish nationalism (there were more non-Turks than Turks among parliamentary deputies). But the historic importance of the rise of the CUP was obscured in 1911 by the Italian invasion of Tripolitania and Cyrenaica (the coastal regions of modern Libya) in September. Italian naval superiority was enhanced by the British decision to declare Egypt, still nominally an Ottoman fief, neutral, which stopped the Turks sending troops overland. In spring 1912 the Italians captured the Dodecanese archipelago off the Turkish west coast. In summer the Turkish government resigned. In autumn the Balkans exploded into war as Turkey's smaller neighbours saw their opportunity in Ottoman discomfiture. Montenegro declared war on October 8, and Bulgaria, Greece and Serbia on the 18th, all hoping for territorial gain. On the same day, however, some relief was provided by a settlement with the Italians, which led to the signature of a peace treaty by diplomats of the two sides in Switzerland. Cyrenaica and Tripolitania were ceded to Italy, and Turkey was supposed to be given back the Dodecanese. Representatives of the leading powers met in London under the chairmanship of Sir Edward Grey, the Foreign Secretary, in an attempt to mediate which was more remarkable for the spirit of cooperation and sense of common purpose exhibited by such rivals as Britain and Germany than for the results achieved in the Balkans. Turkey signed an armistice with Bulgaria and Serbia on December 3, but Greece and Montenegro carried on fighting. Early in the new year Bulgaria reopened hostilities, in the hope of capturing the vital city of Edirne in Thrace.

On the pretext that Kemal Pasha, Grand Vizier again since July 1912, was planning to give in to the Bulgarians, two of the most powerful men in the CUP, Enver Bey and Talaat Bey, led a violent coup against him and installed a new government under Mahmud Tewfik Pasha, on 23 January 1913. But Edirne fell all the same, on March 26. Subsequent peace talks led to a cessation of hostilities and a treaty on May 30. But there was still no peace in the Balkans as Turkey's enemies fell out among themselves over their gains from the crumbling empire. The Bulgarians attacked Greece and Serbia on June 29 and on July 10 Rumania attacked Bulgaria in the hope of a quick profit. The Turks, as a sort of consolation prize for all they had lost in Africa and the Balkans (and the Dodecanese, which the Italians cynically kept until 1946), took advantage of the disarray among their estwhile enemies by sending troops under Enver to recapture Edirne on July 22. The Treaty of Bucharest of August 10 finally put an end to the Balkan Wars. The Ottoman Empire now consisted of the small European enclave round Constantinople, the Levant, Arabia and the Turkish heartland of Anatolia; and its control over its Arab subjects was at best shaky.

The German connection survived all these upheavals in and around Turkey, not just unscathed but actually enhanced. The CUP after its rise to power in 1908–9 turned to western Europe for whatever help it could get in modernizing the Ottoman state. Italian engineers, French financiers, communications experts, German constructors and others moved in; the British were invited to modernize the Turkish Navy and the Germans the army. But the influence of Germany remained predominant after the Kaiser's visit in 1898; Britain was the only power in a position to displace the Germans, thanks to its naval supremacy and a long history of friendship. The British, however, as we have seen, lacked motivation, and, as the threat of a general European war grew, limited their aim in Turkey to achieving a benevolent neutrality in Constantinople. The Germans were playing for much bigger stakes. Looking to their own strategic interests, the Germans saw the modernization of the Turkish Army as their principal task but soon found it to be a most daunting one. The only military commodity available in abundance was the courage and formidable fighting spirit of the Turkish soldier, but he lacked equipment, training, organization and leadership. The German Military Mission, led from June 1913 by the gifted General (later Field Marshal) Otto Liman von Sanders, was unable to affect the outcome of the wars against Italy and in the Balkans, but the ruse of reoccupying Edirne was a German idea.

The regeneration of the Turkish Navy was also a Sisyphean task for the British Naval Mission, originally led by Rear-Admiral Sir Douglas Gamble and from April 1912 by Rear-Admiral Arthur Limpus. Abdul Hamid had allowed the navy to decline from the world's second largest at the beginning of his reign to a collection of useless hulks thirty years later, the result of a combination of inertia and fear of a revolt in which naval guns might be trained on Constantinople. The British gained enough headway to enable the navy to make a modest but useful contribution in the disastrous Balkan Wars, but one cannot escape the impression that the overall task was too much for them, leading to a certain demoralization. When the Germans took over this role, they discovered that the old battleship *Messudieh* had been fitted with a pair of lovingly carved wooden guns in place of her main armament of two 9.2-inch pieces, which the British had promised, but inexplicably and protractedly failed, to replace! The British had made so little progress that the Germans believed them to have been guilty of deliberate procrastination if not outright sabotage. When the Germans offered to sell the Turks two pre-dreadnought battleships cheaply to strengthen their navy after the Balkan Wars, Admiral Limpus hurriedly asked the Admiralty in London to make a better offer. Churchill, the First Lord of the Admiralty, was in favour though no enthusiast for Turkey; Battenberg, the outstandingly able First Sea Lord who also had a blind spot as far as Turkey was concerned, was against. In the end neither country delivered any ships because the First World War supervened.

But in May 1911, the Turks had placed contracts with Armstrong and Vickers on the Tyne for two super-dreadnought battleships, each of 23,000 tons (the second to be armed with ten of the latest 13.5-inch guns), for delivery in September and December 1914. This was a considerable coup for the naval mission, which was in place not only to exert British and counter German influence but also to win as many orders as possible for British shipyards. It was also a considerable financial and psychological investment by the Turks, who had gathered the money for these immensely powerful vessels from private subscriptions donated by people in all walks of life. The pair of ships became a symbol of resurgent national pride after the debacles of 1911–13 and their delivery was awaited with a keenness bordering on passion. British blindness not only to the strategic significance of Turkey but also to the new Turkish nationalism led to an appalling error, based on ignorance and arrogance, over these ships, which had cost the Turks £7.5 million. The first, the *Sultan Osman I*, was completed in May 1914, and the second, the *Sultan Mehmet Rechad*, in July. Only minor fitting-out remained to be done, and as the war approached, a Turkish captain and 500 sailors were waiting on a transport in the Tyne to take delivery of the first ship. But on the very eve of war, on July 28, Churchill sequestered both ships; they were later renamed HMS *Agincourt* and *Erin* respectively. Apparently the addition of two capital ships to the Royal Navy was regarded as outweighing the drastically underestimated importance of Turkish goodwill or neutrality.

The only man among British leaders who might have stopped this foolishness was Admiral of the Fleet Lord 'Jacky' Fisher, but he had retired from the post of First Sea Lord in 1910 after his radical reconstruction of the Royal Navy. As early as 1904, Fisher had been almost alone in pressing not just for an understanding with Turkey but for bringing it into a quadruple entente with Britain, France and Russia. Fisher, whose foresight on so many matters verged on the uncanny, saw more clearly than almost anyone else the importance of Turkey's position across lines of communication with Russia and its still important claim to lead Islam (there were more Muslims in the British Empire than in the Ottoman). In the meantime Turkey's significance in terms of naval strategy had, ironically, increased as a result of her defeats. Italy, still a member of the Triple Alliance with Germany and Austria-Hungary, had gained potentially vital naval advantages in North Africa and the Dodecanese, and nobody could be entirely sure before the war what Italian intentions were. Fisher was recalled from retirement in October 1914 for his second term as First Sea Lord, but by then it was too late.

The *coup d'état* by Enver and Talaat, the most committed pro-Germans as well as the leading figures in the CUP, had led to the appointment of Mahmud Tewfik Pasha as Grand Vizier on 23 January 1913. Sir Louis Mallet, the

British Ambassador to Constantinople, described the new government as having a 'distinct German colouring'. When Tewfik was assassinated on June 11, this picture did not change. Said Halim Pasha took over as Grand Vizier (he remained in office until February 1917) and the CUP set about eliminating serious opposition by banishment and hanging.

Although Turkey had become accustomed over many years to the humiliation of having other powers intervene in its affairs, its leaders had developed the art of playing them off against each other, a ploy whose effect was, if anything, enhanced by the long tradition of vacillation and factionalism in Constantinople. The Germanophiles might be in the ascendant now, but there were also Anglophiles and Francophiles close to the new centre of power. The driving force behind the eventual commitment to Germany was Enver. He was born in 1881 and educated for a military career and by 1903 he was a captain on the staff of the Third Army Corps at Salonika. His dynamism enabled him to rise rapidly in the councils of the CUP, which attracted many go-ahead young officers, so that he played a leading role in the revolution of 1908–9. His reward for that was the plum post for a progressive officer of military attaché in Berlin. The brief tour of duty there powerfully reinforced his conviction that the Germans were the nation of the future and the right people to side with in the event of international conflict. As a lieutenant-colonel he led the force that retook Edirne, an easy triumph because the Bulgarians had thinned down their garrison to meet threats elsewhere, but all the more glittering for being an isolated one. He was therefore promoted to brigadier-general (which brought with it the title of 'Pasha') and at the beginning of 1914 he was appointed Minister for War. Talaat, Minister for the Interior and political boss of the

CUP, a strong character with an appetite for work, was also a convinced pro-German. But the overwhelming majority of influential and politically aware opinion believed that Turkey's only chance of survival in a general international conflagration was to remain neutral. Enver and Talaat were the driving forces of the CUP and the government but they were in a small minority of pro-Germans. The Grand Vizier, Halim, a less forceful character, favoured neutrality but allowed himself to be won over, though he found it easy to restrain his enthusiasm. Halil, the Chairman of the Chamber of Deputies, and Jemal Pasha, the Minister of Marine, were also won over. But all this was of itself not enough to swing the government as a whole behind Enver's reckless pro-German policy. As recently as 1911 Turkey had actually asked Britain for an alliance, a request Churchill was delegated by the cabinet to turn down.

As the war clouds in Europe turned black, Berlin was seized by a sudden sense of urgency to clinch an alliance with the Turks at any cost. On 28 July 1914, the day Britain commandeered the two Turkish battleships and also the day Austria declared war on Serbia, the German faction led by Enver secretly but formally asked Berlin for an offensive and defensive alliance against Russia, the culmination of much hard work by the Germans in Constantinople. Secure in the knowledge that the Kaiser was on the verge of panic in case Turkey, wavering as ever, slipped out of reach, Chancellor Theobald von Bethmann-Hollweg replied by cable the same day with a short draft treaty. The haggling and the vacillation continued in Constantinople as the energetic German Ambassador, Baron von Wangenheim, pressed for a commitment and the Turks argued among themselves. On August 2 the Enver faction lost patience and took the law into its own hands. The Grand Vizier was persuaded to sign, and the only others who were in the know were Enver, Talaat and Halil. The *fait accompli* provoked a furious row within the Turkish government, but it was too late.

The treaty contained eight brief clauses. Both parties agreed to remain neutral in the conflict between Austria and Serbia (although the Germans were already committed to standing by the Austrians). If Russia intervened on the Serbian side (as it was determined to do), thereby obliging Germany to support Austria in keeping with her alliance obligation, Turkey would come under the same obligation. The German Military Mission was to stay in place and to play an active command role if Turkey entered the war. Germany undertook to help Turkey militarily against external threat. The purpose of the treaty was defined as mutual protection against adverse international developments and it was to remain in force until 31 December 1918. It would be renewed for another five years unless either side gave six months' notice of termination. It was to be ratified within one month by the Sultan and the Kaiser. Finally it was to remain secret until both parties agreed to reveal its existence. Austria became an associate party to the treaty.

The day before his diplomatic triumph, Wangenheim cabled Berlin to ask that the *Goeben* be sent to Constantinople to help the Turkish fleet prepare for an attack on the Bosporus by the Russian Black Sea Fleet (a possibility of which Austrian sources had warned). On August 2 the Foreign Office replied that the Kaiser did not feel able to spare the *Goeben*, but on the 3rd Admiral Tirpitz, creator of the German Navy and head of the Imperial Navy Office, told the Foreign Office that the *Goeben* and the *Breslau* had been ordered to go to Constantinople after all, and that the Turks could be told that Admiral Souchon was at their disposal to lead the Turkish fleet.

In response to the Austrian declaration of war on Serbia, Russia mobilized on July 29. On its refusal to stop this process, Germany declared war on Russia on August 1, and on France on August 3. Despite the existence of the secret pact with Germany, Turkey announced on the 3rd that it would adopt a position of armed neutrality. All the diplomatic and other missions of the rival powers stayed on in Constantinople, and the British and the French believed that the all-important line of communication with Russia via the Straits and the Black Sea was therefore assured. Britain meanwhile decided to enter the war in support of France, at midnight GMT (1 A.M. Central European Time) on the night of August 4. The sooner the Germans could produce the Turkish card from their sleeve, the better for them. It was to be a frustrating task, but in the end it was the *Goeben* alone that made it possible.

2

Naval dispositions for war in the Mediterranean

The German Navy burst into the Mediterranean, where the other relevant maritime powers had been scheming and building for decades, on a sudden whim of the Kaiser in November 1912. The creation from scratch in almost indecent haste of the Mediterranean Division did not unduly disturb the other powers, especially since there had been some easing of international tension thanks to shared concern over the great crisis in the Balkans. A single battlecruiser, even if she were the biggest and the fastest in the Mediterranean, escorted by an even faster but lightly armed small cruiser, could hardly make much difference to the overall imbalance of forces which so favoured the Entente Powers. Most of the French Navy was concentrated there, making France the leading naval power by a large margin. Also present was a strong British Mediterranean Fleet. Italy and Austria, the other important naval powers, though both members of the Triple Alliance with Germany, were engaged in a naval arms race of their own and adding dreadnoughts to their fleets. The Kaiser's action was prompted by a call from the Grand Vizier of Turkey at a conference of ambassadors in Constantinople for the dispatch of an international fleet, when it seemed that the Ottoman capital might be overrun by the Bulgarians, opening the way for their Russian friends to achieve the dream of a millennium by advancing to the Mediterranean. The Turkish appeal was addressed to all the nations which had taken part in the Congress of Berlin in 1878, when Russia had once again been turned aside from seizing Constantinople. Nine countries decided at once to send ships to protect their interests, including Russia. When Britain informed Germany that it had decided to send two cruisers, the Kaiser to his chagrin had to admit that he had no ships in the area. This must have been a humiliation for a ruler whose guiding principle in international affairs was that Germany should always play a role commensurate with her deserts as a great power, whatever that might mean (his interventions were often made for their own sake, without a strategy, or even a clear objective, behind them.) That the host country of the Congress could not, apparently, play its part when even the Netherlands was sending a cruiser redoubled the embarrassment. But, as ever, Admiral Tirpitz, the father of the vastly expanded Imperial Navy, was on hand to press the interests of his service. He pointed out to the Kaiser that the *Goeben*, the latest battlecruiser, was already on her sea trials, and the *Breslau*, the newest light cruiser, had all but completed hers. A maiden voyage to the Mediterranean would not only help both ships to 'shake down' but would also enable Germany to show the flag in splendid style. The Kaiser at once fell for the idea and signed the relevant 'order from the All-Highest' assigning the two ships temporarily to the Mediterranean and creating for them the new command of the Mediterranean Division, under the flag of Rear-Admiral Trummler and the direct orders of Wilhelm himself. After frantic preparations, the *Breslau* set sail on November 5 and the *Goeben* from Wilhelmshaven the following day. When the two cruisers reached Constantinople on November 15, German honour was more than satisfied. The great, gleaming *Goeben* was the mightiest and most impressive ship on view by far, and the only dreadnought. Nobody was to know that the overhasty commissioning of the magnificent ship had led to serious boiler trouble; this was hidden from the eyes of the admiring spectators, dazzled by this dramatic display of German power. But for that, Germany would, like the United States, have been represented only by the gunboat it kept on station at Constantinople. The international fleet, led by the senior officer present, a French vice-admiral, was there to protect European and American lives and property should the Bulgarians break through from the west and enter Constantinople, as they were then on the point of doing. On November 18, sailors and marines went ashore to the distant thunder of the artillery menacing the city, but the Turkish line managed to hold. The ships of the ten foreign navies stayed into the new year.

After such a spectacular entrance with all its benefits to German prestige, it was inevitable that the Mediterranean Division should become permanent. It could go on showing the flag, and as Turkey acquired ever greater weight in the minds of the Germans and their contingency plans for war, a presence in the Mediterranean might well have other advantages. It was not as if the Kaiser could ill afford to detach the two ships, even if the flurry surrounding their initial dispatch might suggest otherwise. German naval strength was overwhelmingly concentrated in home waters, the North Sea and to a lesser extent the Baltic. The High Seas Fleet had been built up virtually from scratch since 1898, when Tirpitz persuaded the Kaiser that Germany should have a navy worthy of the world's leading military and industrial nation. It should be large enough to give pause to the world's greatest naval power, Britain (at which it was really aimed); even if it could not hope to defeat the Royal Navy in a fleet action, it could hope to inflict such damage as to destroy British world supremacy at sea in the event of war (the 'risk theory'). It might also erode British naval strength by concentrating superior force against detached elements of the British

fleet, destroying them piecemeal. This early version of
the theory of deterrence with which we have had to
become only too familiar in the nuclear age led to a
gigantic naval arms race between Germany and Britain
and became one of the principal causes of the First World
War. Even the British invention of the dreadnought, the
fast, heavily armoured, 'all-big-gun' battleship and its
battlecruiser variant in the first decade of the century,
which rendered all other capital ships obsolete at a stroke,
did not stop the race: the other major navies simply
followed suit as fast as they could. The British won the
race, but it forced them to reconsider and eventually
abandon their policy of isolation from alliances with other
powers. The Entente Cordiale can now be seen as the
start of Britain's long decline. The Germans meanwhile
assembled an enormous new fleet, second only to the
British; and apart from a Far East Cruiser Squadron to
protect German colonies and the occasional detachment
of a light cruiser or two to show the flag around the
world, imperial naval strength stayed at home. Now
the Germans had established a small presence in the
Mediterranean which could work with the navies of their
partners in the Triple Alliance, Austria and Italy, and
use their bases. It was another piece on a large board,
but not one which worried the French and British commanders in the Mediterranean, who continued to focus
their war plans on dealing with the Italian and Austrian
fleets. If was, after all, only to be expected that Germany
as a major power with interests in the area should give
some attention to the Mediterranean: if this was a threat,
it was containable.

The creation of the Mediterranean Division, seen by
Germany's main maritime rivals, Britain and France, as a
minor phenomenon, was to alter the course of history.
Ironically, another event concerning the Mediterranean

which they saw as epoch-making, the Anglo-French Naval Agreement of 10 February 1913, had few effects on the course of events there (as distinct from elsewhere) when war came, and most of those were adverse. The agreement gave the bulk of the French fleet overall responsibility for the Mediterranean and allotted the British a secondary role, which naturally seemed to be a major shift at the time, as the end of a long tradition of British domination. The real significance of the pact was that it enabled Britain to concentrate superior naval force in home waters against the Germans, covering the French Channel and Atlantic coasts in the process. Thus the agreement was the foundation of ultimate victory, thanks to the distant blockade it made possible; yet the Mediterranean side of it proved to be a fiasco. But before examining the dispositions of the powers in the Mediterranean on the eve of war it is necessary to consider the historical background which led to them.

The Europe which slid into war in 1914 had been shaped in the main by the creation of the German Empire in 1871 after the Prussian Army's smashing defeat of France. More than four decades of peace, however uneasy at times, ensued, the Balkans always excepted. (Bismarck predicted that if a new war came, it would arise over 'some damned foolish thing in the Balkans'.) The German and Italian questions seemed to have been permanently resolved by unification in each case, and with the exception of Austria-Hungary and its irksome jumble of nationalities, the principal European powers turned their attention to new colonies. France was isolated by its defeat and was alone in refusing to swallow its relegation from first place in the list of leading European military powers at the hands of Germany, something which rankled even more than the loss of Alsace and Lorraine.

As the sole opponent of the new balance of power, France alone could find no ally for twenty years, while the pattern of understandings and rapprochements among the other five major European states shifted around it.

Until his dismissal in 1890, Bismarck was the prime mover of European diplomacy. Germany concluded the Dual Alliance with Austria in 1879 because it could not allow the creaking Habsburg Empire to fall prey to Russia, but successfully opposed Austrian attempts to recruit Britain and Italy into an alliance with Germany against Russia. The Austrians and the Russians were already competing for control of the southern Slavs in the Balkans. In 1881 Austria joined the Three Emperors' Alliance with Germany and Russia, having got nowhere with the British. In the following year, Austria, Germany and Italy concluded the Triple Alliance. This provided for Italian neutrality in the event of war between Austria and Russia, as well as for Italian assistance to Germany if the latter were attacked by France. Italy added a special protocol allowing it to stay out of a war with Britain. The Three Emperors' Alliance fell apart in the late 1880s over Austro-Russian rivalry in Bulgaria, but the Mediterranean agreements concluded in 1887 by Austria, Britain, Italy and Spain against any French and Russian designs in the Mediterranean gave the Austrians, for the time being, relief in the Balkans. German-Russian relations having deteriorated over trade and finance, Germany joined this 'Mediterranean Entente' by 1894. France saw her opportunity to break out of isolation and concluded financial and military agreements with Russia, also by 1894. Russia's vital interest in extending its influence in the Ottoman Empire was based on the need to keep open the Straits between the Black Sea and the Mediterranean through which its grain exports passed. Austrian policy wavered between understandings with the Russians to frustrate revolutionary nationalism in the Balkans and trying to contain Russian influence there. Britain meanwhile was probably more concerned in the dying years of the nineteenth century about Russia, both because of its expansionist designs in Persia and Afghanistan and because its interest in the Ottoman Empire might lead to a threat to the Suez Canal, the imperial lifeline. (This perceived double Russian threat to India won Austria much sympathy in London, at least until Anglo-Russian differences in Asia were settled by their 1907 agreement.) The unbroken threads in this bewildering pattern of diplomatic manoeuvre were Austro-Russian rivalry in the Balkans, Germany's commitment to Austria, French hostility to Germany and British distaste for continental entanglements. At the turn of the century this left three power-blocs in Europe: the Triple Alliance of Austria, Germany and Italy, the Dual Alliance of France and Russia, and still-isolated Britain, which viewed the latter as a greater threat than the former. In 1897 Austria and Russia arrived at an understanding, shelving their differences in the Balkans, but not resolving them.

The new factor that changed all this was the shift in German policy which followed the accession of Wilhelm II in 1888 and the dismissal of Bismarck two years later. The new Kaiser was much less adept at power politics than the old Chancellor and under him Germany became something of a cuckoo in the European nest, always demanding, never satisfied and usually dangerously unpredictable. The traditional British fear of one-power domination of Europe was aroused when the continent's leading military and economic state began to expand its navy at an alarming rate. The Royal Navy was the bulwark of British strength which held the empire together while protecting the island kingdom from any European threat. Bismarck had won Germany its 'place in the sun' without a significant navy (a fact which was lost on the Kaiser). The only motive Germany could have for becoming a major naval power was to challenge Britain and inhibit its freedom of action. The answer was for Britain to seek an accommodation with France. The two countries settled their differences over Morocco (defined as being in the French sphere of influence) and Egypt (British), which paved the way for the Entente Cordiale in 1904. Germany's ill-judged and gratuitous challenges to French domination of Morocco strengthened the ties between the Channel Powers to such an extent that they began, in great secrecy, naval and military 'conversations' on cooperation in the event of war between both and Germany. The two admiralties held discussions at the turn of 1905–6, in 1908 and in 1911. As we have seen, Britain settled her differences with Russia in the East in 1907, and although Europe was not mentioned in the agreement, it meant that the British were now on good terms with France's ally, completing the Triple Entente.

The Anglo-French talks led to an agreement that a British army would be shipped to France in the event of war with Germany, to fight on the French left; meanwhile the naval discussions, which went on in the period of 1912–14, resulted in the understanding that the French fleet would concentrate in the Mediterranean to protect British and French interests there, enabling the British to build up their strength for the principal maritime struggle in the North Sea. These naval dispositions were completed in advance of the outbreak of war.

The naval agreement of February 1913 for 'combined action in the Mediterranean' in the event of a joint war against the Triple Alliance left the British free to provide as much or as little naval force as it could afford in the light of its overriding responsibility to cover the 'decisive theatre of naval operations', the North Sea. But the agreed minimum British presence in the Mediterranean in peace and war alike should be enough to 'fight, with reasonable chances of success, the Austrian fleet if this came out of the Adriatic.' The guiding principle was to be that the two fleets would operate separately, the French in the Western and the British in the eastern basin of the Mediterranean (west and east of Italy). The French would take on the Italian fleet. In the event of a junction of the Austrian and Italian fleets, the British and French would cooperate in fighting them, though not to the extent of trying to form a single line of battle. But if the British were obliged to withdraw ships to the North Sea to such an extent that they could no longer tackle the Austrians alone, *the remaining British vessels would come under French command in time of war*. Each power had free use of the other's bases in the event of war. The most important immediate wartime task identified in the agreement was the transport of the French Army's XIX Corps (the 'Army of Africa') from Algeria and Tunisia to France, to take up its assigned place in the line opposing Germany. In this way the two allies, as they now were, planned to cover their strategic interests in the Mediterranean, keeping open the south-to-north route vital to the French Empire and the west-to-east route no less vital to the British. Shared communications and a joint signal-book were provided to facilitate cooperation once war began. It is noteworthy that the agreement, of which the foregoing is a full summary, made no mention at all of German ships, let alone what to do about them.

Once Rear-Admiral Wilhelm Souchon took over the command of the Mediterranean Division, he became the driving force in achieving agreements on potential joint action with the Austrian and Italian navies in case of a war between the Triple Alliance and the Entente. As soon as he arrived at the end of October 1913 he made it his business to explore every corner of the Mediterranean he could reach, to learn as much as he could about his likely enemies and to work out how he could most effectively deploy his small command to cause maximum disruption. No doubt the massive panoply of potential opposing forces concentrated his mind wonderfully; but he also happened to be far and away the best naval commander in the Mediterranean, the most professional, decisive and resolute admiral afloat there, whose quality was accentuated by the unusual capacity for under-achievement of those lined up against him.

Wilhelm Anton Theodor Souchon was born in Leipzig on 2 June 1864. His first sight of the sea at the age of seven on an excursion to the coast was 'an amazing experience' which he never forgot; from then on his obsession was to go to sea. After his father, also Wilhelm, a portrait-painter of Huguenot descent, died when the boy was only twelve, his mother, Clara, *née* Naumann, a Berlin banker's daughter, put him in the care of a privy councillor in Weimar called Genast. He had already started studying there in 1873 at a *Gymnasium* (grammar school). His scholastic performance was poor until it was pointed out to him that education was essential for a naval officer. He promptly moved to the top of the class and comfortably passed the examination for admission to the Kiel Naval School in 1881. Passing out top of his year he went on to the Naval Academy as a sea-cadet; his dissertation while there on the Strait of Gibraltar was so outstanding that it was published in the leading German naval magazine. There it was spotted by the bilingual Battenberg, the future British First Sea Lord, who person-ally translated it for publication in a British naval period-ical. A series of training and junior staff posts followed, including a spell in charge of the British section of the Naval High Command, interspersed with occasional tours of duty at sea. As the German Navy expanded, so Souchon's promotion accelerated. Whereas it took him twenty years to become a lieutenant-commander (1901), in which rank he served in the plum job of chief-of-staff to the Cruiser Squadron in East Asia, he became commander in 1905 and captain eighteen months later, at the end of 1906 – whereupon he got his first command, the battleship *Wettin*. When he returned from the Far East in 1904 to work in the foreign warfare section of the Imperial Navy Office, he was personally welcomed by Tirpitz, the head of the Office, and publicly praised for his staff work on the China station. In 1901 he became chief-of-staff to the Baltic command; two years later he made the great leap from captain to rear-admiral and became second-in-command of the Second Squadron of battleships. He was the first man to be offered the command of the Mediterranean Division but made so bold as to decline the Kaiser's invitation (based on the recommendation of Tirpitz) because his first marriage was on the verge of collapse. He retained his posting in home waters and was divorced at the end of 1912. When the Mediterranean command was offered a second time in 1913, he jumped at it, having remarried in the meantime.

Those who served with Souchon in his early days noted his even temper, self-control, cheerfulness, versatility and capacity for hard work. He also had a gift for which the German national character is not normally renowned – tact, which soon, together with his good manners and modest demeanour, earned him the nickname of 'the Diplomat'. As his responsibilities grew, he also showed a capacity to delegate which sat well with his inclination to take the broad view, as a commander should. His subordinates regarded him as strict but fair and above all loyal to them.

The small, square-cut admiral bursting with energy, who seldom drank alcohol and never smoked, spent the first few days of his new command buried in the files. He then wrote a letter home from which one sentence demands to be quoted for the insight it offers into his philosophy of command:

Everything is so new for me, though, and needs much thought, so that I take the right course without becoming dependent on [our] own diplomatic representatives or the Admiralty Staff in Berlin.

His command, as we have seen, consisted of just two ships. SMS *Goeben* was Germany's third battlecruiser of the seven that were completed and the second and last member of the *Moltke* class. She was ordered from the Blohm & Voss yard in Hamburg in April 1909, launched in March 1911 and handed over in May 1912. On her trials she exceeded her specified speed by a remarkable two and a half knots, reaching 28 knots on the measured mile and an average of 27.2 knots on a forced voyage of six hours. Unlike her British counterparts, she carried armour that was almost up to the standard of a new battleship, with an 11-inch belt around her vital amidships and 10 inches on her five gun turrets. A skirt of subsidiary armour plate below the waterline and inside the hull gave protection against torpedoes and mines, which was to save her more than once. Some 5,000 tons had to be added to her displacement (22,640 tons) for the extra armour and the larger turbines needed for her high speed in consequence. Decidedly superior to all British battlecruisers in armour and with a distinct edge in speed over the first generation of ships of this type in the Royal

Navy, the *Goeben* had a main armament that was on paper inferior (ten 11-inch guns compared with the original British norm of 12-inch). But the German barrels were of higher quality, delivered a higher muzzle velocity, used better ammunition, had better rangefinders and were sited on a ship nearly twenty feet broader in the beam, which made her a much steadier gun platform. A full ten-gun broadside from the *Goeben* weighed 6,600 pounds, compared with the 6,800 pounds fired by the eight 12-inch guns of the first British battlecruisers. The German guns had an effective range of 18,500 yards and, all in all, were not noticeably inferior to the British 12-inch. She was 610 feet long, 97 feet broad and had a draught of 27 feet.

All this made her the most formidable warship in the entire Mediterranean when war broke out. But she had her weaknesses, the worst of which was a very high rate of leakage in her boiler tubes, which had been made of inadequate metal. As with all German capital ships, designed for work close to home in the North Sea and North Atlantic, her range was relatively short. With her normal load of coal she could sail at top speed (theoretically) for just over nineteen hours and a distance of about 520 nautical miles; at her optimum cruising speed of 19 knots and with her bunkers full (3,000 tonnes, three times the normal load), she could cover about 3,500 miles, and at her economical cruising speed of 12 knots, about 4,250 miles. The Mediterranean is about 2,200 miles long. For her crew of 1,100 men she was extremely uncomfortable on a long cruise, being designed for brief operations (German sailors lived ashore in barracks and were not used to long periods at sea). The ventilation and lighting were poor, the messes primitive and over-crowded and before the war a request for a second air-cooling machine had been turned down on grounds of economy. But the low priority given to comfort enabled the shipbuilders to give her a hull of remarkable strength with extra watertight bulkheads.

SMS *Breslau* by contrast had the elegance of all the latest German light cruisers, with four tall and slender funnels slightly raked. She was launched at the Vulkan yard in Stettin (now Szeczin in Poland) in May 1911 and was designed for service in home waters as a destroyer flotilla-leader or for reconnaissance with the battle fleet. She was 455 feet long but only 44 feet wide with a normal top speed of 28 knots which she may well have exceeded in short bursts. She carried a crew of 373 men and ten 4.1-inch guns, displacing 4,550 tons. She was very lightly armoured and heavily outgunned by British light cruisers of the same vintage, which carried 6-inch guns; but she had the legs of them. She too offered her crew little comfort, tended to roll excessively in heavy seas despite a modified keel, and vibrated severely at high speed. Her range was somewhat greater than that of the *Goeben*, but her coal consumption was, of course, far lower. She gave her name (from the now Polish city of Wroclaw, formerly Breslau) to a class with three other members. The battle-cruiser was named after General August von Goeben, the able commander of an army corps in the Franco-Prussian War of 1870–1.

From the moment Souchon hoisted his flag on the *Goeben* in Trieste on 23 October 1913, he concentrated on getting to know his operational area. The seemingly endless round of courtesy calls at friendly, neutral or potential enemy ports was used to acquire detailed information on channels, currents, anchorages and anything else of relevance. On his first visit to the Sicilian port of Messina, which was to play a pivotal role at the outbreak of war, Souchon found the French battleship *Voltaire*, then the flagship of Vice-Admiral Augustin Boué de

Lapeyrère, the French Commander-in-Chief, in port and took the opportunity of a personal meeting (November 1913). He was not impressed. He never got the chance to meet Admiral Sir Archibald Berkeley Milne, the British C-in-C, because the British pursued a policy of one-upmanship. They made a point of calling at foreign ports as soon as possible after the Germans in order to impress the natives with a grander show of force and cap any effect that might have been achieved. The Kaiser elegantly described this ploy as 'spitting in the soup'. In the first few days of his term of service, Souchon called on Admiral Haus, the Austro-Hungarian Commander-in-Chief, at Pola on the Adriatic, the Austrian fleet's headquarters. They agreed that in the event of a war between the Triple Alliance and the Entente Powers Souchon would come under Haus's command. In December 1913 the German commander called on the Italian C-in-C, Vice-Admiral Prince Lodovico, Duke of Abruzzi, while both were visiting Alexandria; Souchon followed this up with a visit to the Admiralty in Rome in January 1914. It was mainly due to him that the staffs of the three navies produced a common signal-book, ciphers, recognition signals and tactical plans. Messina was agreed upon as the gathering point for joint action. In March 1914, Haus and Souchon agreed that the first objective of the German ships in war would be to disrupt the transfer of French troops from North Africa to France.

But in May Souchon was so concerned about the state of the *Goeben*'s twenty-four boilers that he sent a message to warn Tirpitz that the flagship would cease to be fit for sea in two months. She was due to be replaced by the *Moltke* in October, but in June the chief engineer said at least two weeks in port for emergency repairs were needed before she could sail home. This did not prevent the crew of the *Goeben* from vastly increasing Turkish goodwill towards Germany and its navy at a stroke. The ship was on a routine visit to Constantinople on May 22 when a major fire broke out at an infantry barracks there. The call for volunteers was answered by 150 German sailors who raced, scantily clad and covered in coaldust, through the narrow streets of the city (they had been coaling their ship) to perform Herculean feats in bringing the blaze under control. Three Germans died and four were injured. Many thousands of people turned out for a great funeral ceremony to show their appreciation of the sailors' sacrifice. In June arrangements were made for the *Goeben* to put into Pola in mid-July. German shipbuilders and a large consignment of boiler tubes were sent there from home. By the last few days of July, nearly 4,500 tubes were replaced, a great improvement which, however, did not eradicate the problem. On July 29 the flagship left Pola for an official visit to Trieste followed by some gunnery practice; on the 30th she left there, southward bound. At this time, the *Breslau*, free of mechanical troubles, was in Durrazzo as part of an international naval force supporting the new (German) royal house in Albania, independent from Turkey since 1912, against a rebellious population upon whom it had been thrust by the Central Powers. She sailed away on July 31; only a few days before, her officers had the honour of entertaining Rear-Admiral Ernest Charles Thomas Troubridge, flag officer commanding the British First Cruiser Squadron. They found him lively, jovial and full of self-confidence.

In France, *Que fait donc l'armée navale?* was a question that was to be repeated with increasing volume and urgency as the war began. The French Navy had in fact done a great deal to modernize itself in the prelude to the war. After a period of neglect in the first few years of the century, something which may, by reducing the traditional Anglo-French naval rivalry, have made it easier for the British to reach an accommodation with France, the navy experienced a revival from 1909. The man responsible was Admiral Lapeyrère, who then began a two-year term as Minister of Marine. With apparently tireless vigour, he shook up all departments and brought about a considerable reduction in shipbuilding times. Using his wide powers, which also covered the shipyards, he increased administrative efficiency by reorganization, reduced tension and unrest in the fleet and ashore, and raised morale all round. The keel of the first French dreadnought, the *Courbet*, was laid in September 1910 and she was launched just a year later. France was to have four by the outbreak of war. Her last pre-dreadnought, the *Voltaire*, had needed nineteen months between the laying of the keel and the launch, and four years altogether to complete. In September 1911 the French felt confident enough to tell the British that they could take on the Austrian and Italian fleets combined. Lapeyrère's reward was to be appointed Commander-in-Chief (*Admiralissime*). It turned out to be a classic case of over-promotion, or perhaps it came too late in the career of an undoubtedly distinguished sailor.

Lapeyrère was showing his age, having been born in 1852. He was a man of impressive physical presence, large, gruff, sometimes taciturn to the point of rudeness, with a raw, florid complexion and a grey-white beard. He was known to his men as 'the Seawolf' (*loup de mer*) and sometimes succumbed to irritation and arrogance. In his younger days he had acquired a reputation for keenness and energy. When he was serving in China under Admiral Courbet (after whom his flagship was named), his chief described him as the most gallant of his captains. He was autocratic and worked his men and his ships hard (at any rate in peacetime), to the limits of their endurance, especially on manoeuvres. But he was respected and under him before the war morale was high. When Souchon called on him, he refused to speak English (the *lingua franca* of the sea just as it is of the air today) and told the German admiral, in French, that his role in war was to knock out the Austrian and Italian navies; he did not deign to mention Souchon's ships, but this is unlikely to have been out of courtesy.

At the outbreak of war, his command consisted of two dreadnoughts, including the *Courbet* (fleet flagship); the First Squadron of six 18,000-ton battleships, the Second, of five slower 15,000-ton battleships; the First Light Division of four armoured cruisers of 13,000 to 14,000 tons each, the Second, of three more of 13,000 tons each, and a Reserve Division of four old battleships of 12,000 tons; a Special Division of two even older battleships, four armoured cruisers and three light cruisers; six flotillas of destroyers (thirty-six in all) and two of submarines (sixteen in all). The fleet's weaknesses included a general shortage of speed and the questionable value of the older ships. The flagship was the fastest, and could make just 20 knots. The destroyers were judged satisfactory but the submarines were of little use in the open sea. One of the dreadnoughts, the *Jean Bart*, had been detached to take President Raymond Poincaré and the Prime Minister, M. René Viviani, on a state visit to St Petersburg, from which they hurriedly returned only on July 29. Another new dreadnought, the *France*, went along as escort. On the outbreak of war, the fleet was in the main French naval base at Toulon.

At the head of the British Mediterranean Fleet was Sir Archibald Berkeley Milne, an unimaginative dandy who owed his unmerited advance to full admiral to friends at court. His nickname in the navy was 'Arky Barky' but the names Lord Fisher called him on his appointment in April 1912 to what had traditionally been the plum command afloat were rather more pungent, the shortest being 'Sir B. Mean.' Later Fisher was to refer to him as 'Sir Berkeley Goeben'. Writing to Churchill from retirement, he told the First Lord that 'I consider you have betrayed the navy . . . *You are aware that Sir Berkeley Milne is unfitted to be the senior admiral afloat . . . I can't believe that you foresee all the consequences!* The results would be IRREPARABLE, IRREMEDI-ABLE, ETERNAL!' The emphases are Fisher's; his literary style ranged from the wild to the explosive. He accused Churchill of toadying to the court and described Milne as 'an utterly useless commander'. Unlike Fisher, Milne was born with a veritable canteen of silver cutlery in his mouth, in his father's official apartments in the Admiralty building (his father attained the supreme rank of Admiral of the Fleet with a baronetcy thrown in). His early naval service was pampered enough, but in 1882, at the age of twenty-seven, he began a long career in various posts in royal yachts, culminating in his appointment as rear-admiral in charge of all of them in 1903. A snappy dresser and a ladies' man, he never married and became a special friend of Queen Alexandra while she was still Princess of Wales and the future Edward VII was busy being unfaithful to her.

His second-in-command, Rear-Admiral Troubridge, also did a tour of duty in a royal yacht and inherited the finest social connections. The only other thing they had in common was the uniform they wore. Troubridge bore with pride a name glorious in naval and military annals. His great-grandfather, the first baronet, was Rear-Admiral Sir Thomas Troubridge, a close friend and colleague of Nelson who fought at the Battle of the Nile, one of the 'band of brothers' who led the navy in its days of greatest glory. His son, Sir Edward Troubridge, also had a distinguished naval career in the Napoleonic Wars and after, and also attained the rank of rear-admiral. The third baronet was Colonel Sir Thomas Troubridge, who exhibited superhuman courage in the Crimea, losing his left foot and right leg at the Battle of Inkerman. Our admiral was the third son of the gallant colonel. Ernest Troubridge was born in 1862 and took up the career of a naval officer as to the manner born, his name giving him automatic access to the highest social circles; but he was no courtier. He took his work seriously and became a professional. While his social background gave him the confidence to speak his mind and must have helped his career, he did actually have something to say: the 'right people' recognized a genuine talent for leadership and a young man full of ideas. His physical courage won acclaim when he was twenty-six. He was serving aboard a torpedo-boat when he won the Royal Humane Society's silver medal by diving from its deck at night to save a sailor who had fallen into the sea as the ship was sailing at full speed off Crete.

Three years after that, as a dashing lieutenant with prospects after seven years in the rank, Troubridge wed Edith Duffus in 1891. The future admiral was unlucky in love, or more precisely in marriage (he seems to have been the kind of sailor who had a girl in every port). After bearing one son and two daughters, Edith died tragically young in 1900. If his first marriage was a personal tragedy, his second, in 1908, was a social catastrophe. The neurotic daughter of a genteel womanizer, Una Taylor had artistic leanings but no talent. The increasingly ill-suited couple had a daughter, but as the war began Una indulged another leaning by supplanting a female cousin in the affections of one Radclyffe Hall.

Neither an obscure Oxbridge college nor the setting for a Brontë pastiche, Radclyffe Hall was not a man either but an indifferent writer who gained an undeserved fame with a turgid novel about lesbianism called *The Well of Loneliness*. One of the least attractive satellites of the overblown Bloomsbury group, which in any case produced more transient scandal than lasting literature, Hall, styling herself John, took Una to live in Rye, where they were wont to have public rows culminating in exchanges of scones at point-blank range. When her understandably long-since estranged husband was knighted, Una took childish pleasure in further scandalizing the Troubridge family by availing herself of the title Lady. But his marital misfortunes did not apparently interfere with his accelerating career, which took him to captain in 1901 and commodore in 1908.

As naval attaché in Tokyo in the rank of captain he witnessed some of the action in the Russo-Japanese War of 1904–5, and wrote invaluable reports on a conflict which changed naval strategic and tactical concepts. The natural seaman also proved to be a natural staff officer, serving as Naval Secretary to Churchill's predecessor as First Lord, Reginald McKenna, and then as the first Chief of Staff at the Admiralty when the decision was made to set up a naval War Staff, in 1912. Last but not by any means least, one of his warmest admirers was the mercurial Lord Fisher, with whom Troubridge, in earlier days before the great admiral's retirement, had not been afraid to cross swords in argument. Fisher was an autocrat but could not abide 'yes-men'. The navy's fondness for nicknames also extended to Troubridge, whose full head of wavy white hair earned him the soubriquet of 'the Silver King'. He was indeed a majestic figure with a broad, open, ruddy face, set off by a direct and jovial manner – a man you could rely on who had the rare good fortune to be loved by his subordinates and admired by his superiors. He could bear his name with pride; but in the unique stress of war it was to become a burden.

The two British commanders were, in their decidedly different ways, heirs to a naval tradition which had become ossified in a century unusually peaceful for Britain, which had not been involved in a major naval battle since Nelson's time. The navy was obsessed with the concept of the 'line of battle' which had proved itself in Nelson's day (the fact that Britain's greatest fighting admiral abandoned it when it seemed appropriate was suppressed). The intricacy of movement and the complicated manoeuvres involved in manipulating the line led to a centralization of command, not only in the battle fleet at sea but all the way up to the top in the Admiralty. It is hardly surprising that this rigidity of thought produced so few commanders of talent; and it was compounded by the bewildering succession of far-reaching technological developments which swamped the navy in a great rush before the First World War: steam and iron, then steel and armour, bigger and better guns, range-finders, centralized gunnery control, turbines, torpedoes, mines and submarines – and wireless, a tactical blessing but also a means of extending detailed interference from the Admiralty round the world. Small wonder amid all this that most naval officers clung to as much unthinking routine as they could in a world full of disturbing changes. This is not the place to diverge too far into these matters, though they must be mentioned because Milne at least was an extreme example of what the system could produce. But there is one incident which bears retelling here, as an extraordinary illustration of the attitudes which still dominated the navy whose most glamorous post he occupied in 1914, and which are central to what follows. On fleet manoeuvres in 1893, the battleships were sailing in two parallel lines. The commander, Vice-Admiral George Tryon, an officer whose genuinely exceptional qualities did not include agility in mental arithmetic, ordered the two columns to reverse course by turning inwards. His flagship, HMS *Victoria*, at the head of one line, and the *Camperdown*, leading the other, began to execute the order. Unfortunately, the distance between the two ships was less than the combined diameters of their turning circles. HMS *Camperdown* therefore rammed the side of the *Victoria*, which went down with great loss of life, including Tryon's. Neither Rear-Admiral A. H. Markham on the *Camperdown* nor any other officer dared to oppose an order whose inevitable consequence became clearer with every second that passed. From this the Admiralty of the day does not seem to have drawn the obvious lessons, such as that admirals should make use of the expertise of people like ship's captains and navigation officers or that juniors should be encouraged to speak up when their seniors appeared to be in error. Instead, the only conclusions that seem to have been drawn were that experiments like the fancy turn which turned into disaster were dangerous, and that absolute obedience to an order excused anything. Twenty years later, naval officers were still held in thrall by two rules of thumb: follow the senior officer's motions, and when in doubt request instructions. Strategy and tactics were very much secondary to mastering the intricacies of new ships and equipment. Thus on the outbreak of war the Royal Navy was uniquely strong in officers specializing in seamanship and other technical skills, supported by all-regular sailors of the highest standard of training. But beyond the rank of captain there were few outstanding leaders. When the German General Max Hoffman made his immortal remark about the quality of the British fighting man, he was referring to the army on the Western

Front, but he could just as well have been speaking of the navy. In general the sailors were indeed 'lions led by asses'.

Milne's command on the outbreak of war consisted of the Second Battlecruiser Squadron of just three first-generation dreadnoughts (but with less armour and fewer guns than battleships, for the sake of extra speed). They were HMS *Inflexible* (his flagship), *Indomitable* (sister-ships of the *Invincible* class) and the slightly larger and more modern *Indefatigable*. All three had a design speed of 25 knots and eight 12-inch guns. The first two named had main armour 7 inches thick and a displacement of 17,250 tons; *Indefatigable* had 8-inch armour and displaced 18,750 tons. Also under command was the First Cruiser Squadron, led by Rear-Admiral Troubridge and consisting of four broadly similar heavy or armoured cruisers: *Defence* (flag), *Warrior, Duke of Edinburgh* and *Black Prince*. Their design speed was 22 to 23 knots and their main armament the 9.2-inch gun (*Defence* had four, the others six each); the flagship displaced 14,600 tons and the others 13,550 tons, and all had 6 inches of main armour. It is worth noting that this type of ship had fallen out of favour and none had been ordered since 1905; there was no real tactical role for them between the capital ship and the nimbler light cruiser. Of the latter type, Milne also had four: *Chatham, Dublin, Gloucester* and *Weymouth*, each of around 5,000 tons with a main armament of 6-inch guns. Finally there were sixteen destroyers of various ages, and three submarines at Malta. On the eve of war, Milne concentrated his fleet there.

The Austrian fleet, at Pola, consisted of three dread-noughts, thirteen armoured cruisers, three fast light cruisers, thirty-six destroyers and six coastal submarines. Italy announced her neutrality at the outset.

From the point of view of the Entente, the Mediterranean on this basis looked capable of being converted into an Anglo-French lake, provided only that the mouth of the Adriatic were properly sealed before the Austrian fleet could pass through. Italy's long-established friendliness towards Britain suggested it would stay neutral (as it was entitled to do under the terms of the Triple Alliance, which required it to come to the aid of Germany only if that country were attacked by France). The French Navy was in any case strong enough to hold the Austrians and the Italians even without the considerable British presence. Without Italy, the Germans could make use only of Austrian bases, entailing the risk of being trapped in the Adriatic cul-de-sac. The flaw in the Anglo-French arrangements, which were strategically unimpeachable and completed in good time, was their vagueness at the tactical level. There was no formal alliance and no established mechanism for detailed liaison between the two Admiralties. Their initial errors owed as much to a failure of communication as to faults in command, and in the first week of the war, more so. There was also a gross failure of imagination: nobody gave a thought to Turkey.

PART TWO
The Evasion

He who hesitates is lost.

Proverb

Where lies the land to which yon ship must go?

William Wordsworth
Miscellaneous Sonnets, part 1, xxxi

3

Admiral de Lapeyrère and the French Fleet

The success of the *Goeben* has always been regarded as an essential British failure. All the accounts ever published, whether long or short, British or German, take this view; even the contemporary British Admiralty, whatever it may have said in public to exonerate itself and its admirals, regarded the whole affair as a purely British matter. The French press of the day also blamed the British. There can be no doubt that the German evasion was of itself a miserable blunder at the very outset of the war at sea, even if its catastrophic consequences are ignored; there can be no doubt that it remains one of the great black marks on the record of the Royal Navy. What is overlooked in all this is the undeniable fact that it was the French Navy that had, and missed, the first opportunity of catching Souchon, and that it made no attempt at all to rectify its error while there was still time. France, after all, had been allotted overall responsibility for the Mediterranean. It would be wrong to seek to shift the whole burden of blame to the French, but the level of bungling incompetence in their naval movements at the very beginning of the war (and for a long time thereafter) earns them an equal share, as some honest Frenchmen were prepared to admit at the time. No comprehensive account of the *Goeben* affair can afford to ignore them; the record needs to be set straight.

Que fait donc l'armée navale? Its orders were both sound and clear, having been worked out with the active assistance and concurrence of Lapeyrère, the C-in-C, well in advance. The first priority for the French in the event of war with Germany was the transport of the Army of Africa, XIX Corps, from their North African possessions via Marseilles to its place in the line, as rapidly as possible. This was exhaustively discussed in the Supreme Council of National Defence, usually with Lapeyrère present. For the sake of speed, it was specifically and unmistakably agreed that no time should be wasted on the formation of convoys: the ships carrying the troops should sail one by one as soon as they were full and at top speed. The navy would in the meantime cover this operation by establishing its mastery of the Mediterranean with a vigorous offensive against every enemy ship afloat, in concert with any British forces. The French fleet, concentrated, but for some light forces, in the Mediterranean during 1913, had the strength to seize control. This arrangement was included in general orders to the C-in-C which he himself had a hand in drafting. Shortly before the war Lapeyrère declared in a lecture at the French Naval School that his plan was to seize the mastery of the sea in the opening days of a general war by tackling first the Italian and then the Austrian fleet. Geography in fact decreed that an aggressive French sweep eastwards would impose this programme upon him unless the Austrians and Italians managed to effect a junction before this could happen. The Italian fleet was the more formidable proposition with four new dreadnoughts mustering a total of fifty-one 12-inch guns and with a design speed of up to 23 knots. These were supported by older battleships of at best moderate value, considerably inferior to the more numerous French equivalents, as indeed were the smaller ships. But in the immediate prewar days Italy showed not the slightest sign of mobilizing; by July 30, the British were convinced she would stay neutral and passed this on to the French.

On July 28, Lapeyrère suddenly revealed that he had

grave doubts about his orders. In a letter to Dr Gauthier, the Minister of Marine, he proposed the formation of convoys escorted by his squadrons to ferry the troops. The government in Paris was taken aback. The ministry sent a telegram saying there was no question of modifying his orders, and backed this up with a long and detailed letter. This patiently explained that the Ministry of War was fully aware of the risks involved in allowing transport by solitary ships, but deliberately accepted them in the interest of the fastest possible movement of the three divisions to the frontier with Germany. This plan was the result of careful study in which the admiral himself had taken part; convoys had been totally excluded from the start; speed was paramount; the navy was mistress of the sea and had been ever since the orders were formulated (at a Defence Council meeting of 7 April 1914). The letter concluded:

The risks you mention, nobody doubts it, were foreseen and weighed [up] with you in good time; you are covered for them by your instructions and the discussions in which you took part which served as a basis for them; this is no longer the moment to discuss, but to act.

The reply reached the admiral by special messenger at Toulon on July 31.

It was remarkable that anyone in Paris could find the time to write at such length because the capital was in uproar, and not only within the administration. President Poincaré and Viviani, Prime Minister and Foreign Minister of just six weeks and head of the tenth French Cabinet in five years, returned from Russia on the *Jean Bart* on July 29, having cancelled a visit to Copenhagen they were to have made on the way. The Austrian ultimatum to Serbia on July 28, which led to war between them, had been deliberately timed by Vienna to catch the French leaders at sea. General Joffre, the army commander, told them on their return that the Germans were on the move at the frontier and demanded immediate general mobilization. The government hedged. Its overriding concern now that war seemed inevitable was to ensure that France did not have to fight without immediate British support. To this end it was determined to do everything it could to show up Germany as the aggressor, come what may. On July 30, therefore, to Joffre's horror, the government took the startling step, timid or reckless or possibly both, of ordering a general retreat of all troops along the frontier to a distance ten kilometres inside French territory. Viviani's idea – and it was his – was to eliminate the possibility of an 'incident', a clash of patrols, an accidental straying across the German border, that the Germans could seize upon as an excuse. There was also the desperate hope that war might still be averted even in these last minutes of the last hour of peace. The streets and cafes of Paris meanwhile were awash with people and wild rumours; the tension was palpable, fear and excitement were in the air everywhere.

At 7 P.M., Central European Time (one hour ahead of GMT), on July 31, the German Ambassador, Baron von Schoen, went to the Foreign Ministry and presented Viviani with an ultimatum: France was to state within eighteen hours whether she would stay neutral in the event of war between Russia and Germany; he would call for the reply at 1 P.M. the next day. That was in fact only half the story; the Ambassador was a man of honour and could not, for shame, deliver the rest of the message, which demanded the surrender of the key French fortresses of Verdun and Toul as a guarantee for such neutrality (to be returned in mint condition after the war). But the French had intercepted the wireless message from Berlin containing his instructions and already knew the worst. It was an intolerable demand, but Viviani limited himself to saying that he would give his answer in due time. The German ultimatum to Russia had been delivered in St Petersburg at the same time. The cabinet went into another prolonged and emotional session full of argument; late in the evening, the shocking news reached it that Jean Jaurès, the pacifist socialist leader, had been shot dead in a Paris café by a demented 'super-patriot'. The sensation further electrified an already unbearably tense and neurotic city but there was still no definite news of war. The political and diplomatic discussions went on into the night.

A no less nervous and depressed Baron von Schoen called two hours early at the Foreign Ministry for Viviani's reply. It consisted of one sentence, worked out with Poincaré and the cabinet: 'France will act in accordance with her interests.' Given the terms of the ultimatum, this could only mean '*non*'. At 3.30 P.M. on August 1 general mobilization was ordered, to begin at midnight. Lapeyrère was of course informed and prepared to set sail with the fleet the next day.

But on that 2nd of August there occurred a hiatus in the flow of communications to the fleet which, as we have seen, was led by a man with new doubts about his general orders. It was discovered in Paris that Gauthier, the Minister of Marine, had forgotten to issue instructions to the French torpedoboats earmarked for duty in the Channel. General Adolphe Messimy, the Minister of War, concerned to move XIX Corps at once, questioned the competence of the navy. Gauthier, overcompensating for his lapse, now proposed attacking the German ships in the Mediterranean, even though war had not yet been declared; on the edge of a nervous collapse he challenged Messimy to a duel. The two men almost had to be prised apart, and Gauthier was persuaded to resign, on the quite accurate grounds of ill-health. He was replaced on August 4 by M. Victor Augagneur.

At 6.53 P.M. GMT on August 2, meanwhile, Lapeyrère received a message aboard his flagship, the *Courbet*, from the French naval station in Bizèrta, Tunisia, that the *Goeben* had been clearly heard wirelessing in Tunisian waters. Quite reasonably believing that the Germans would try to interfere with the transport of the Army of Africa just as or even just before hostilities officially began, the French admiral sent orders at 7 P.M. to Bizerta and also Algiers to stop the departure of all troopships until naval escorts arrived. Since the fleet was still sitting in port, this implied a serious delay of at least two days for XIX Corps. Lapeyrère told Paris of his action an hour later, adding that he now regarded convoys as essential. Fifty minutes after that, the *Courbet* logged receipt of a message from the Ministry of Marine in Paris (put together by the cabinet in the absence of an effective Minister of Marine), drafted in the late afternoon:

Goeben and *Breslau* arrived at Brindisi during the night of July 31 to August 1. Set sail, and if you are signalled hostilities commenced, stop them. Cabinet has again declared that special troop transport to proceed in isolated ships. War Department accepting all risks thereof.

What could be clearer? This message had been drawn up some time before the alert from Bizerta, but it came from Paris, which was likely to be better informed about enemy movements, with all the intelligence sources at its disposal and a staff trained to sift them. If both messages were right (in fact the one from Bizerta was a false alarm), together they suggested that the Germans were heading west along the North African coast. Assuming they had left Brindisi at first light on the 1st and had taken the shortest route to a point somewhere off Bizerta, a distance of about 600 nautical miles, they would have been travelling at an average speed of about 16 knots. Assuming further that they were making for the western exit of the Mediterranean by Gibraltar, Lapeyrère, by setting sail *at once* with his strongest ships at the same speed, could have expected to cut them off before they reached Oran. If they paused on the way to shell the coast, so much the worse for them; if they expended more time looking for troop transports, they would not find any because they were held back in their ports by his order. But all this is academic because the admiral did not set sail. Instead he waited for an answer to his 8 P.M. message to Paris. When none came, at 11.20 P.M. he sent another:

Before receipt of your telegram, conforming with the powers provided in my instructions I telegraphed to Bizerta and to Algiers not to let transports leave before arrival from Toulon of protection squadron. This squadron will be at Algiers during afternoon of August 4. Fleet leaves Toulon tonight and, following your order, will be on coast of Algeria to seek signalled cruisers. I regard as indispensable formation convoys to assure security of transports and am making dispositions in consequence.

At 1.30 A.M. on the 3rd, still in Toulon, Lapeyrère received a short message from Paris reporting (correctly) that the *Goeben* and the *Breslau* had arrived in Messina on the afternoon of the 2nd. That being so, the Germans could not possibly have been off Tunisia, as reported, seven and a half hours earlier. The French fleet finally set sail at 4 A.M., the C-in-C's messages still unanswered.

The fleet was now divided into three sections. By far the largest was Group A under Vice-Admiral Chocheprat, consisting of the First Squadron of battleships (six of

the pre-dreadnoughts), the First Light Division of four
armoured cruisers and twelve destoyers – a good half of
the fleet – under orders to sail to Philippeville (now
Skikda), Algeria. Group B was led by Lapeyrère in the
Courbet with the Second Squadron of five older battleships (Rear-Admiral le Bris), the Second Light Division
and various smaller ships, bound for Algiers. Group C,
made up of the elderly Reserve Division with one extra
old battleship and four destroyers, had been sent out of
Toulon ahead of the rest at 8 P.M. on the 2nd and had
reached the vicinity of the Balearic Islands. From there it
was ordered to Oran. Now all three groups were sailing
at a stately and less than urgent 11 to 12 knots, Group A
to the east, Group B in the centre and Group C to the
west, as befitted their respective destinations. All three
formations were in close order: no thought was given to
putting out screens of cruisers to reconnoitre, an elementary precaution and standard tactics in war, which was
known to be imminent. The ships of the mistress of the
sea were tiptoeing across the Mediterranean like a gaggle
of schoolgirls lost in a forest, huddled together in groups
as if for comfort in the dark.

On the afternoon of the 3rd, Lapeyrère received this
message from Admiral Milne:

Admiralty desires combination between French and British
forces. How can I best assist you? I have three battlecruisers,
four armoured cruisers, four light cruisers and sixteen
destroyers.

During the night of the 3rd to the 4th, the French C-in-C
remembered to send a reply:

I thank you for your kind message. Presently occupied in
western Mediterranean to assure passage of the troops; if
you can watch, in Adriatic, movements Italian, Austrian and

German fleets, I should be most grateful to you for it. You will be informed as soon as I have regained my freedom of movement.

The same evening Lapeyrère received a message saying that Italy had announced her neutrality; at midnight he was informed that the German ships had left Messina and were being hunted by the British. And at 1.10 on the morning of August 4 he was handed the text of a new message from Paris which had taken an incredible *five hours* to unscramble and decode:

Government has every confidence in your vigilance for assuring all possible security for troop transports. But, conforming with view of War Department, it determines that convoys should not be formed and that ships shall leave at fixed time, isolated and with all speed. You should thus consider as null and unreceived paragraphs 6 and 7 of your instructions of April 7. On request of British admiral, act in concert with him to increase security troop transports and destroy German cruisers, hostilities with Germany being now declared.

Germany, having received no further reply to its ultimatum to France, declared war with effect from 6 P.M., Central European Time, on August 3. The paragraphs of general orders referred to in the message envisaged the eventual formation of convoys but only if this did not delay the sailing of the troops, a condition which could only have been met with several days' warning. There was no time now, and for the third time in eighty hours the C-in-C had been unmistakably ordered not to do it (and at the same moment got his second order in less than thirty hours to tackle the German ships). Lapeyrère's response was to continue as before, making haste slowly and issuing no instructions. He was now quite clearly acting in contravention of his orders.

At 4.55 GMT on the morning of the 4th, soon after

first light, he was given a message to say that the Algerian
port of Bône (now Annába) had just been bombarded by
an enemy ship. Here at last was solid and immediate
information on the exact whereabouts of the Germans,
which was not adversely affected by a mistake in the
message that followed at 6.15 A.M., reporting the bombardment of Philippeville, some sixty nautical miles to
the west of Bône, and adding that the enemy *cruisers*
(note that plural) made off to the west afterwards. As the
distance between the two shelled ports was more than
twice as far as the distance the Germans could travel at
their utmost speed in the single hour between the two
bombardments, it ought to have been obvious that they
had parted company and must be more than an hour's
top-speed sailing time apart. Whether heading west, east
or even north after their attacks, at least one of the two
ships must now lie across the path of Chocheprat's Group
A, bound for Philippeville. Unfortunately Admiral
Chocheprat was still some eighty miles north of his
destination because mechanical trouble had developed on
the battleship *Mirabeau* of the First Squadron; a
destroyer, the *Carabinier*, was also playing up. Lapeyrère
allowed the pace of the bulk of the fleet (Group B as well
as Group A) to be dictated by the reduced speed of one
of his thirteen battleships and one miserable destroyer. So
at 6.35 A.M. the C-in-C cancelled his order to Chocheprat,
telling him instead to head south-west for Algiers 'as fast
as the *Mirabeau* lets you.' But the *Goeben*'s north-
westerly course from Philippeville had been a routine
feint, as a sharp observer at Cap de Fer, midway between
the two bombarded ports, saw at 6.30 A.M.: he noted a
large plume of smoke from a big ship moving *eastwards*.
This information reached Lapeyrère at 9.15 but he chose
to ignore it – it ran counter to his conviction that the
Germans must head for the west in the end. As it was,

the left wing of Group A, westward bound, appears to have passed within forty nautical miles of SMS *Goeben*, heading east, in a sea of a million square miles of water, at about 7 A.M. GMT on 4 August 1914. If Chocheprat had put out the usual cruiser screen, if his very modest average speed from Toulon had been less than two knots faster, or even if he had not been told to change course, he must have seen her on a morning offering ten miles of visibility. It was by this narrowest of margins that the bulk of the French fleet missed the first chance to attack the *Goeben*, for which, contrary to orders, it was to make no effort to search. In fact, the failure was even worse than this, as we shall see.

The diversion of Group A to Algiers followed from Lapeyrère's fixed idea that the Germans must come west. He therefore wanted to assemble the bulk of the fleet in the waters off Algiers to stop them. But it was still entirely acceptable to him that the fleet should be held down to the ridiculously low speed of its slowest component, the *Mirabeau*, which did eventually manage to work herself up to 15 knots. Hanging back to enable just two faulty ships, of no use for anything in their condition, to keep up instead of detaching them as soon as their problems became known seems at least eccentric. This extraordinary and misplaced solicitude, if such it can be called, was not the action of a man impatient to confront the enemy; as we shall see, Lapeyrère produced other reasons for his overall tardiness at an inquiry. It was just as extraordinary that no greater effort was made to involve the British in concerted action against the Germans, especially after the hard evidence of their whereabouts provided by the bombardments (and after news during the night from Paris that the British were looking for them west of Sicily following their departure from Messina). But Lepeyrère had done nothing about the

British since sending his acknowledgment to Milne, a message which airily left the entire work of policing the Mediterranean to a secondary force not yet at war, while the French fleet slowly prepared to carry out a task it had specifically been forbidden to perform. He simply left them out of his calculations.

There is a tantalizing postscript to the story of the failure of the French fleet to catch the *Goeben*, to be found in the evidence given by Troubridge to the court of inquiry and at his court-martial. On both occasions the British rear-admiral referred to his meeting with Lapeyrère on August 16 at Malta, where he placed himself under the Frenchman's command. Arguing that Milne, the British C-in-C, should have blockaded Messina, Troubridge said at the first hearing:

Others, I know, thought it. Admiral de Lapeyrère had blocked the west between Sardinia and Africa: *he himself had actually sighted the* Goeben *with his flagship with the First Division* of the French fleet. He was only an hour and a half behind her himself and *actually saw her smoke* on the horizon; this he told me [author's italics].

The French sources put the flagship *Courbet* with Group B rather than Group A, which passed very close to the Germans, as we have seen. At his trial, Troubridge added a little more detail about his discussion with Lapeyrère:

He told me that he himself, in the *Courbet* with some battleships in company, had sighted the *Goeben*'s masts and smoke at a distance of twenty-five to thirty miles from him on the morning of August 4. *He at once decided it was futile to endeavour to close her* and took measures with the fleet under his command to ensure that the other and important objectives he had been given were fulfilled [author's italics].

All this indicates that the Germans passed even closer to Group B than to Group A, which included the bulk of the fleet. Troubridge is so specific that we may conclude that Lapeyrère deliberately threw away the chance to tackle the Germans which he had explicitly been told to do. This puts the worst possible light on his conduct. On this evidence, he could have encircled them.

Later in the morning of the 4th the C-in-C decided to take the minuscule risk of increasing speed, leaving the First Division of the First Squadron, including the limping *Mirabeau*, and the Second Flotilla of destroyers, including the *Carabinier*, to follow as best they could, under Chocheprat. Group B was off Algiers at 3 P.M. and was joined by the rest of Group A a few hours later. Group C arrived at Oran the same afternoon. On the way to Algiers, Lapeyrère had ordered Chocheprat to change course again and make for Philippeville after all, to escort the transports waiting there to France with his sound ships. At 8.35 P.M. the C-in-C may have got another delayed message informing him that British ships had sighted the two German vessels north of Bône in the morning and had started to follow them (Britain was still not at war). He was to deny receiving it, however.

There is something decidedly odd about Lapeyrère's decision to head for Algiers in order to block the Germans' passage westwards (a reasonable guess at their intentions at the time the decision was made). His intelligence placed the Germans some 200 miles east of that point while he was 160 miles north of it. Given the known advantage in speed of the German warships over his own fastest major vessels, he was at least as likely to miss them as to meet them. What is more, by the time the C-in-C sent his second message to Chocheprat, ordering him to Algiers, the Germans, had they in fact been going westwards, would have had a fifty-mile start over Group A which, at the time of the bombardment, had been about the same distance away from Algiers as the faster Germans were. Most of the components of the great trap to be set off Algiers would have been a good ten hours behind the Germans had the latter been making a dash for the Atlantic at their best speed!

During the night of the 4th to the 5th, Lapeyrère was told that the British had lost touch with the Germans somewhere in the Sardinia-Sicily-Tunisia triangle (which suggested they had gone east after the bombardment). At 12.30 P.M. on the 5th, he learned that they had definitely been heading east. But the C-in-C had not been idle overnight. He had created a new formation consisting of his flagship, the *Courbet*, and two battleships from the Second Division of the First Squadron (*Condorcet* and *Vergniaud*), with light escorts, to hunt the enemy – Group D. This aggressively minded spearhead of the fleet left the waters off Algiers at 8.25 A.M. – north-*westward* bound. It was fifty miles north of Algiers, at 12.30, when the information arrived that the Germans had been heading *east* when last seen. But Lapeyrère, because he had heard that a German collier had been spotted lurking in the Spanish Balearic Islands, resolutely turned his face to the west and sailed on. Admiral Amadée Bienaimé, who led a parliamentary inquiry into the naval conduct of the opening period of the war (see chapter 7), commented: 'The chase, which in these conditions could only appear a camouflaged retreat, was to make Group D pass between Majorca and Ibiza in the night [of the 5th to 6th].' Lapeyrère was clearly still absolutely convinced that the Germans must eventually head westwards, and in fairness it must be said that he was far from alone in making this miscalculation. After dark on the 5th, meanwhile, Group A was approaching Philippeville, Group B was still off Algiers, waiting for the transports to come out to join it, and Group C was doing the same off Oran. B and C duly left in the very early hours of the 6th with their convoys; Group A limped into Philippeville at 5 A.M., left the damaged ships behind and set off again at 7.40 A.M. – solemnly escorting precisely *one* troop transport and bound for Ajaccio in Corsica. Limited by the speed of its one-sheep flock to eight knots, Group A reached Ajaccio at noon on the 7th, found two more military transports there and set off again with its final total of three charges for Toulon, which it reached at 7 A.M. on the 8th.

Group D arrived there at about the same time, considerably augmented. The *Jean Bart* and another brand-new dreadnought, the *France*, had come from Brest via Gilbraltar and joined the C-in-C north-west of Ibiza. Group B meanwhile led its convoy on a route which took it between the Balearics and the Spanish mainland, where it linked up with the C-in-C on the 7th. Lapeyrère with Group D took over the duty of escorting the transports and sent Group B back to Algiers to collect some more. They parted company at 6 P.M. But twice in the course of the 6th, Lapeyrère had been told that the *Goeben* and the *Breslau* were once again at Messina. The slow minuet of the French fleet and the convoys held up the arrival of the Army of Africa at the front by four days. Not one of the 49,000 troops and 11,800 horses conveyed in eighty-nine transports across the Mediterranean was lost; but the greatest danger to which they had been exposed was boredom. On the way to Toulon, the following message reached the C-in-C at half past midnight on the morning of the 8th:

Cease immediately all escort of troop transports. Reserve Division and Special Division alone will be charged with watching. Gather all the rest of the fleet as soon as possible at Bizerta, having completed with coal. Your mission is to join your efforts to those of the British fleet to prevent Austrian squadron forcing Dardanelles and entering the Black Sea, but you will intervene with force only if the Austrians try to get through it.

As the French fleet was not ready to move coherently again until August 10, the day Souchon left the Mediterranean by its eastern exit, it passes out of this part of the story. The foregoing account of its conduct may be held to speak for itself, but before turning to the actions of the British Mediterranean Fleet we may consider some of the things the French did not do, without lapsing too deeply into unfair hindsight.

The announcement of impending general mobilization on the afternoon of August 1 by a reluctant French government should have galvanized Lapeyrère into putting to sea at once. There could have been no clearer indication of the imminence of war and the entire strategy of the fleet was based on seizing mastery of the Mediterranean in the opening days, recognized as the best means of protecting the troopships. He should also have set up a close watch of the channel between Sardinia and Tunisia – half a dozen light vessels would have sufficed to watch a waterway through which any westbound ship was obliged to pass – immediately. The C-in-C appears to have thought of this, for on July 31, when the Second Submarine Flotilla of six boats was sent to Bizerta to collect torpedoes, he asked Paris if he could also send the Reserve Division there with its light escorts. This was refused on the grounds of the 'need' to keep the forces of the navy concentrated. But as a last resort he had the submarines, which could have watched the channel, at least in the good weather then prevailing. Correctly anticipating a German move against the troopships or their embarkation ports, and aware since July 31 at the latest that Souchon was coming out of the Adriatic, implying an eventual westward course, Lapeyrère would have lost nothing by an early move at high speed towards the Adriatic on the 1st; he knew then that all three of his potential enemies, including the two German ships that suddenly loomed so large in his thoughts, were east of Sardinia. He cannot be blamed for his obvious uncertainty about British intentions, despite Milne's friendly message, because they were a mystery for everybody until late on August 4, when it became known that Britain would be at war with Germany from midnight GMT that night. The French C-in-C cannot be especially blamed for not envisaging the possibility that Souchon's ultimate plan was to make for the Dardanelles because nobody else on the Allied side did so until it was too late. But he should have concerted his actions with the British from the 5th onwards because he knew that the conditions under which the French would have overall command in the Mediterranean existed: the ten capital ships the British had there when the February 1913 Naval Agreement was concluded, capable of tackling the Austrians on their own, had been whittled down to three in order to reinforce the North Sea. The fact that Milne outranked him might have been temporarily embarrassing but could hardly override an international agreement. The idea that the Germans might be his first problem was not new to Lapeyrère either, because the May 1914 fleet manoeuvres had as their theme the tactics to be used in preventing them getting at the troop transports!

There was one other curious incident in Paris of which the C-in-C could not have known. On August 3, as the Ministry of Marine tried to pull itself together after the upheaval of losing its minister, it passed a message to the Admiralty staff for transmission to Lapeyrère. It contained the simple order: 'Attack with your armament any German ship.' But President Poincaré, not the man to feel constrained by the purely symbolic nature of his office in a country where the Prime Minister was head of government, happened to be there and stopped it being sent. In view of subsequent events at sea it is unlikely that this message would have changed Lapeyrère's conduct. But Poincaré's action on the afternoon of the 3rd reflected government concern to ensure that Germany, not France, would clearly be seen as the aggressor. France could not risk firing the first shot. The government was as hesitant as its admiral.

The French admiralissimo, as the British called him, was, however, clearly guilty of delay, disobedience and disregard of elementary strategic and tactical requirements. It is a terrible irony that the famous French élan, dash in attack summed up by the old motto '*courir sus à l'ennemi*' (charge at the foe), was missing in the navy, which was so well placed to indulge in it, but not in the army of 1914, which rushed up in close order and brightly coloured uniforms to be scythed down by German machine guns. The navy chose to skulk. Admiral Bien-aimé said of Lapeyrère's conduct:

When one assumes responsibilities going as far as formal disobedience to orders received, one has no excuse but in success. But the facts have shown that it is precisely because he did not execute them that the German cruisers were able to escape.

He missed a priceless opportunity of inflicting an early defeat on German arms at the very start of the war. But he was not the only one to do so.

4

Admiral Milne and the British Mediterranean Fleet

ADMIRALTY [LONDON] TO C-IN-C
[MEDITERRANEAN]
[Time of origin] 3.10 P.M. [30 July 1914] Received 8 P.M.

Should war break out and England and France engage in it, it now seems probable that Italy will remain neutral and that Greece can be made an ally. Spain also will be friendly and, possibly, an ally. The attitude of Italy is, however, uncertain, and it is especially important that your squadron should not be seriously engaged with Austrian ships before we know what Italy will do. Your first task should be to aid the French in the transportation of their African Army by covering, and, if possible, bringing to action individual fast German ships, particularly *Goeben* who [sic] may interfere with that transportation. *You will be notified by telegraph when you may consult with the French admiral.* Do not at this stage be brought to action against superior forces, *except in combination with the French, as part of a general battle. The speed of your squadrons is sufficient to enable you to choose your moment.* We shall hope later to reinforce the Mediterranean, and you must husband your forces at the outset [author's emphasis].

This message reached Admiral Sir Berkeley Milne, the British Commander-in-Chief in the Mediterranean, aboard his flagship, the battlecruiser HMS *Inflexible*, at Valetta, Malta, where the fleet had been ordered to concentrate in preparation for war. The First Lord of the Admiralty, Mr Churchill, that acknowledged master of the English language (and also a minister who poked his nose into everything going on in his department), had a decisive hand in drafting it. It is quoted in full here because it was to assume a disproportionate and central role when the time came for the Royal Navy to examine its failure to catch the German ships in the Mediterranean. One does not look for literary quality in a naval signal but only for clarity: the old adage about 'clear thoughts clearly expressed' translates into military terms on the lines of 'clear strategy clearly ordered.' In these terms this crucial text is both curious and an interesting subject for the linguistic analyst: it is not difficult to imagine it being used in an English language examination (or a test for naval officers) followed by the dread word, 'discuss'. What was made of it will become clear later, particularly in chapter 9, but a few points may usefully be made here. The first is its sheer prolixity, given the difficulties of transmission at the time – the use of morse code and cipher and the need constantly to repeat messages to ensure they got through in those early days of wireless, the atmospherics, the garbles and the like. It was of itself an important message regardless of its later role, which justifies the use of flowing language rather than the cablese which was already much in favour to save words and therefore time and money. Nonetheless it is full of unnecessary words and repetitions. The opening lines could be boiled down to the following: 'If England and France go to war, Greece and perhaps Spain could become allies. Italy will probably be neutral but until this is known avoid major engagement with Austrian ships' – thirty words for sixty-seven and also a great saving on treacherous punctuation! To point this out is not to quibble: it cannot be denied that the formulation and transmission of orders is one of the main tasks of the staffs of the armed services. So far the message is merely verbose. But the central sentence ('Your first task . . .') is carelessly drafted, raising all manner of questions. Is the admiral not to engage German ships unless they are both 'individual' and fast *and* interfering with the French troop transports? Is he not to cover them if they, there being only two anyway, are sailing together? The last part of the signal ('Do not at this stage . . .' to the end) appears to tell the admiral both that he may join the French in a general action and that he should maintain the strength of his forces, two instructions which could without distortion be seen as potentially irreconcilable. Lastly it should be noted that the phrase 'superior forces' is not defined.

Churchill later wrote of this text (in *The World Crisis*): 'So far as the English language may serve as a vehicle of thought, the words employed appear to express the intentions we [the First Sea Lord and himself] had formed.' In that case it would be interesting to know why he made so many alterations to the above text (taken from contemporary Admiralty records) in the process of reproducing it in his book. He reconstructed three sentences, tidied up the punctuation and changed '*Goeben* who' to '*Goeben* which'. The reordered sentences he quoted as follows:

It now seems probable should war break out and England and France engage in it, that Italy will remain neutral and that Greece can be made an ally . . . Except in combination with the French as part of a general battle, do not at this stage be brought to action against superior forces . . . You must husband your forces at the outset and we shall hope later to reinforce the Mediterranean.

These changes certainly make the signal read better and do not alter the meaning; but there is one clear change of emphasis, resulting from the transposition of clauses in the second of the three sentences he altered. The instruction 'do not at this stage be brought to action against superior forces' loses some of its own force by being tucked behind the adverbial phrase qualifying it. One cannot make a federal case out of this, as an American might say; but the comment of the great American historian of the Royal Navy, Arthur J. Marder, on *The World Crisis*, made in a footnote to his brief account of the *Goeben* affair, is worth quoting here: 'I wish I could remember who it was that said of this history of the war (with all its self-justification and errors of fact an indispensable source), "Winston has written an enormous book about himself and called it *The World Crisis*"!'

Before returning to the events at sea we may note that Milne read this order as meaning that the protection of the French transports should be his absolute priority; and that he passed on the gist of the rest of the message to his second-in-command, Rear-Admiral Ernest Troubridge, flag officer of the First Cruiser Squadron, in the following form:

The Admiralty have informed me that, should we become engaged in war, it will be important at first to husband the naval force in the Mediterranean and, in the earlier stages, I am to avoid being brought to action against superior force. *You are to be guided by this should war be declared* [author's italics].

This quotation is taken from the contemporary Admiralty record of Milne's written sailing orders to Troubridge at Malta of 2 August 1914.

Milne's own standing instructions from the Admiralty were contained in War Orders No. 2 for the C-in-C, Mediterranean, sent to him on 1 May 1913 in the light of the naval agreement with France of the preceding February. These mentioned the issue of a common signal-book to aid communication between British and French ships, to be kept sealed in 'Secret Package A'. If in a period of tension that could lead to war joint Anglo-French action were to be decided, the admiral would be sent a cipher telegram. A further such signal would be sent to order the actual opening of hostilities alongside the French.

On 27 July 1914 Milne was at Alexandria on the coast of Egypt with most of his fleet as part of a general cruising programme. One battlecruiser and a handful of smaller ships were at Malta for maintenance. Troubridge was at Durrazzo with his flagship, the armoured cruiser *Defence*, and a destroyer, as part of the international squadron watching Albania. In the late afternoon Milne received a signal which was not the official warning telegram of imminent war between the Triple Alliance and the Triple Entente but might just as well have been, ordering him to return to Malta at normal speed to fill up with coal and stores and to warn Troubridge. Milne set sail the next morning and reached Malta on the morning of the 29th; late that evening the official warning telegram arrived and Milne recalled Troubridge to join him. The dockyard at the main British naval base in the Mediterranean became a scene of unprecedented activity as one ship after another took on coal and supplies, last-minute running repairs were completed, ammunition loaded and 'luxury' items not required in wartime taken ashore. Milne's reply on July 31 to the signal quoted at the beginning of this chapter made the point that efforts to protect commerce would endanger individual warships, and therefore that he proposed to keep the entire fleet at Malta, ready to assist the French fleet to protect the troop transports. But he decided to detach the light cruiser *Chatham* to watch the southern entrance of the Strait of Messina, between Italy and Sicily (an obvious port of call for any Austrian, German or Italian ship coming from the Adriatic). By the afternoon of Saturday, August 1, the fleet was ready for sea. Late that evening it became known that the *Goeben* and the *Breslau* had been at Brindisi taking coal.

On the afternoon of Sunday the Admiralty sent this order to Milne:

Goeben must be shadowed by two battlecruisers. Approach to Adriatic must be watched by cruisers and destroyers. Remain near Malta yourself. It is believed that Italy will remain neutral, but you cannot yet count absolutely on this.

The German ships, having spent the night of July 31 to August 1 at Brindisi, on the eastern or Adriatic side of the 'heel' of Italy, moved on to Taranto on the inner, western side of the heel and a British consular officer reported their arrival to London on the afternoon of the 2nd. The *Goeben* in particular, with her high fuel consumption, was anxious to accumulate coal wherever possible.

HMS *Chatham*, one of Milne's four light cruisers, moved out of Valletta on the Sunday afternoon on her special task of checking the Strait of Messina. After dark Troubridge took the bulk of the British fleet to sea to watch the mouth of the Adriatic. In addition to three of the four armoured cruisers of his own squadron, the light cruiser *Gloucester* and eight destroyers, he also had under his command for the time being the battlecruisers *Indomitable* and *Indefatigable*. These had been assigned the task of shadowing the *Goeben*. On the same evening the Admiralty put out a message to all relevant British naval commanders round the world, including the C-in-C Mediterranean, which ordered:

You can enter into communication with the French Senior Naval Officer on your station for combined action in case Great Britain should decide to become ally of France against Germany. Situation very critical. Be prepared to meet surprise attacks.

Milne reacted with typical, time-consuming caution:

At present I have no cipher in which to communicate with French admiral, can contents of Secret Package A be used as cipher?

This should have been obvious from his general orders mentioned above, but he waited passively for a reply which took more than twelve hours to arrive and was in the affirmative. It was thus only on the afternoon of the 3rd, getting on for twenty-four hours after the order to contact the French had been issued, that Milne sent his friendly message to Lapeyrère, who at that stage would have been some 150 miles south of Toulon. The French admiral's reply, however, never reached Milne, who therefore decided that evening to send the light cruiser *Dublin* (Captain John Kelly) to the French naval station at Bizerta with a *letter* offering cooperation!

As the *Chatham* and the reinforced Troubridge set off on their respective missions on the evening of the 2nd, another query from Milne reached London. If the German ships left the Adriatic, he wanted to know, should those of Troubridge's ships not assigned to shadowing them maintain watch on the mouth of the Adriatic, or should they be brought back to rejoin the residue of the fleet to help carry out the order of July 30 on assisting the French troop transport operation? Churchill wrote the reply in the early hours of the 3rd:

Watch on mouth of Adriatic should be maintained, *but* Goeben *is your objective*. Follow her and shadow her wherever she goes and be ready to act on declaration of war, which appears probable and imminent. Acknowledge [author's italics].

The Strait of Messina which the *Chatham* was now approaching from the south lies between the south-western extremity, or 'toe', of Italy, and the north-eastern

tip of the great island of Sicily. The port of Messina lies
on the western or Sicilian side of the Strait, a few miles
south of the narrowest, northernmost part of it – the
Scylla and Charybdis of Homer's *Odyssey* – which is
barely two miles wide. The merest glance at a map shows
that a ship at Messina, which the *Goeben* and the *Breslau*
reached on the afternoon of August 2, would proceed
northwards out of the Strait if she intended to head
westwards across the Mediterranean, and southwards if
she wanted to enter the sea's eastern basin: the shape
and size of Sicily impose this logic. The *Chatham* duly
passed right through the Strait in daylight on the morning
of August 3, checking the port of Messina on the way
and seeing nothing of interest. She was about six hours
too late to sight the German ships. They had turned left,
or north, on leaving the harbour, which meant they were
currently headed westwards across the Mediterranean.
Milne was told in the early hours of the 3rd that they had
been located at Messina and passed the news on to
Troubridge, who immediately asked whether he should
go ahead with the watch on the Adriatic. Milne replied:
'Yes, but *Goeben* is primary consideration.' Troubridge,
now off south-eastern Sicily, then asked: 'Shall I send
battle cruisers to westward of Sicily passing by south of
Sicily?' Once again Milne was cautious: 'Should delay
until you get authentic news of the *Goeben*.' When
Chatham reported at about 7 A.M. on the 3rd that the
German ships were not at Messina, Milne took barely
half an hour to order her to sail westwards along the
northern coast of Sicily, and then to tell Troubridge to
leave the light cruiser *Gloucester* and his eight destroyers
to mount the watch on the Adriatic and proceed with his
heavier ships, including the two battlecruisers, westwards
along the south coast of Sicily. It must be said at this
juncture that these dispositions were absolutely correct

and in full conformity with the flow of orders from London. Milne was not only right but also entirely logical in guessing that the German ships were heading west; he did not know what the French were doing but knew they must be a long way to the west; and he had sent the bulk of his firepower after the Germans. With any luck he would trap Souchon between the French fleet and his own. Even his afterthought at lunchtime on the 3rd, which led him to order Troubridge to take the three armoured cruisers he had with him and join the light forces in covering the Adriatic, leaving the faster battle-cruisers to press on westwards unaccompanied, made no difference to the strategic position at this stage of the chase: the pursuing force outgunned the Germans by a large margin and need no longer be held back by the lumbering heavy cruisers, which could barely manage 20 knots. The fourth of this type and four more destroyers were sent from Malta in the evening to join Troubridge. Milne kept his flagship, *Inflexible*, the third battlecruiser, as well as the light cruiser *Weymouth* and the last four destroyers at Malta in reserve. The same evening, the Admiralty ordered Milne to send the two already westward-bound battlecruisers at high speed to Gibraltar. He did so, at the same time ordering *Chatham* to turn back and rejoin Troubridge. The Admiralty obviously assumed that the Germans would attempt to break out into the Atlantic, and the Gibraltar naval station had been ordered to patrol the Strait with destroyers. The two detached battlecruisers, *Indomitable* (Captain Francis Kennedy) and *Indefatigable* (Captain Charles Sowerby) stepped up their speed from 14 to 22 knots on receiving the order to make for Gibraltar; Kennedy, higher on the captains' list, was in command. Fortune thus placed them due north of Bône at 9.32 A.M. GMT on August 4, when a lookout on the *Indomitable* reported a light cruiser on the starboard bow, heading east at high speed. Two minutes later, another lookout reported a capital ship on the port bow, to the south, also steering eastwards at high speed.

The electrifying message from Kennedy went out to Milne at 9.46 when the two ships had been identified beyond doubt:

Indomitable to C-in-C. Enemy in sight in latitude 37°44' north, 7°56' east, steering east, consisting of *Goeben* and *Breslau*.

But the signal was inaccurate in one important respect: the Germans were not, as yet, the enemy. The explanation for that frustrating and inhibiting fact lay in London, as the *Goeben* lay across the sights of sixteen mighty 12-inch guns, at the optimum range of less than 10,000 yards.

That the Admiralty had been firing off streams of messages into the ether for several days suggests that Britain had already decisively changed gear from 'if' to 'when' in its preparations to enter the war. If the actions of the navy alone are studied, the impression is fully understandable. By an extraordinary stroke of luck the bulk of the Royal Navy was off Portland on July 26 at the end of extensive manoeuvres and mobilization practice, planned long before the crisis between Austria and Serbia blew up, as it now did. The ships' crews were up to full wartime strength but the fleet was due to disperse on the morning of the 27th. Churchill, the First Lord, and Battenberg, the First Sea Lord, told the ships to stay put. The value of the measure was exploited by releasing it to the press, which ensured that it prompted sobering thoughts in the chancelleries of a Europe on the brink of continental conflict. The next move, no less important, was to order the Grand Fleet to its war stations at Scapa Flow in the Orkney Islands and on the east coast of Scotland on the 28th. The line of grey steel eighteen miles long passed through the Channel on the 29th, heading north at speed, leaving the Channel Fleet on full alert in its wake. Any plan for a surprise attack by the German High Seas Fleet in the North Sea had been foiled in advance and the Royal Navy was in position to operate the strategy of 'distant blockage' of Germany upon which the Admiralty had finally pinned its faith. Churchill then persuaded Asquith, the Prime Minister, to let him send the official warning telegram.

None of this meant that the British government as a whole was ready to declare war or was even in favour of doing so in response to the increasingly urgent and angry pleas for a decision from M. Paul Cambon, the French Ambassador. The cabinet was split between peace and war parties, and the neutralist tendency had a two-to-one majority. Asquith, Grey (Foreign Secretary) and Churchill were among the minority. Further, the government was distracted by the Irish Home Rule crisis and the threat of mutiny over Ulster by the army officers stationed at the Curragh, all of which had served to relegate the European war scare to second place on the main news pages of the papers. As Britain was a co-guarantor of the integrity of Belgium, Grey artfully sent telegrams to Berlin and Paris on July 31 asking for assurances that both would respect Belgian neutrality. The French gave theirs at once; the Germans did not reply (their strategy for a two-front war being to strike overwhelmingly at France through Belgium to knock out the French before concentrating against the Russians – the Schlieffen Plan). At the cabinet meeting on August 1, vacillation continued to rule. Four ministers threatened to resign when Grey sought support for honouring the naval agreement with the French by covering their Channel and Atlantic coasts, denuded for the sake of the Mediterranean. Churchill was overruled when he demanded mobilization of all naval reserves. Asquith's main concern was to keep the cabinet together on whatever decision was finally taken, to avoid a damaging public row which might affect recruiting to the all-volunteer army and navy in the event of war. That night it was learned that Germany had declared war on Russia, France's ally. Grey promised Cambon that the Channel would be closed to the German fleet, come what may, and Churchill called up the naval reserves, both without cabinet approval. The one issue that would now produce a solid cabinet majority in favour of war was Belgium. On the evening of Sunday, August 2, the Germans gave the Belgians twelve hours to agree to the passage of the German Army through their territory to the French frontier. At the end of the twelve hours, on the morning of the 3rd, the Belgians said no, and King Albert took personal charge of bracing his small country for the almighty blow from the world's greatest military power. It was the Bank Holiday weekend which the retired First Sea Lord, Fisher, had predicted would bring war, but the cabinet stayed in London for one meeting after another. On Sunday, at the cost of two resignations, it reluctantly and retroactively underwrote the naval measures taken without its authority the previous day; on the Monday (the 3rd) the news of Belgium's defiance burst upon another session. In the unbearable tension, two more ministers (temporarily) resigned but Lloyd George, the Chancellor of the Exchequer and the rising star in the government, who had been sitting on the fence, came down on the side of the war group. It fell to Grey, not the world's most convincing orator, to make the all-important statement in the House of Commons. He began by revealing the naval arrangements with France but centred his argument on Belgium, a British invention, and the danger of one-power domination of the continent. The House cheered him to the echo. Stilted speaker or no, later that evening, after Germany had declared war on France, Grey made the portentous remark for which he is now best remembered: 'The lamps are going out all over Europe; we shall not see them lit again in our lifetime.' It was not to be very long before they went out in the Near and Middle East as well.

The Germans marched over the Belgian border on the morning of August 4. At noon King Albert appealed to Belgium's other guarantors for help. Britain then at last issued its ultimatum to Germany demanding withdrawal from Belgium, in the absence of which a state of war would exist between the British and the German empires from midnight that night (GMT), the 4th.

In the Mediterranean Admiral Milne, having paused only to order HMS *Dublin*, the nearest available reinforcement, to leave Bizerta and rush to join the two battle-cruisers, now signalled the Admiralty at 10 A.M. GMT that they had found the German ships and were shadowing them. Unfortunately he forgot to add that the Germans and their pursuers were steaming *east*. Churchill's reply was staccato but still managed to reveal his jubilation: 'Very good. Hold her. War imminent.' (The 'her' was of course the *Goeben*.) He then sent hastily scribbled notes to Asquith and Grey asking permission to add to the brief message while it was being transmitted again and again, the order: 'If *Goeben* attacks French transports, you should at once engage her. You should give her fair warning of this beforehand.' This was sent fifty

minutes later. But the cabinet, meeting shortly afterwards, overruled this decision, and at 2.05 P.M. the
Admiralty wirelessed to all ships:

The British ultimatum to Germany will expire at midnight GMT
August 4. No act of war should be committed before that hour,
at which time the telegram to commence hostilities against
Germany will be dispatched from the Admiralty.
    Special addition to Mediterranean, *Indomitable*, *Indefati-
gable*. This cancels the authorization to *Indomitable* and *Indefatigable* to engage *Goeben* if she attacks French transports.

It was galling; it was appalling; it was impeccably correct.
'At the Admiralty we suffered the tortures of Tantalus,'
wrote Churchill. But so long as the faintest hope of
avoiding war remained, the cabinet had no choice but to
adhere to the terms of the ultimatum. In any event,
the Germans had no intention of attacking the French
troopships; they had made their demonstration on the
Algerian coast (as the British at sea and in London
now knew) and had other plans. To add to Milne's
preoccupations as he waited to hear from the pursuing
battlecruisers, he received another signal which was to
prove profoundly important:

The Italian government have declared neutrality. You are to
respect this neutrality rigidly and should not allow any of HM
ships to come within six miles of the Italian coast.

When the *Indomitable* sighted the *Goeben* on her port
bow, the distance between them was estimated aboard
the British ship to be 17,000 yards. The German vessel
'was cleared for action but her guns were laid fore and
aft,' Captain Kennedy reported a few days later. Her
speed was about 20 knots, and at this stage the two ships
were travelling in opposite directions, so that when the
Goeben turned to port she appeared to be deliberately

closing the gap or even preparing to cross the British bows. The *Indomitable*, the lead ship, turned a little to starboard and the *Goeben* a little further to port, so that the two ships passed at a distance the British calculated at 8,000 yards. The German guns did not move; the British broadside was trained on her and followed her movement. Now both British battlecruisers began a gradual turn to port at speed until they fell in astern of the *Goeben* in parallel, keeping at a distance of 7,000 to 11,000 yards as the German ship settled on a due easterly course. The *Breslau* meanwhile had turned north and was lost to view at about 10.30 A.M. GMT. Three hours later she rejoined her flagship as the chase continued. The *Dublin* appeared at 2 P.M. and Kennedy ordered her to take a position on the starboard beam of the *Goeben* but out of range of her guns.

Even in these conditions of acute tension, after hours at action stations, British sangfroid and hallowed tradition were not lightly to be cast aside. 'Sent hands to tea,' wrote Kennedy laconically, 'and *Indefatigable* to go to tea after us.' But as the light refreshments were being digested by those who had the time to consume them (which did not include the stokers and others below decks as they tried to coax more speed from the engines), the Germans began to pull away noticeably. By 3 P.M. GMT the *Goeben* could only just be discerned from the *Indomitable*, although the newer and larger *Indefatigable* and also the outrider *Dublin* were still keeping up. Not only did the British ships all have a lower design speed than the German; the battlecruisers' crews were not up to wartime strength, particularly below decks, where each was ninety men short. The *Indomitable* had just begun her annual refit at Malta when the emergency caused it to be cancelled. The boilers of both battlecruisers failed to perform at peak efficiency. First the *Indomitable* (at 3.35

P.M.) and shortly afterwards the *Indefatigable* lost sight of
the Germans altogether and the light cruiser *Dublin*
became their eyes, reporting the Germans' adjustments
of course so that the battlecruisers could change theirs. A
little over two hours later, however, the *Dublin* too lost
sight of the fleeing Germans in a light fog which had
come down as they approached the waters off the north-
western tip of Sicily. Milne recalled all three ships westwards, then southwards, in case the Germans doubled
back. Like the French, he knew that a German collier
was waiting at Palma, Majorca, in the Balearics, and he
remained convinced that the Germans must make for the
west in the end. The fact that he also knew Souchon had
found colliers at Brindisi, Taranto and Messina and might
have others to draw upon did not occur to him. The three
frustrated hunters eventually linked up with Milne and
his flagship off the island of Pantelleria south and a little
west of the western end of Sicily, at 10 A.M. GMT on
August 5. Milne had been in the channel between Malta
and Sicily when the order to open hostilities against
Germany reached him just after midnight GMT and
headed north to meet them. He was now placed to block
the most likely route west to the Germans, the channel
between Sardinia and Tunisia; with this in mind he chose
Bizerta as the port to which to send the *Indomitable* to
refill with coal, accompanied by three destroyers. The
Dublin was sent to Malta to refuel, with orders to join
Troubridge, still covering the Adriatic. Troubridge, in
response to an order from Milne, had detached the
Gloucester (Captain Howard Kelly, brother of the
Dublin's commander) to watch the Strait of Messina from
the south. As the light cruiser arrived at the southern end
of the funnel of water leading into the Strait at 4 A.M. on
the 5th, SMS *Breslau* had just entered it from the north.
Shortly after 5 A.M. unbeknown for the time being to the

—

British, both German ships were beginning their second visit to the port of Messina in less than three days. *Gloucester* could get no nearer to the harbour than about ten miles: to go any closer would have meant coming within six miles of the shore on one side or the other of the narrowing Strait, and like all other British ships she was under orders not to do that. The Germans, who also knew of Italy's decision to remain neutral, showed no such delicacy. But the British cruiser was the first to report the Germans' whereabouts. Her wireless operators picked up powerful signals and divined the truth, ten hours after she took up station. Her alert, however, got through to the *Inflexible* nearly half an hour later than a message to the same effect from the British consulate at Reggio di Calabria, opposite Messina on the Italian mainland. In Italy generally the news spread very swiftly. The British Embassy in Rome was tipped off by what must have been an excellent bush telegraph system at about 10 A.M. GMT on the 5th, with a story which prompted it to send this unusual message to the Foreign Office (unfortunately it took seven hours to get through):

Following sent to Consul at Messina: 'Urgent. Have learnt privately that German ship *Breslau* is attempting to procure coal from British collier at Messina. Captain should be warned to supply no coal to belligerent. If force being used protest to local authorities.'

Leaving the *Gloucester* to her lonely patrol, Milne decided on the afternoon of the 5th to take all his ships in company to the waters off Bizerta, warning the French admiral there of his approach, and that four of his ships would need coal. After these were in harbour, Milne during the night began to patrol northwards with the rest, back towards Sicily, as the messages placing the Germans in Messina came in from several sources. At 6.30 A.M. on the 6th he reached the north-western tip of Sicily and turned east for a slow sweep along the northern coast of the island in case the Germans returned westwards. Having heard nothing new all day about them, he decided in the afternoon to block the northern exit of the Strait of Messina and picked up speed, sending his two light cruisers, *Chatham* and *Weymouth*, ahead, and following with his two battlecruisers. The third, *Indomitable*, was still stuck in Bizerta, having wasted twelve hours while Captain Kennedy sought permission to requisition coal from colliers – a good example of lack of initiative of the kind described in chapter 2. Admiral Milne had now made his first major error. Disposing of sufficient forces to be able to block both exits from the Strait of Messina with combinations of ships each of which would have been superior in firepower to the Germans (he could have asked Troubridge to send reinforcements), he allowed his *idée fixe* that Souchon must go west to commit him to the northern exit, leaving just one light cruiser at the other end.

At ten minutes past five in the afternoon, Greenwich Mean Time, His Majesty's Ship *Gloucester* signalled urgently that the *Goeben* had come out of Messina towards her, 'steering east'.

Admiral Troubridge and the
British First Cruiser Squadron

The solitary vessel which now took up the chase of the
Goeben with zest and skill was less than well equipped
for the task. The *Gloucester* had a design speed of 25
knots (three slower than the *Goeben*'s escort, the *Breslau*,
which was very similar in dimensions), but had surpassed
this by more than one knot on her trials, in 1911. Her
armour was negligible and her most formidable armament
was two 6-inch guns sited fore and aft; she also had ten 4-
inch guns (five on either side) and two 18-inch torpedo
tubes. She displaced 4,800 tons and carried a crew of 376
men.

In the course of her patrol in the southern approaches
to the Strait of Messina on August 6, she began in the
early evening to make a pass northwards as if to sail
through. At 5 P.M. GMT, when she was making 12 knots
at a point some fourteen miles south-west of the nearest
part of the Italian mainland, she saw the *Goeben* coming
out of the Strait, passing along the Italian shore and less
than three miles out (so within Italian territorial waters).
Ten minutes later, as the alert was being signalled to the
British fleet, the *Breslau* appeared, following her flagship
at a distance of about two miles. The *Gloucester* accelerated to 23 knots and turned to starboard so as to bring
herself on a parallel course with the *Goeben* but 16,000
to 18,000 yards off, on the edge of the enemy ship's gun
range. The British light cruiser stayed abreast as the
Germans, still sticking close to the shore, steamed round
the toe of Italy in the fading light, into which their ships,
with the land behind them, gradually merged, so that by

6 P.M. they could no longer be made out. This did not prevent Captain Howard Kelly from confidently predicting to his C-in-C by wireless that the *Goeben* would round Cape Spartivento, on the south-eastern extremity of the Italian toe, at 6.20 P.M.. The all-important wireless office was in the hands of an extremely competent chief operator, Petty Officer Telegraphist Theodore Perrow, who saw to it that none of the long series of crisp messages to Milne and Troubridge, amounting to a running commentary on the pursuit, took longer than fifteen minutes to get through.

By the time Milne got the *Gloucester*'s triumphant view halloo at 5.10 P.M. he had reached a point roughly one third along the length of the northern coast of Sicily from its western end. His reaction was to abandon his idea of blocking the northern exit of the Strait of Messina and to turn *west*, taking the long way round Sicily. The shortest route for following the Germans would have taken him through the Strait of Messina which, as has been noted, was only two miles wide at its narrowest point: but he was still under orders not to go within six miles of the Italian coast. Notwithstanding the fact that the Germans had not allowed themselves to be put off by such considerations, he obeyed. He was also still absolutely convinced that the Germans must eventually come west, whatever they might be up to in the Ionian Sea for the moment. But if this were not to be the case, by taking the long way round Sicily he had added considerably to the distance he would have to cover to support the *Gloucester* if the chase did continue eastwards. That, however, was not his immediate intention. As he wrote in his special report to the Admiralty about the chase:

The reports [from *Gloucester*] which followed [her first signal] showed that *Goeben* and *Breslau* intended to go eastward, so the battlecruisers returned to Malta, arriving about noon on August 7 and completing with coal with all despatch in order to continue the chase.

There is an interesting puzzle here. Captain John Creswell, RN, who made a special study of the chase of the *Goeben* and wrote and lectured about it between the wars, calculated after close examination of ships' logs and other records that all three battlecruisers at this stage, including the *Indomitable* which had been sent to Bizerta, had enough coal in their bunkers to be able to get to the eastern end of the Mediterranean and back, even at high speed. Creswell, as quoted by Marder, observed:

If he [Milne] followed up hard he would only be a few hours astern. But throughout the period he seems to have been obsessed by *Goeben*'s superior speed as displayed on August 4 and considered that mere chasing was out of the question . . . But the fact remains that you will never catch a ship if you don't chase her, and that it is only by making the utmost use of every second of time available that one can hope to bring an unwilling enemy to action.

As it was, Milne took a leisurely seventeen hours from his about-turn north of Sicily to get to Malta, a distance of around 250 miles which he covered at an average speed of under 15 knots. He linked up with *Indomitable* and the three destroyers, which had been in Bizerta, at Valletta. On his way, long after it had ceased to be relevant, Milne received just before 10 A.M. on the 6th a message from the Admiralty which had been sent for transmission three hours earlier: 'If *Goeben* goes south from Messina, you should follow through the Straits, irrespective of territorial waters.' If Milne was slow, he was not alone in this failing. But HMS *Dublin*, the light cruiser commanded by Captain Howard Kelly's brother, John, and two destroyers, the *Beagle* and the *Bulldog*, had left Malta at 2 P.M. on the 6th to join Troubridge in the Adriatic. As Milne headed south that evening he signalled to *Dublin*:

Get position, course and speed of *Goeben* from *Gloucester*. If possible sink him [sic] tonight.

Having got this information from his brother, Captain John Kelly saw that he could not hope to catch up with the Germans until mid-morning the next day if they stayed on the same course. But, on the basis of never knowing what might turn up, he at least showed the proper sense of urgency and ordered full speed ahead.

Back aboard the *Gloucester* meanwhile, Captain Howard Kelly, having lost sight of the Germans in the gloom and fearing that they might double back in the shadow of the land, turned in towards the coast himself at 26 knots. Engineer-Commander Malcolm Johnson and his men below decks had managed by working to their utmost to surpass the ship's official maximum performance. The moon was due to rise at 6.45 P.M. GMT, and Kelly wanted to place his ship between the *Goeben* and the land so that his ship and her smoke would be obscured while the *Goeben* and hers would become clearly visible to him in the moonlight, with the sea as background. The manoeuvre carried the risk, if the Germans were indeed doubling back, of propelling the little cruiser well into the range of the big ship's guns. But Souchon was still on course for the entrance to the Adriatic, now steering north-east, and the *Gloucester*'s pass across his wake had the desired effect of bringing him back into view, at 7 P.M. Doubtless feeling relieved, Kelly settled down to following the *Goeben* from a position between her wake and the land to take advantage of the moon. Just over an hour later, however, the *Breslau*, astern of the *Goeben*, tried the same trick and headed westwards towards the land. *Gloucester* countered the move by doing the same, until she began to run out of sea-room. The *Goeben* meanwhile was pulling away. As she was Kelly's objective, he went up to full speed again and changed course towards the battlecruiser. The *Breslau* now altered her course to the eastward to cross the bow of the *Gloucester*. The two light cruisers were now heading full tilt towards each other at a combined approach speed in excess of 50 knots. Kelly shifted slightly to port to put himself between the *Breslau* and the land, to have the advantage of the moon in the event of a fight. His men were at action stations, the guns loaded and aimed, as the two vessels passed one another at a range of between 3,000 and 4,000 yards. Always mindful of his true objective, Kelly decided not to open fire unless fired upon, but the *Breslau* passed in silence, eventually sailing out of sight to the south-east. The *Gloucester* once again settled down to following the *Goeben*, now steaming at between 17 and 21 knots, her course north-easterly in the direction of the Adriatic. But shortly after 9.30 P.M. she made a major alteration to starboard and the south-east, away from the Adriatic. At 9.46, *Gloucester* signalled: 'Urgent. *Goeben* altering course to southward.'

If Souchon stayed on this new course for any length of time, he would place himself within striking distance of the *Dublin* and a night torpedo attack, as both the Captains Kelly quickly realized with some relish. John Kelly now calculated on sighting both German ships, which he guessed were intent on joining up again, at half past midnight GMT on the morning of August 7.

He put his two destroyers, *Beagle* and *Bulldog*, in line ahead on his starboard side and a little astern of his light cruiser. Both smaller ships were 'flaming' – their funnels

exuding showers of sparks and flame in the effort to catch
up with the Germans, a fact which made the small
pursuing group exceptionally visible at night. Kelly tried
a small reduction in speed but when this made no appreci-
able difference he threw caution to the winds and returned
to full speed. At 11.45 P.M. he ordered action stations;
five minutes later *Beagle* almost vanished in a cloud of
her own steam as one of her boiler tubes gave out
under the strain. Somehow the destroyer kept station and
maintained speed on four boilers. Dead on midnight
smoke was sighted ahead to port from the bridge of the
Dublin, soon deduced to be coming from the *Breslau*.
Kelly made a series of course alterations aimed at closing
the gap and at reducing the disadvantage of being caught
between the enemy and the bright moonlight, losing sight
of the *Breslau*'s smoke several times in the process. At
1.20 A.M. Kelly thought he saw a torpedo track pass some
thirty yards to port but continued the chase. There was
still no sign of the *Goeben*, which meant that Kelly's
guess about the enemy ships joining up had been premature. But it was the big ship that he was after, and he set
out to find her on the basis of information fed to him by
the no less stubborn *Gloucester*. He came to the conclusion that the *Goeben* must be somewhere astern of his
original course and turned a few degrees to port so as to
be down the moon from the battlecruiser when they met.
At 2.10 A.M. he changed course from north-east to north-
west, expecting to sight the *Goeben* ahead at 2.30; five
minutes after that he indeed sighted smoke, to starboard
but somewhat behind him. He could not determine at the
relevant distance whether it came from the *Goeben* or
the *Gloucester*; if it were the German ship, she was a
long way off and had the advantage of the moon, nor
could she be attacked from ahead in the dark, as Kelly
had planned, but only from astern in daylight, by the

time he would be close enough to fire torpedoes. John Kelly assumed that the *Breslau* had warned the *Goeben* to evade his attack and with chagrin he gave up his attempt, altering course to rendezvous with Admiral Troubridge as originally intended.

Much work was subsequently done on plotting in detail the courses of the various ships involved in the chase of the *Goeben*, initially for court purposes and later by historians. Any captain reporting on a mission would enclose a chart showing his ship's movements with times. Correlation of these indicates that the *Dublin* and the *Goeben* passed within sight of one another some time before Kelly saw smoke to the east at 2.35 A.M. One theory is that the British had concentrated all the attention of their lookouts to the port side from which it was expected the German flagship would be sighted, but the *Goeben*, having altered course slightly after the *Breslau*'s warning, in fact passed on the starboard side, perhaps less visible than she might have been because of the position of the moon. There is no mention in the *Goeben*'s log of sighting the *Dublin*, for which she would have been looking after hearing from *Breslau*. Confusion is worse confounded by lack of clarity about times – GMT, CET, local and shipboard. It is also straining credibility somewhat to impute such carelessness to one of the best captains in the Royal Navy, who would surely have had men covering all points of the compass (though those best placed – aloft – may have concentrated on the port side). We are left with a small but tantalizing mystery. One thing we can be sure about is that if Captain John Kelly had managed to get himself into position to attack, he would have done so in spite of the obvious risks involved. Meanwhile his brother Howard aboard the *Gloucester* was still doggedly following the *Goeben* (it

being most likely that it was *Gloucester*'s smoke which
John Kelly saw).

We now need to go back a little in time to consider the
most controversial and dramatic incident in the whole
sorry story of the pursuit of the *Goeben* – the actions of
Admiral Troubridge on the night of August 6–7. It will
be recalled that the admiral left Malta on the evening of
August 2 with the greater part of Admiral Milne's available force: eight destroyers, two light cruisers (*Chatham*
and *Gloucester*), his own squadron of four armoured
cruisers including his flagship *Defence*, and two of the
three battlecruisers (*Indomitable* and *Indefatigable*). The
last named were, as we have seen, detached westwards
early on the 3rd to hunt for the *Goeben*, while Troubridge
sailed on to the mouth of the Adriatic to counter any
move by the Austrian fleet with the rest of his force. Late
in the morning of the 3rd, Milne ordered him to leave the
Gloucester and the eight destroyers to cover the Adriatic
and to take his four heavy cruisers westwards. On August
5 Milne ordered Troubridge to put about and go back to
the mouth of the Adriatic, to watch not only for the
Austrians but also for any German attempt to join them.
By that time Troubridge had sent his destroyers off to
coal and on the evening of the 4th he detached the
Gloucester to mount guard over the southern entrance to
the Strait of Messina, again on Milne's orders. On the
afternoon of the 5th he learned that the German ships
were at Messina and decided to place his ships between
Cape Spartivento on the toe of Italy and the entrance to
the Adriatic to cover a move by the Germans in that
direction. He hoped for a night action, but on the 6th
Milne ordered him to leave a night attack to the
destroyers. On the same day Troubridge made a sweep

as far south as Cephalonia in the hope of capturing a German collier reported in the area, but drew a blank.

At 5.15 P.M. GMT the rear-admiral picked up the *Gloucester*'s report that the Germans were heading east, and then that they were rounding Spartivento. He therefore, not unreasonably, concluded from the north-easterly course of Souchon's ships that they were on their way to the Adriatic. He ordered all destroyers that were ready for sea to leave their coaling station at Santa Maura Island (now Levkas, north of Cephalonia) and set up a screen across the mouth of the Adriatic at its narrowest point, between the Italian Cape Santa Marie di Leuca to the west and the little island of Fano (now Othonoi) to the east. Troubridge led his cruisers northwards from off Cephalonia with the same destination, hoping to sight and engage the *Goeben* between 2.30 and 3 A.M. GMT, preferably in the narrow waters north of Corfu and round Fano, where the lack of sea-room would help to offset the German capital ship's obvious advantages in speed and armament. In his report to Milne dated August 16, Troubridge tried to explain his thinking:

The problem of fighting the *Goeben* with the First Cruiser Squadron has been most exhaustively gone into by me, and I had come to the conclusion that the only circumstances in which I could engage her successfully with the squadron would be (i) by night, (ii) in half light, or (iii) in navigation waters.

It was plain I could never bring her to action in the open sea. Her speed – 27 knots – her effective gun range of 14,000 yards against our speed – a doubtful 19 – and effective gun range of 8,000 yards ensures her escape at any time if she so desires, or, alternatively, a position of great advantage at a range which we could not hope to hit her, while making four good targets for her long range fire. I did not propose to put this squadron in such a position unless circumstances imperatively demanded it, which circumstances at the early stages of the war as indicated in paragraph two of my instructions do not now prevail.

The reference at the end of this somewhat convoluted passage, interesting for being the first considered apologia by Troubridge for his actions made just nine days afterwards, is to his orders of August 2 from Milne, which passed on the Admiralty's instruction not to take on a superior force.

Firmly convinced that the *Goeben* was headed for the Adriatic ('I could not in fact conceive of any mission she could have in the eastern Mediterranean'), Troubridge thought at first that the Germans were feinting when the *Gloucester* reported their change of course from northeast to south-east. But by midnight 'I realized from other signals that the approach towards the Adriatic was the feint and her real course was to the southward.' So, echoing Milne, he ordered the *Dublin* and her acolytes to try to intercept, called his own destroyers to him and altered course to the south in the hope of crossing the Germans' path at 3 A.M. GMT. So far so good: the admiral's dispositions were unimpeachable. Unfortunately the run south offered time for reflection to the sleepless Troubridge as he tried to doze on the bunk in his chart-house, below the bridge aboard the *Defence*. At 1.45 A.M. GMT there was a knock on the door. It was Captain Fawcet Wray, RN, commander of the flagship and ex-officio flag captain to the squadron commander, a double-edged privilege: theoretically such a man is as much the master of his ship as any other captain, but, with an admiral aboard, his room for independent thought, let alone action, is minimal. If he pleases the admiral, his career will benefit; if he does not, it will probably suffer and meanwhile life can be decidedly unpleasant. Wray, however, from the photographs a handsome, compact, even dapper figure, got on well with his flag officer, an outgoing man who had clearly taken him into his confidence.

Wray asked: 'Are you going to fight, sir? Because, if so, the squadron ought to know.'

'Yes,' said Troubridge. 'I know it is wrong, but I cannot have the name of the whole of the Mediterranean Squadron stink.' He then dictated a message for the captain to have transmitted to the cruisers:

I am endeavouring to cross the bows of *Goeben* by 6 A.M. [local time] and intend to engage her if possible. Be prepared to form on a line of bearing turning into line ahead as required. If we have not cut him off, I may retire behind Zante [Island] to avoid a long-range action.

About three-quarters of an hour later, Troubridge was still awake in the unlit chartroom. There was another deferential knock: it was Wray again, seeking permission to speak.

'Yes, what is it?'

'I do not like it, sir.'

'Neither do I; but why?'

Wray then rehearsed a number of doubts which had arisen in his own mind – the failure of the *Dublin* to damage, even to find, the *Goeben*, the uncertainty about Milne's movements and intentions, the all too clear visibility.

'I do not see what you can do, sir,' said Wray, who was a gunnery specialist. 'There are two courses open to the *Goeben*: one [is] directly on sight of you to circle round you at a radius of the visibility at the time, and another course [is] for her to circle round you at some range outside 16,000 yards, which her guns would carry and which your guns will not. It seems to me it is likely to be the suicide of your squadron.'

'Are you sure that we cannot close in to the range of our guns?'

'No, sir, but we will send for the navigator.'

'I cannot turn away now – think of my pride.'

'Has your pride got anything to do with this, sir? It is your country's welfare which is at stake.'

The navigation officer was summoned and went to the admiral's room. A few minutes later he appeared on the bridge to report to Wray: 'The admiral wishes us to alter course to south 30 east.' Thereupon, at 2.55 A.M. GMT on the morning of August 7, just as the *Dublin* gave up the hunt, the First Cruiser Squadron sheered off and headed for the shelter of Zante. Wray went below yet again to Troubridge and said:

'Admiral, that is the bravest thing you have ever done in your life.'

There was no reply. By this time Rear-Admiral Sir Ernest Troubridge, flag officer commanding the First Cruiser Squadron, was weeping inconsolably.

In his report to Milne he explained:

At 4 A.M. [local time] I reduced speed, finding from the *Goeben*'s position that I could not come across her till 6 A.M., two hours after daylight, with a visibility of from twenty to thirty miles, and eighty miles from land.

I had already decided that that was a condition under which it was not in my power to bring her to action unless in company with a battlecruiser, and one so advantageous to the enemy, that I did not think it proper practically to ensure the defeat and possible loss of HM Squadron without any corresponding injury to the enemy or advantage to our arms.

I reluctantly gave up the chase, convinced that my personal desire and that of my squadron to endeavour to engage at all costs should be sacrificed to the general objectives of the war in the Mediterranean as emphasized in Their Lordships' instructions.

Troubridge was to pay a high price for placing discretion above valour. As we shall also see, Fawcet Wray too was to be punished, in his case without trial, for counselling caution at the moment of truth. Now there was nothing to stop the Germans so long as they kept going east.

Troubridge drafted a signal for his C-in-C, Milne, at 3.05 A.M. GMT, reporting that he had abandoned the chase on the grounds that the *Goeben*'s guns outranged his own and that the Germans were 'evidently' going for the eastern Mediterranean. More than four hours later Milne asked by wireless: 'Why did you not continue to cut off *Goeben*? She only going 17 knots and so important to bring her to action.' Troubridge replied as follows with a case he made at greater length in his written report to Milne of August 16:

With visibility at the time I could have been sighted from twenty to twenty-five miles away and could never have got nearer unless *Goeben* wished to bring me to action which she could have done under circumstances most advantageous to her. I could never have brought her to action. I had hoped to have engaged her at 3.30 in the morning in the dim light but had gone north first with the object of engaging her in the entrance to the Adriatic.

It was too late to intercept her when she altered course to the southward. In view of the immense importance of victory or defeat at such an early stage of a war I would consider it a great imprudence to place the squadron in such a position as to be picked off at leisure and sunk while unable to effectively reply. The decision is not the easiest of the two to make I am well aware.

But there was still one solitary British piece in play – HMS *Gloucester*, skilfully commanded by the younger of the Kelly brothers, last heard from in this narrative reporting the *Goeben*'s crucial change of course on the evening of August 6. As the German battlecruiser headed south-east during the clear night at an average speed of 17 knots, the British light cruiser hung on, picking up speed occasionally to keep the enemy's smoke in sight, then falling back, then probing forward again, following resolutely at a distance of between four and seven miles, well within the range of the *Goeben*'s main armament. As dawn broke on the 7th, Howard Kelly was able to fall back to the safer distance of nine to fifteen miles without losing sight of his quarry. At 4.52 GMT, soon after first light, Kelly was told by Milne: 'Gradually drop astern. Do not be captured.'

Kelly's report to the C-in-C after the chase shows what excellent officer material he was:

. . . as it was almost certain that the *Breslau* was ahead of the *Goeben*, and therefore there was but little danger of being caught between the two ships, and as it was essential to know if the enemy were making for Egypt or for the Aegean Sea, it was considered permissible to continue shadowing.

In other words, he decided to disobey orders on the grounds that he was the man on the spot and he knew better. The phraseology in which this fine example of individual initiative is clothed is delightful; also noteworthy is the clear conviction that the Germans had a mission of some kind to the east: obviously Howard Kelly had no need of hindsight to grasp a fact that was staring him in the face. His guess about the whereabouts of the *Breslau* was soon proved right; the German light cruiser appeared at 9.30 A.M. from well ahead and from southward to take position astern of the *Goeben*. The *Breslau* now tried by judiciously falling back and swinging across the course of the *Gloucester* to enable the *Goeben* to get ahead. Alone as he knew he was, with no hope of early reinforcement, Captain Kelly would not permit himself to be driven off in this manner from his objective, the *Goeben*. He feared that if the battlecruiser did manage to get ahead, she would try to set a trap for the *Gloucester* by hiding behind a headland or an island and using the

Breslau as a lure. How right he was will become clear. Meanwhile, something had to be done:

At 1 P.M. [local time – noon GMT on] August 7, when between Sapienza and Matapan, *Breslau* was dropping so far astern of *Goeben* that it was essential to make her close up or *Goeben* drop back, otherwise *Goeben* would soon have been out of sight. With this object in view, at 1.35 P.M. fire was opened with *Gloucester*'s fore 6-inch gun at a range of 11,500 yards at *Breslau*, then bearing two points on port bow of *Gloucester*. *Breslau*, having at the time her starboard guns bearing, replied at once with two ranging guns, and then went into salvo firing. On *Breslau* returning her fire, *Gloucester* increased to full speed and altered course ten points to port, bringing *Breslau* on her starboard quarter, closing the range at first to about 10,000 yards, then opening rapidly, as it was found the shooting of *Breslau* was excellent, and a whole salvo of hers dropped along the line on the off side of *Gloucester*, none of them being more than thirty yards over. The *Gloucester* at this time was engaging with her starboard battery and both 6-inch. On fire being opened, the *Goeben* altered course sixteen points to rejoin *Breslau* . . . At 1.50 P.M. . . . ceased fire as range was too far and . . . *Gloucester* resumed her original course to follow the enemy, who were now close enough together to be kept in sight.

This splendid attempt to re-enact the story of David and Goliath at sea, a cat-and-mouse game in which the mouse boldly tweaked the tail of the cat, was carried out by an unsupported ship which, as far as her captain knew, was slower than either of her opponents, one of which could have destroyed her with a single shell from well outside her own range. But the *Goeben* did not (as Kelly erroneously reported) open fire: apparently the Germans were satisfied with seeing the shadowing ship fall back. The *Gloucester* had fired eighteen rounds of 6-inch and fourteen of 4-inch to the *Breslau*'s seventy-three rounds of 4.1-inch. The British ship was unscathed; the *Breslau* took one hit on her side armour which made a harmless dent. Three minutes before ceasing fire, Kelly received an order from Milne to turn back at Cape Matapan, the southernmost extremity of the Peloponnese. This time Howard Kelly obeyed. The role of shadow had consumed a great deal of coal and his men had been on the alert continuously for two and a half days, working flat out for nearly twenty-four hours. Many, especially in and around the engine-room, had reached the limit of their endurance. As the *Gloucester* headed north-westwards to rejoin the First Cruiser Squadron off the Ionian Islands, Troubridge sent Kelly (with what mixture of feelings we can only surmise) 'my congratulations on your fine piece of work with *Goeben*.' There was also a brief exchange between the flagship, *Defence*, and the returning light cruiser.

'Congratulate you on your splendid feat,' signalled Captain Wray.

'Yes, they are very large,' Howard Kelly replied.

This example of wardroom humour, in the finest traditions of the feeble pun, has no historical significance but may be treasured for one incidental reason: it is about the only joke to be found in all the records of the *Goeben* affair.

Thus, by 3.45 P.M. GMT at the latest on August 7, the German Mediterranean Division was out of sight of its enemies for the first time since leaving Messina, and in the Aegean Sea with its profusion of islands. It was nearly three and a half years before the two ships that got away were next seen west of the Dardanelles.

Although the British Mediterranean Fleet had now lost contact with the Germans, Admiral Milne had not, for all his caution and slow reaction, given up the chase. Just after midnight on the morning of August 8, all three battlecruisers and the light cruiser *Weymouth*, having completed coaling, set off from Malta for the Aegean to search for Souchon's ships, though at a less than impressive 14 knots. As Milne was under way some twelve hours later, there occurred yet another failure for which responsibility must be borne by the British Admiralty itself. A junior official concerned with the drafting of signals left his desk to take an early lunch. A colleague whose sole motive was to be helpful noticed what looked like an important and urgent message lying on the desk and on his own responsibility caused it to be transmitted by wireless to all HM ships. It said simply: 'Commence hostilities at once against Austria.'

Unfortunately, in terms of catching the Germans, this information was decidedly premature: Britain and Austria were not yet at war, though they soon would be. Milne's reaction, which was to strengthen the screen covering the mouth of the Adriatic, was entirely right and proper in the circumstances as he now perceived them. To support Troubridge, still on guard there, and to prevent his Battle Cruiser Squadron from being cut off from Malta by an Austrian sortie, he made a northerly adjustment to his course, ordering Troubridge to move south to join him, leaving two light cruisers in place as scouts. Two hours after the disastrous message, which had been drawn up as a routine contingency matter, came the correction: 'Negative my telegram hostilities against Austria,' which reached Milne at 3 P.M. GMT. Now the Admiralty's carelessness in failing to forestall such a crass error combined with Milne's over-cautious nature to produce an exponential growth of the delay in resuming the hunt for Souchon. In his report to the Admiralty of August 20, Milne wrote of the corrective message: 'As this appeared to me to be peculiar, I signalled for confirmation which I received at 6 P.M.' It struck him as odd that only the last

three words of it had been in cipher, obviously a procedure designed to save time in transmission but which,
given Milne's nature, had the effect of causing hours of
deliberative and passive delay. At 4.35 P.M. he signalled:
'Am I to understand Admiralty telegram 372 cancels
orders to commence hostilities against Austria?' More
than an hour went by before the reply came: 'Re your
telegram 407. Yes.' But this was followed within half an
hour by another message from London: 'With reference
to the cancellation of telegram notifying war on Austria,
situation is critical.' One cannot but feel sorry for Milne
at this juncture as the recipient of such confusing information from his superiors, especially as he now became
bogged down in a series of 'housekeeping' exchanges
with Troubridge about coaling which are too tedious to
bear repetition but which illustrate perfectly how little
leeway the Royal Navy and its admirals allowed subordinate commanders. What with all this, Milne did not
resume the search for the Germans until lunchtime on
the 9th, after receiving a direct order to do so from
London: 'Not at war with Austria. Continue chase of
Goeben which passed Cape Matapan early on 7th steering
north-east.' The three battlecruisers and the *Weymouth*
once again tried to pick up a trail which had grown
ominously cold. By the time they rounded the Peloppon-
nese, they were *fifty-nine hours* behind Souchon. Like
everybody else, Milne had no idea about Souchon's
intentions, so he positioned the battlecruisers between
the Peloponnese and Crete to block a German move
back to the west (again!), while the *Weymouth* searched
for signs of the Germans, with the newly arrived *Chatham*
(light cruiser) in support. Eventually all five ships made a
sweep of the southern Aegean on the morning of the
10th.

At 9.30 A.M. Milne was encouraged by the interception

of enemy wireless traffic, correctly attributed to the *Goeben*. As radio direction-finding was then an art awaiting invention, this did not help the British to locate Souchon but at least gave them some encouragement that they were getting warm again, although the Aegean offered an impossible proliferation of hiding places, especially in the Cyclades Islands where they were now. The search continued fruitlessly all day and all the next night until finally, at 10.30 A.M. on the 11th, Malta relayed an Admiralty message: 'Information received from Dardanelles that *Goeben* and *Breslau* arrived there 8.30 P.M., August 10. You should establish a blockade of Dardanelles for the present, but be on the lookout for mines.' The original tip on the true destination of the German vessels came from the British vice-consul at the Dardanelles, Mr C. E. S. Palmer, who got off a cable at 8.30 on the evening of the 10th: '*Goeben* arrived. *Breslau* arrived. Acknowledge this.' The dramatic news took more than fourteen hours to reach London and another hour to reach Milne, who then dithered for six hours and permitted himself another quibble (but a justified one, as the reply shows). He asked: 'Am I to understand all vessels are to be denied egress and ingress to Dardanelles or German ships only? If formal blockade is to be established, will declaration be issued by home government?' The Admiralty answered: 'In reply to your 1624, no blockade intended only to carefully watch the entrance in case enemy cruisers come out.' Which leaves us with the unanswered question why the extremely specific word 'blockade' had been used in the first place. Milne was as much sinned against as sinning.

It thus remained for the hapless Commander-in-Chief to close the stable door, with an interesting variation from the usual procedure in such sterile matters: this time the horse had bolted into the stable and the door was to be closed from the outside. It fell to HMS *Weymouth* (Captain W. D. Church) to try the key on the afternoon of the 11th, some twenty-four hours after the Germans had gone in. As *Weymouth* approached the entrance, two Turkish torpedoboats emerged and took up station broadside-on at the three-mile limit, hoisting the signal, 'Heave to.' *Weymouth* stopped. 'They steamed round my stern, read the ship's name, saluted most politely and dashed off to the mouth of the Dardanelles,' Church reported later, 'paying no attention to my signals applying for a pilot or my signs to them to stop so that I might communicate with them.' Cunningly, Church let his ship drift innocently towards the shore, but after a mile of this the forts there fired two blank warning shots and the guns on both sides were ostentatiously turned on the lone light cruiser. Another request for a pilot was met by a signal from onshore saying, 'Not practicable.' *Weymouth* stayed put. The next morning a torpedoboat emerged and put a Turkish Army lieutenant aboard with a message. In fractured English he announced that the two German ships were at Constantinople and had been purchased by the Turkish government. Church disingenuously asked if he could just take his ship up as far as Chanak (inside the Dardanelles) and was told in no uncertain terms that this was out of the question. 'He also informed me that the names *Goeben* and *Breslau* had been changed to *Sultan Osman* and *Midilli*.'

Hitherto in this history SMS *Goeben* and SMS *Breslau* have appeared as inanimate, sinister grey shapes in the distance, apart from the two occasions on which they showed their teeth, as unseen presences somewhere over the horizon or as crosses on the charts of the two navies which had been ordered but so signally failed to find them and bring them to action. But this, of course, is only one side of the story. The time has come to examine how the great evasion, which for the Germans had an awe-inspiring purpose from the very beginning, looked from their point of view as they darted and dodged across the inland sea with the intention of changing the course of history. For that we need to go back to Messina.

6

Admiral Souchon and the German Mediterranean Division

Rear-Admiral Wilhelm Souchon, chief of the Mediterranean Division, took the two ships of his command to the Sicilian port of Messina, which they reached at lunchtime on August 2, for two reasons. It was the port at which the naval commands of the three members of the Triple Alliance had agreed to gather their ships in the event of joint war; and it was his best chance of completing with coal in readiness for his first war task, to disrupt the French troop movements across the western Mediterranean. Souchon ordered the two ships to meet at Brindisi, on the eastern side of the Italian heel, on August 1. The *Goeben* came racing down from Trieste, the *Breslau* across from Durrazzo: Souchon, unable to predict with certainty which countries would enter the now inevitable war and when they would do so, could not allow himself to risk being bottled up in the Adriatic. Anchoring in the roads outside Brindisi, the Germans asked the Italian port authorities to send colliers out to them but, ominously, were politely refused on the tenuous grounds of rough weather – a clear sign of Italy's impending decision to start the war as a neutral despite her membership of the Triple Alliance (but she was obliged to support Germany only if France attacked, which was not, of course, the way it happened). So the Germans weighed anchor and sailed on round the Italian foot to Messina. There too the authorities at first refused to supply coal and even provisions, and the German consul warned that the whole of Italy was likely to cold-shoulder the Imperial Navy. But for the moment the Sicilians relented and allowed the two ships to draw such coal as they could from Italian government stores, the shoreside bunkers of the great German shipping firm, Hugo Stinnes (there were no colliers in port), and from the handful of German merchant ships present. One of these was the modern and luxurious passenger and cargo liner *General* (Captain Fielder) from Hamburg, owned by the German East Africa Line and asked by Souchon by wireless to meet him at Messina. Since the admiral had heard at about midnight, August 1–2, that the Kaiser had ordered general mobilization twelve hours earlier, he was now empowered to commandeer any vessel under the German flag without further ado. Souchon went aboard in person to ask the passengers to leave, making sure they were given money to continue their journeys by other means or, in most cases, to return home. The liner was then plundered for everything that might be of use, including some of her coal, and also members of her crew who were on the naval reserve list.

The *Goeben* by this means acquired just 173 tonnes of coal, raising the total aboard to 2,042 tonnes or only about two-thirds of her maximum bunkering capacity. The *Breslau* managed to ship 200 tonnes (it was that much easier to load coal on to the smaller ship) to give her a near-maximum load of 1,220 tonnes. Meanwhile a steady flow of intelligence was coming in about the intentions of the various powers and their likely attitudes towards the war, and the positions of the various fleets in the Mediterranean. The crews of the two ships were told of the mobilization order after breakfast and simultaneously on the morning of the 2nd on the way to Messina. An address by each commander (Captain Richard Ackermann of the *Goeben* and Commander Kettner on *Breslau*) was followed by a ceremonial recital of the articles of war, three rousing cheers for the Kaiser and the issue of identity tags. The ships were then readied for war service, which entailed discarding 'luxury' items, readying ammunition and the like, a process which was completed at Messina.

At midnight GMT on August 2–3 the Germans sailed northwards from Messina, which meant they were westward-bound across the Mediterranean. Souchon ordered his two ships to steer for a point south of Cape Spartivento (confusingly, there are two such capes, one on the toe of Italy, the other at the southern end of Sardinia; it is the latter that is referred to here). After breakfast the admiral made his intentions clear to Acker-mann and Kettner by sending them a written order:

Objective: to unsettle the enemy, if possible to cause damage on the Algerian coast and the Bizerta-Toulon line of communi-cation, to prevent him transporting troops away to the mother-land without greater security measures.
Execution: Tomorrow at first light (about 3.30 GMT) *Goeben* stands before Philippeville, *Breslau* before Bône and establishes, under foreign (Russian) colours at first, what lies in harbour. Hoisting German colours, destroy by gunfire, possible tor-pedoes, enemy warships, transport ships, transport installations. Be sparing with ammunition, do not engage in exchange of fire with shore forts. Sail out of sight on westerly course, then join up in the direction of Spartivento (Sardinia).

On the run south from Spartivento to the attack, the log of the *Breslau* records the interception of wireless traffic in plain language between the French battleship *Danton* and the *Descartes*, an old armoured cruiser, loud and clear and apparently quite close (Admiral Chocheprat's Group A on its way to Philippeville), at 1.30 A.M. GMT on the 4th. About an hour later, the sighting of a blacked-out ship to starboard was recorded. What this was is unknown: the German light cruiser, also blacked out, steamed on undisturbed, to bombard Bône for nineteen minutes at ten rounds a minute, starting at 4.05 A.M. GMT. The targets identified included three steamers, shore installations and a nearby signalling station; the Germans could not be sure what they hit and did not stay to find out. For her part the *Goeben* also went to action stations at 4 A.M. but then sighted two suspect steamers coming out to sea from Philippeville and sheered off to avoid detection. She returned one hour later and opened fire at 5.08 with her secondary armament of 5.9-inch guns, expending thirty-six rounds in ten minutes and causing a large conflagration ashore, clearly visible from her position eight miles out. A coastal artillery battery fired back with what appeared to be 8.7-inch shells, but they all fell short of the now retreating battlecruiser, which made no response. After the raid the *Goeben* had just 1,350 tonnes of coal left, a disturbingly low supply for her voracious furnaces in a sea likely to be bristling with enemies. On the way southwards from Sardinia Souchon had received his fateful order to go at once to Constantinople but coolly decided that, having come so far, he would first carry out the planned raid on the Algerian coast: he had not been ordered to abandon it, and the now minor extra loss of time might well be more than compensated for by the confusion likely to be caused among the French, the most numerous of his enemies. That this was indeed the case was shown in chapter 3.

The instruction to make for the Ottoman capital is remarkable for being the only order Souchon received during these first few days of war. Berlin was obviously fully aware of his plans for the first days of a conflict and how he had agreed them with potential allies, and with admirable restraint left him to get on with them, taking the view that he was best left alone to his task. The German Admiralty and also naval attachés, consulates and other sources of intelligence concentrated on sending essential information. This policy of tactical non-interference seems enviable when compared with, for example, the bombardment of telegrams inflicted on Admiral Milne; in fact it reflected the power of the military in the Kaiser's autocratic Germany and was an unmixed blessing only when the commander thus left alone was of high quality, like Souchon. Indeed, the 'independence' shown by certain field commanders in the invasion of France wrecked the effectiveness of the Schlieffen Plan for the swift defeat of the French and, by turning what was meant to be a short war into a long one, made a major contribution to Germany's ultimate defeat. In the democracies there was to be constant tension between the elected politicians who bore the ultimate responsibility for the conduct of the war and the commanders in the field, often with appalling results.

By 9.05 A.M. GMT the German warships had sighted and identified each other, but within ten minutes they saw two heavy smoke-clouds coming westwards towards them from about due east. At first suspected of being French capital ships, they were soon identified as a pair of British battlecruisers of the *Invincible* type (in fact the *Indomitable* and *Indefatigable*). The *Breslau* saw them first and warned the *Goeben* by wireless. Both ships went to action stations but Souchon ordered the *Breslau* to make off north-eastwards at maximum speed: she was still a good distance away from his flagship and would only be a liability in an exchange of fire between the big ships, during which she would be at risk. The admiral had been informed of the likely hostility of Britain but did not yet know whether a state of war between her and Germany actually existed. The *Goeben*'s guns were loaded and her decks cleared for action, the gunnery officer at his post in an armoured tower amidships and seventy men in each of the five-inch gun turrets; the guns themselves however remained aligned fore and aft. The excellent rangefinders, the best in the world at the time, made the distance between the *Goeben* and the two British ships as they passed the Germans to the south, to be 9,000 metres (10,000 yards). Souchon found time to give consideration to the delicate and potentially crucial question of whether to challenge and salute, as naval etiquette in peacetime required. One of the two inter- lopers could well have been Milne's flagship, the *Inflex- ible*, in which case Souchon, as the junior in rank, would make the first gesture; but the British were too far off for it to be possible to discern an admiral's flag at either masthead (in fact there was none). A routine challenge by lamp might, in the atmosphere of palpable tension, be taken for the flash of a ranging gun; the movement of flags at masthead for the hoisting of a battle ensign. The British, too, were cleared for action. Souchon, mindful of his orders and the reason for them, determined not to fire unless fired upon and decided against a salute. The British made no sign either but after passing began to turn at high speed until they were heading east in the *Goeben*'s wake.

There now began for the crew of SMS *Goeben* an appal- ling ordeal, of which an unusually lengthy entry in the crisp war diary of Captain Ackermann for August 4 gives the reason:

Increased speed in order not to let the English come up. To be able to carry this out, the entire war-watch had to be sent into the bunkers, so that it would only have been possible for me to go into action with the off-duty watch, unless the speed were to be reduced from 24 to 15 knots.

Every available man, officers not excluded, was ordered below for the ghastly task of trimming coal, helping the stokers at the furnaces and clearing hot ash. Even off-duty or non-essential wireless telegraphists were not spared, and one of these, Georg Kopp, wrote the only full-length and first-hand account of the *Goeben*'s escape and subsequent career:

Two hours in that hell below was all a man could stand. Smarting and irritating, the fine coaldust in the bunkers penetrated the nose and clogged the throat. Lungs laboured heavily as the men struggled at their work. A crust of coaldust would form in the throat and cause a racking cough. Coffee and lemonade were constantly and greedily gulped down. But the relief did not last. The coaldust would attack the nose and throat worse than before, form a fresh coating and find its way into the eyes, bringing tears and inflammation.

In silence, but pluckily and undismayed, the stokers stuck to their work – half-naked, in nothing but their trousers, they served the fires, tearing open the furnace doors, trimming the coal, drawing out the ash and putting the fresh coal ready. The sweat ran in streams down their gleaming torsos. The searing heat streamed from the furnaces, burning the skin and singeing the hair. And still the work went on in the torrid stokeholds. It was here that the issue was being fought out.

An ever-increasing roar filled the whole ship; it was as though some giant force was being unleashed. A constant quaking, rhythmic quiver shook the whole vessel; turbines raced, propellers whirled – the air drove howling through the ventilators in front of the furnaces; it was an ear-splitting din. The *Goeben* was doing all her turbines were capable of.

At such speed, damage to boiler tubes was unavoidable. The material was not equal to these exorbitant demands. A stoker was scalded dangerously – and he was not the first. A silent, unostentatious heroism was being displayed. Any moment that dreadful, uncanny hissing might be repeated, and spouts of steam and boiling water do their deadly work on men's bare bodies. Yet every man stuck to his job.

This hellish scene, a challenge to the imagination of a Hieronymus Bosch, is an admirable description of what it took to get a coal-fired capital ship up to maximum speed and keep her going. The *Goeben* stored her coal in bunkers along her sides (placed there as added protection against damage). Fuelling the furnaces was not just a matter of shovelling coal out of the nearest bunker; as this was being done, other hands were shovelling coal out of the more distant bunkers fore and aft towards amidships where the stokeholds were. As the men shovelled maniacally, they slid about on the shifting coal in clouds of thick dust, expending enormous muscular effort just to keep their feet and working harder than any coal-miner. Their task was made no easier by the fact that their ship was short of coal; every ounce of black gold had to be dug out and passed towards the insatiable fires. Small wonder that the sailors of the time hated handling coal more than any other duty. It was all too much for one Seaman Westphal, who was overcome in one of the bunkers and died of suffocation some time during the flight from the British battlecruisers. Nor was he to be the only fatal casualty as Souchon and Ackermann worked their men ruthlessly beyond the point of mere exhaustion.

But the murderous pace below soon began to tell: the pursuers infinitely slowly but perceptibly began to fall back, although their huge smoke-clouds showed that they too were piling on coal as fast as they could. It is doubtful whether the *Goeben* exceeded 23 knots or at the very most (and then for short periods) 24, thanks to her continuing boiler trouble – there is much confusion in the records about what speeds were achieved during the chase. Had the British ships been on top form they should just have been capable of keeping up; manifestly they were not, as the *Goeben* began to pull away.

At 1.15 the *Breslau* reappeared from the north and took up station in echelon behind the *Goeben*, well able to keep up with the larger ship. At 1.35 a British light cruiser (*Dublin*) joined the chase, but by 3 P.M. GMT the two British capital ships were no longer in sight: only the *Dublin* remained in contact. At this stage *Breslau* was detached with orders from Souchon to go on ahead to Messina and make all possible arrangements for coaling. The SS *General*, which Souchon had sent to Palermo to load with coal after his first call at Messina, was ordered to return to the latter. As darkness fell, the Germans were able to reduce speed when visibility declined and then a haze developed. There was now no sign of the enemy except for his attempts to jam wireless transmissions.

Breslau reached Messina at about 4 A.M. on the 5th, followed by the *Goeben* nearly three hours later. One and a half hours out, action stations were called again as a flotilla of five destroyers appeared; but they were Italian. Three placed themselves ahead and two astern of the *Goeben* as an escort. Half an hour later Ackermann performed the melancholy duty of supervising the burial at sea of Seaman Westphal. But there was to be no rest for the German crews. The *General* and four other German ships were waiting in the roads outside the harbour and the distasteful and tiring labour of coaling began within minutes of anchoring, one merchantman on either side of the *Goeben*. Lighters of the Hugo Stinnes company brought more coal from the port, and not before time; the battlecruiser was down to a couple of hundred tonnes by the time she got to Messina. It had been a close-run thing.

During the dash to Messina, the war-watch pattern of four hours on, four hours off, had meant for most of the *Goeben*'s crew four hours on followed by four hours trimming coal. Now they were to perform a scarcely less prodigious feat by loading nearly 1,600 tonnes of coal in difficult conditions in little more than twelve hours, in the

August heat of Sicily. Souchon did not stand on ceremony in his determination to get all the coal available as fast as he could. Rails were torn out and holes cut in the decks of the merchant ships to speed up the plundering process. The sailors were given copious drinks, extra rations, music by the ship's band and endless encouragement from the officers working alongside them. As men keeled over from exhaustion, they were given a few hours' sleep in the comfortable bunks of the *General* and the chance to take a bath. Then it was back to work, if they could. In the end, the men's reserves of energy ran out well before all the coal available could be taken aboard; Souchon reluctantly showed a little mercy and called a halt when the *Goeben* had some 2,100 tonnes aboard, two-thirds of capacity. He had to let the crew have a few hours' proper rest before leaving, as he had resolved to do, as soon as possible.

A small legend arose about this coaling operation, in which the *Breslau* also took 495 tonnes to make a load of 920 tonnes. It concerns the humble British collier, SS *Wilster*, 2,759 tons. It was the British Embassy in Rome that sounded the alarm about this unremarkable vessel, which happened to be in Messina with a load of coal destined for the Middle East, as described in chapter 4. But the telegram took seven hours to get through, by which time the question was academic. Not, however, to the Admiralty in London. On its instructions the *Wilster* was arrested by the Customs and Excise when it called at Brixham in Devon on 28 November 1914 to top up a load of coal she was carrying from Newcastle upon Tyne to Port Said. The owners, a West Hartlepool, County Durham, tramp-steamer firm, protested by telegram to the Admiralty the same day: 'Please say why she is detained and how long she may be detained.'

A later German account in the newspaper *Stettiner Abendpost* explains the Admiralty's concern in the course of a long report of Souchon's escape:

The coal supply . . . *General* proved to be insufficient; no other good coals could be obtained except from an English collier in port. The British consul of the port was well aware of the fact and with the assistance of the harbour police kept a strict watch on the captain. To seize her cargo would mean a serious breach of Italy's neutrality, so it only remained for him to buy the coals from the master. This appeared impossible, when a young lieutenant of giant bodily capacity and equipped with a bottle of whisky proceeded on board and paid the English captain a visit. The silly old skipper got as drunk as an owl and sold him the cargo.

The name of the 'silly old skipper' does not seem to have been recorded, but the man who talked him into selling his coal to the German Navy was Souchon's chief-of-staff, Lieutenant Commander Wilhelm Busse, 'though not in the way that legend has suggested, by drinking the English captain under the table,' as Souchon himself wrote later. At Brixham, Royal Navy investigators established that the unnamed master was German by birth (aha!) but British by naturalization; what was more, the *Wilster* was owned by the Trechmann brothers, also of suspiciously Teutonic origin (no laughing matter at the time, as many unfortunates with German-sounding names, discovered to their cost, from Battenberg, the First Sea Lord, downwards). The records do not show what explanation the captain gave, but on November 30 he was allowed to proceed on his voyage. It seems clear that the *Wilster*'s cargo was brought to the German warships by lighters from the port to their anchorage.

While the coaling was going ahead, wireless traffic reached a crescendo too, Souchon using the *General*'s transmitter to confuse the enemy. Berlin ordered: 'Report position daily. It is specially important to mask movements eastwards if possible.' The beleaguered admiral decided to appeal for help to Germany's one ally (knowing Italy would remain neutral), Austria-Hungary. He therefore had messages sent to the German naval attaché in Vienna and the Admiralty in Berlin to use their influence on his behalf, saying that British ships blocked his escape from Messina. He also wirelessed Admiral Haus, the Austrian naval C-in-C at his base in Pola, in the Adriatic:

Appeal to you urgently to fetch *Goeben* and *Breslau* from Messina as soon as possible. English cruisers stand before Messina. French forces are not here. When can I expect you in the vicinity of Messina in order to [be able to] run out?

Berlin replied: 'Press on. Austrian help very doubtful.' Later on the 5th came a faint and garbled reply from the Austrians themselves. Only the last few words, but with them the message, were clear: '. . . cannot come, Admiral Haus.' In fact Austria, not yet at war with Britain or France, was experiencing difficulties with mobilization in an arthritic empire whose peoples had little taste for the war it had begun by its declaration against Serbia. Haus himself later explained to Admiral Pohl, his German opposite number, that when he and Souchon had agreed on plans for the Mediterranean, they had not reckoned on Italian neutrality. Haus also felt that while he could take on the British forces in the region, he could not handle the French as well; so, although he had gone so far as to put to sea, he had decided he was unable to intervene.

Souchon now knew he was alone, that France and Britain were definitely at war with Germany and that

Italy was neutral and would help him no more (the Italian government had said it would not allow him to coal in its ports again). He busied himself by drawing up an order for the breakout: 'I assume that enemy forces are in the Adriatic and that both the exits from the Strait of Messina are watched.' The order continued:

Objective: To break through to the east and reach the Dardanelles.
Execution: *Goeben* runs at 5 P.M. [local time], speed 17 knots. *Breslau* follows at distance of five miles, joins up at dark. I shall initially seek to create the impression that we are bound for the Adriatic, and if that appears achieved, to get a start towards Cape Matapan during the night by a surprise starboard turn at maximum speed, and to get rid of the enemy contact-keeper when possible.

Coal steamers had been ordered to three rendezvous points in the eastern Mediterranean and Aegean, including one off Cape Malea at the south-eastern extremity of the Peloponnese. These were German ships summoned from neutral ports. The *General* was also ordered to leave two hours after the warships, in the first instance for Santorini (Thira) in the Cyclades to await further instructions, either from Souchon or from the German naval post in Constantinople.

There now came a new complication in an already highly uncertain and threatening situation from the isolated Mediterranean Division, in the form of a message from the Admiralty in Berlin, sent on the 5th and received by Souchon on the morning of the 6th: 'Entry Constantinople not yet possible at present for political reasons. Minister lifting ban on passage of Straits.' This message, which originated from the German Foreign Office, reflected the disarray in the still deeply divided Turkish Cabinet about the newly concluded secret treaty with

Germany, though the Minister of War, Enver Pasha, had apparently succeeded in obtaining permission for the German ships at least to enter the Dardanelles. At best, therefore, Souchon's welcome by the Turks looked likely to be equivocal; at worst he was putting his head in a noose because he could hardly hope, once he had entered the Straits, to be able to turn round and come out, to run the gauntlet of a presumably growing concentration of pursuers. Casting all doubt aside, Souchon wirelessed to Berlin: 'I shall break through to the east.' If necessary he would do so against the will of the vacillating Turks.

Given that acceptance of internment in neutral Italy was for him out of the question, Admiral Souchon did not have much choice; nor had he been ordered to abandon the attempt to go to Constantinople, whatever problems may have arisen there. The Adriatic seemed even less appealing to him now. He recognized the odds against him but on his experience of the enemy so far they did not seem unacceptable. He had got away from the British battlecruisers, which led him to gamble that the enemy had not divined the secret of the *Goeben*'s treacherous boilers. He had a low opinion of contemporary British admirals, which led him to believe that they would not tackle him unless they could bring distinctly superior force to bear. He was convinced that, whatever might lie in his chosen path, the British would not have enough strength afloat to the east to be able to stop him: they were bound to have placed a screen across the mouth of the Adriatic but this was unlikely to be a serious deterrent. (Here at least, in Souchon's reflections as he later recorded them, is a form of backhanded corroboration for Troubridge.) He knew the French were all to the west. But above all he relied on a complete failure on the part of the enemy to guess his intention of heading east instead of trying to run for home westwards across

the Mediterranean. We have already seen how right his
calculations were, perhaps more right than he himself
dared to hope. Thus the most burning question for the
German admiral now, as the last preparations for the
breakout were hurriedly completed, was what might be
waiting for him at the southern (eastbound) exit of the
Strait of Messina. When he saw just one light cruiser, the
Gloucester, his relief can be imagined.

The spectators on shore were fully aware of the great
drama they were witnessing as pandemonium surrounded
the two grey shapes outside the harbour of Messina.
Small boats weighed down with salesmen, the curious of
all classes, thieves and even serenading musicians mobbed
the German ships both during the coaling and the afternoon's rest prior to sailing. The local newspapers made a
three-course meal of the coming adventure: 'Towards
death and glory: the bold venture of *Goeben* and *Breslau*,'
cried one front page. 'Into the jaws of death,' yelled
another. It was a very good story.

After a five-hour break from coaling, during which
both ships carefully raised enough steam for full speed,
just thirty-six hours subsequent to their arrival in Messina
for the second time in three days the German men-of-war
set sail, the *Goeben* first, then the *Breslau* twenty minutes
later. As he rounded the other Cape Spartivento on the
Italian toe, Souchon tried one more appeal to Admiral
Haus: 'British cruiser following. Where are you? What
do you know of enemy?' There was, of course, no reply.

Relieved though the Germans were to find only one light
cruiser waiting for them, she still had to be shaken off,
preferably before the planned change of course during
the night of the 6th to 7th revealed that their move
towards the mouth of the Adriatic was a feint. Not
without admiration for the *Gloucester*'s dogged pluck,

they soon found this exceedingly difficult. Summoning up new reserves of stamina they did not know they possessed, the men of the *Goeben* once again braved the horror below and the menacingly hissing boiler tubes and gave their utmost to maintain a high speed. The extra man-oeuvring in the battlecruiser's wake by the *Breslau* caused her crew to work just as hard, even though they at least had no need to fear tube breaks or boiler failures (the *Goeben* had as many as three boilers out of action at a time on a number of occasions during the run east). As the Germans hugged the shore to round Cape Sparti-vento, they saw the enemy light cruiser (whose name they did not learn until much later) fall in behind. At 7 P.M. GMT the *Breslau* was ordered to try to lead the contact-keeper away so that the *Goeben* could ease off, fall back and change course to get away; Souchon gave Santorini as a rendezvous. At 7.18 came a more impatient order, to drive the shadow off. About an hour later the *Gloucester* changed course for the *Goeben*, having obviously divined the *Breslau*'s ruse. Commander Kettner made so bold as to complain in his official war diary that he had managed to keep the shadow's concentration on his ship for about an hour: had the *Goeben* taken the opportunity of pulling away at top speed during that period and then changed course, the planned feint would have worked. In the margin at this point is a note in Souchon's handwriting pointing out that the state of the big ship's boilers ruled out such a spurt in advance. Certainly the *Breslau* would have been able to escape because she had the edge on any British light cruiser of the day. As it was, the enemy hung on. The two light cruisers were now on roughly parallel courses. At 8.30 P.M. Kettner ordered maximum speed and turned towards the enemy, who responded in kind; the *Breslau* changed course again to keep herself between the *Goeben* and the shadow. In his war diary Kettner also criticized himself: 'At this point the ship should have been sent in to the attack. But this became clear to me too late.' At 8.48 Souchon ordered an attack, but it was indeed too late; the procession continued, and Souchon made his change of course at 9.30 regardless; the Germans did their best to jam the *Gloucester*'s radio when they heard her signalling at this crucial juncture. Just before midnight another British light cruiser (the *Dublin*) escorted by two destroyers was seen by the *Breslau*, but disappeared within two and a half hours. During the hours of darkness the two German ships remained in contact but well out of sight of one another; it was only at 7 A.M. on the 8th that they sighted each other again. Just over an hour later, the *Breslau* was ordered once more to position herself between the *Goeben* and the shadow, a manoeuvre which took an hour to achieve. The light cruiser then began to sheer off gently to port of the *Goeben*'s course and eventually made a smokescreen to try to draw off the relentless pursuer, although the Germans had no way of knowing that it was the same ship as had trailed them from Messina.

Now certain that the enemy was not overwhelmingly superior, Kettner (who for a while had thought her to be a heavy cruiser of the *Defence* class) was determined to attack at last, and at noon signalled by searchlight to the *Goeben* his intention to do so. He was told to wait. Half an hour later, however, the British ship pulled out to starboard and ten minutes later opened fire with some accuracy. Within a minute the *Breslau* was shooting back. After a few more minutes the *Goeben* put about in a half-circle and the enemy, recognizing the threat, prudently fell back. Souchon signalled: 'Well done. Close up.' The Germans were now approaching Cape Matapan. Two hours later the shadowing ship, still watched with concentration by the aching eyes of the *Breslau*'s lookouts, was seen to be falling back to the edge of visibility. Just before 3 P.M. GMT and now past Matapan, the *Breslau* put on a spurt and closed up to the *Goeben*. The Germans could not afford to relax, however, and at 3.50 Souchon drew up a plan to trap the shadow should he reappear. He signalled:

In case contact-keeper follows further, *Goeben* will go ahead, pass to starboard round Cape Spathi [on the north-western tip of Crete] and wait behind land while *Breslau* moves on to Cape Malea [the south-eastern fingertip of the Peloponnese]. *Goeben* will make the attempt by surprise forward thrust to within shooting range to bear down on contact-keeper astern. *Breslau* to support this by wireless signal to *Goeben*, 'Attack,' when moment is apparently opportune.

It was a sound scheme, straight out of the tactical manual, and we have already seen that the *Gloucester* anticipated such a move exactly. But we have also seen that the plan proved to be superfluous.

Notwithstanding the distant comfort of an exhortatory message from the Kaiser ('His Majesty is confident that *Goeben* and *Breslau* will break through with success') received on the 7th, Souchon still had a great deal on his mind. As usual, one of his first thoughts concerned coal, which ought to be topped up once more before the last stage, the run to Cape Helles at the gate of the Dardanelles: it will be remembered that the *Goeben* had not been able to load more than two-thirds of her capacity at Messina. The boilers had been playing up, as he reported to Berlin: 'Owing boiler leaks prospects damage enemy Mediterranean bad. Will strive for Black Sea.' Stoker Friedrich List was killed during the night of the 7th to 8th by scalding when a tube broke, and had to be buried at sea in the morning. To Lieutenant-Commander Hans

Humann, head of the German naval post (*Eteppe*) in Constantinople, he signalled:

Militarily unavoidably essential to attack enemy in Black Sea. Do all in your power so I can pass Narrows immediately with Turkish government permission, if necessary without formal consent . . . Set up wireless link at once.

This message was sent via the steamer *General*, which had made good her escape from Messina as ordered and reached the vicinity of the Cyclades in good time by the direct route. On the morning of the 8th the admiral made new dispositions. He told Captain Ackermann to keep the *Goeben* in the Cyclades until a wireless connection with Constantinople had been set up. The *General*, unseen but somewhere in the vicinity, was ordered to position herself off Smyrna (Izmir in Turkey) and to be ready to act as a forward communications post both for wireless-relay purposes and via shore telegraph. *Breslau* was told to go to Cape Malea to search for the German collier that should be waiting there and bring her to the tiny island of Dhenousa in the Cyclades, due east of Naxos, so that both warships could coal from her on the 9th. The choice of this remote spot for coaling is an illustration of how minutely Souchon had studied the geography of the Mediterranean: any pursuer coming from the west would have most of the Cyclades islands to search before reaching Dhenousa. The *Goeben* kept slowly on the move in the vicinity of Andros, a larger island in the north-west of the Cyclades due east of Athens, conserving coal and giving as many men as possible the chance to rest after their latest ordeal. Even so, in twenty-four hours the capital ship consumed another 300 tonnes of coal just idling (but with steam up in case of emergency). During the night of the 8th to 9th, the *Breslau* reported that she had found the collier *Bogador* of the German Levant Line (repainted to pass as the neutral Greek ship *Polymytis*, just as the *General* had turned herself into a Rotterdam-Lloyd mail steamer). The disguised German coal ship had been sighted briefly on the voyage round Cape Malea and told to stay put; she had not been disturbed since.

Just after 4.30 A.M. GMT as darkness was fading, SMS *Goeben* nosed warily into the natural harbour of Rousa Bay, Dhenousa Island. Elaborate precautions were taken. Men were sent ashore in the steam pinnace to set up a signal station on a high point from which they could watch the approaches; Telegraphist Kopp says that the men on the pinnace wore British naval cap-bands acquired during friendly prewar exchanges, and that the lookouts were done up as hikers in civilian clothes! What the few local inhabitants would have made of such a vision is beyond imagination, but there was no sign of them. Aboard ship below, enough pressure was kept in enough boilers to be ready for sea in half an hour, while further attempts were made to repair faulty tubes with on-board resources. At 7 A.M. the *Goeben* was down to 860 tonnes of coal, barely a quarter of capacity. Just after eight, the *Breslau* appeared and dropped anchor.

August 9 was a Sunday, and at 10.30 A.M. GMT, while they waited for the collier, those men who were not otherwise engaged were summoned to the deck of the *Goeben* for a church service in these most unlikely circumstances. After that, work went on, tidying up the two ships and carrying out such running repairs as were possible, until at 2.45 P.M. the *Bogador* arrived. One warship took up station on either side of her and once again the loathsome task of taking on coal began. In twelve hours the *Goeben* was able to take on just 450 tonnes of coal and the *Breslau* 150 tonnes. It was the best they could do.

At 4.45 A.M. on the morning of Monday the 10th, after intercepting coded British wireless traffic that seemed to be getting steadily louder, the ships of the Mediterranean Division weighed anchor and headed due north, three miles apart, the *Goeben* in the lead, bound in the first instance for the tiny island of Antipsara in the middle of the Aegean west of Chios. On the way a message from Humann in Constantinople was relayed by the *General*:

Enter, demand surrender of fortress, take Dardanelles boom-pilot. Turkish fleet under command of English officers called away . . . do not leave Aegean Sea before August 11.

But from Berlin there came:

It is of great importance that *Goeben* enters Dardanelles as soon as possible. Acknowledge.

Souchon, resolved to brook no further delay with the British once again trying to pick up his trail, signalled back to Humann:

Will be before Dardanelles August 10, 5 P.M.. Make preparations for entry.

The two ships moved on, their next rendezvous a point three miles west of the island of Tenedos (now Bozcaada), just a few miles south-west of the goal, the entrance to the Dardanelles. At 4 P.M. GMT (5 P.M. local time), still without definite news that he could pass into the Straits at once and unopposed, with the ancient lands of Troy visible to starboard, Rear-Admiral Wilhelm Souchon ordered action stations and halted his ships five miles off the entrance to the strategic waterway which divides

Europe from Asia and joins the Mediterranean to the Black Sea. All primary and secondary armament which could be brought to bear was loaded and aligned on the forts protecting the Dardanelles, which were soon seen to be responding in kind with their own artillery. By flag, by lamp and by wireless, SMS *Goeben* signalled:

Send me a pilot immediately.

For all his success in pinning down the Turks long enough to persuade them to sign the secret treaty of August 2, the German Ambassador in Constantinople, Baron von Wangenheim, had been on tenterhooks ever since as the Turkish leaders argued amongst themselves and the Entente Powers sought to assert their own influence. The Germans and Austrians needed the active participation of Turkey in the war on their side (especially when it became clear that Italy would remain neutral). The advantages to them were clear. From Turkish territory the Suez Canal, Cyprus and Aden, all vital British strategic assets, were within easy reach. The Sultan's claim on the leadership of Islam had important implications for the millions of Muslims in the British and French Empires, the Balkans and southern Russia. But most far-reaching of all was the irreplaceable nature of the lifeline which the Dardanelles and the Bosporus constituted for Russia and which Turkey controlled from both sides. Without this, the capacity of Russia's allies in the war against the Central Powers to help her with supplies was reduced to negligible proportions: there was no hope of making good the loss via Russian ports in the cold far north or the hugely distant Russian Far East, from which communications with the heartlands were tenuous at best. The closure of the Black Sea also strangled Russian exports, crippling the economy and the financial capacity to fight. Without Turkey the Central Powers were effectively surrounded by their enemies and the Russians could throw the bulk of their strength (in manpower verging on the infinite) to the west; with Turkey on their side, the Germans could cut off Russia and take a great deal of pressure off Central Europe. The Entente Powers, by contrast, wanted peace in the Middle East and a neutral Turkey. This would give them access to Russia, peace in their Muslim colonies and a better chance of stirring up trouble for Austria in the Balkans. Britain and France regarded the likely price of a Turkish alliance as too high for their empires; the Russians had a war plan as late as spring 1914 to advance to Constantinople as soon as hostilities began (in keeping with their ancient ambition), but decided that an Entente victory in Europe would enable them to rearrange the Near East in their favour afterwards. For the Entente then, the neutrality of Turkey was not only entirely sufficient: it was also simpler and cheaper.

For the Turks, on the defensive against encroachments by the other powers for centuries and accustomed to playing them off against each other, the outbreak of war all around them presented the prospect of a restoration of mobility in their policy. The chance had at last arisen for making a profit instead of endless losses. The only question was in which direction the maximum advantage lay: in continuing to play off one side against the other or picking the likely winner and plumping for him (a highly risky course but one that could bring larger gains). As only one side wanted an alliance, the latter course boiled down to Germany. Even after the Enver faction forced the issue in Germany's favour, the argument continued, undiminished by the secret treaty which would have settled such a dispute anywhere else. The pro-Entente and neutralist elements believed that there was still a lot to be played for so long as the treaty remained secret and it was not activated.

For the moment it suited the Germans too to keep the treaty secret. On August 3, the Foreign Office in Berlin instructed Wangenheim to ensure Turkish silence so that Souchon's movements in the Mediterranean would not be unnecessarily jeopardized. Had it got out the British and the French might have guessed his ultimate destination in time to stop him. He was also urged, in view of the likely intervention of Britain against Germany, to try to forestall any attempt by Admiral Limpus's British Naval Mission to immobilize the Turkish fleet. On the same day, as we saw in chapter 1, the Ambassador was told that the *Goeben* was on her way. Also on the same day, Wangenheim reported to Berlin that Enver and General Liman von Sanders, the head of the German Military Mission to Turkey, were in favour of the earliest possible Turkish declaration of war against Russia; but the Grand Vizier, Said Halim, was against. So was Wangenheim. He pointed out that the Turkish mobilization in support of the declared posture of 'armed neutrality' had barely begun; the Turks were worried about the unclear attitude of their recent enemy, Bulgaria, which was well placed to take advantage of a Turkish war with Russia. On the 4th, Wangenheim was able to report that Turkey had granted German and Austrian warships the right of passage through the Dardanelles, but added that the Grand Vizier had asked them not to make use of this concession before Bulgaria's position became known: hence Berlin's message to Souchon on the 5th saying that entry to Constantinople was not yet possible, for political reasons. The Turks were also concerned about the possible attitude of Rumania. But on the 6th the Turkish Cabinet was swung round to temporary unanimity by Enver and agreed without a dissenting vote to allow

German ships into the Dardanelles. 'Turkey will not declare war,' Wangenheim reported, 'but will for the time being refer to her right to call the fleets of friendly powers to help.' Meanwhile Turkish troops were slowly being massed on the Anatolian border with Russia. From the 7th onwards, Berlin repeatedly sent the message to Souchon to go to the Dardanelles at once, which he finally received on the 10th, by which time he had made up his mind to go anyway. On the 7th also, Wangenheim reported that Constantinople was rife with rumours that the German ships had been bottled up in Messina and even that they had been sunk. He appealed for an official denial and once again that the ships should arrive as soon as possible.

Residual affection for Britain, the old ally which had lost interest, ensured that her declaration of war on Germany made a great impression in Constantinople, as Wangenheim reported without undue concern on the 6th. The news was offset by encouraging hints from Bulgaria: the Turks hoped that the Bulgarians would be drawn into the war on Austria's, and therefore Germany's, side against Serbia, for the sake of territorial gain. Germany still had the upper hand, but had yet to persuade the Turks to take the next step, which was to allow the ships to sail on from the Dardanelles across the Sea of Marmara to Constantinople. As the divided Turks fought to keep their dwindling options open, Enver and Humann, the German naval post commander, worked out the ruse whereby Souchon was asked to demand the surrrender of the forts at the entrance: this would make his entry look like a unilateral forcing of the issue.

When he arrived he made no such demand. Instead, within a few minutes a Turkish torpedoboat emerged from the Dardanelles, flying a flag-signal which said simply: 'Follow me.' She led the *Goeben* and the *Breslau* slowly in line astern round the minefields to Chanak (now Canakkale), about halfway up the Dardanelles on the Asian shore, where they dropped anchor two and a half hours later. Souchon's division was now out of reach of the enemy unless they forced an entrance; even if the Turks were weak enough to let in the British, they could hardly hope to get past the *Goeben*, which was now well placed at the mouth of the Narrows to thwart any such move. But Souchon could not regard his mission as accomplished until he had got through to Constantinople, still some 140 miles away to the east.

On receiving the news that the German ships were at the Narrows, the Turkish Cabinet went into what proved to be an all-night sitting on the evening of the 10th. The dilemma was acute as the first demands from the Entente Powers came in, requiring the expulsion or the internment and disarmament of the German ships with the removal of their crews. A refusal implied a breach of the neutrality declared a week before; acceptance meant a breach of the secret treaty with Germany. As a further complicating factor, the Germans got wind on the 10th of a Russian proposal to Turkey for a military alliance, which the Turks neither accepted nor rejected out of hand, old habits of procrastination doubtless dying hard. In a moment of doubt or duplicity, Enver had offered the Russian military attaché such a pact before he knew the German ships were coming. Eventually the exhaused ministers thought they had found the answer to their dilemma, and with it something of a recompense for the British seizure of their dreadnoughts: they would announce that Turkey would buy the German ships for 80 million marks as replacements. Under the circumstances it was little short of a masterstroke: as a sovereign state Turkey was unquestionably entitled to buy warships, and she had the added moral advantage provided by

Churchill's short-sighted sequestration of the two ships she had bought from Britain. There was, for all the misgivings of the Entente Powers, no need yet to declare openly for Germany. Indeed on August 13 and 14 the Turks went so far as to renew their declaration of armed neutrality through their ambassadors in London, Paris and St Petersburg; they promised to return the crews of the ships to Germany and not to use the vessels in the Black Sea or the Mediterranean; they even asked the British to leave the Limpus naval mission in place. The cabinet meanwhile had resolved not to allow the German ships to enter the Bosporus under any circumstances. The Entente Powers did not declare war, and the Turks once more deferred the issue of fulfilling the terms of the treaty with the Germans, who were less than pleased. The Turks told them they would not fight unless Bulgaria actively entered the war. The Germans angrily said they would have nothing to do with what they called 'this sham purchase'; they would neither disarm the ships nor change their flags, nor send home the crews. All they would do if pressed to explain was to say nothing, Wangenheim told the Grand Vizier.

Shortly after Souchon's ships dropped anchor at Chanak, the admiral received a welcoming message from Enver, who asked him to move them on through the Narrows to an anchorage at Karabiga Bay, on the southern shore of the Sea of Marmara. At Chanak there were several French and British steamers which had been prevented from passing into the Mediterranean, including two French ships with more than 4,000 army reservists aboard. During the night of the 10th to 11th, the SS *General* arrived safely; as the Turkish patrol boats were not on duty at night, Captain Fiedler coolly took his ship round the edge of the minefields alone. The big, well-equipped steamer was to prove invaluable to Souchon for

administration, supply and accommodation purposes. On
the morning of the 11th, Wangenheim asked Souchon,
through Humann who was now in permanent touch with
the warships by wireless, on no account to take them to
Constantinople as this would create difficulties for the
Turkish government. They should go to Karabiga, where
Turkish torpedoboats would seal off the bay. The German
steamer *Corcovado* arrived to ferry the admiral to Constantinople for consultations while the *Goeben* moved on
to the allotted anchorage. The *Breslau* stayed at Chanak
to watch the Entente Powers' ships and stop them leaving.
Kettner, the captain, kept in touch with Souchon as he
sailed east, informing him that the Turks in Chanak had
required him to leave the Entente ships alone and that,
to judge by wireless traffic, there was a substantial build-
up of British warships in progress off the Dardanelles.
Souchon ordered Kettner to immobilize the French troopships by removing vital parts from their engines, but
Kettner had to refrain when the Turks protested that
this course would embarrass them. Later the *Breslau*
forwarded a message from the Berlin Admiralty she had
picked up: 'HM the Kaiser expresses to you [Souchon]
All-Highest recognition.'

On the following day, the 12th, a signal from the
Admiralty sent on the 10th finally reached Souchon:

It is of great importance to go to Constantinople as soon as
possible in order to press Turkey to declare for us on basis of
concluded treaty. Ambassador has been directly informed.

This was soon followed up with another message from
Berlin:

If not possible remain Constantinople, following comes into
consideration. (1) With tacit consent or without serious opposition from Turkey, breakthrough Black Sea to attack Russia or

(2) Attempt breakthrough Adriatic Sea. Report as soon as ready to sail out, so that Austria [can] make move [on] Otranto [at the mouth of the Adriatic].

The German admiral meanwhile was busy with meetings and drafting his first detailed report on the evasion for transmission to Berlin. In this he made the interesting miscalculation that the real reason why he was followed by just one British light cruiser was because of the success of the German jamming of her wireless: he was clearly surprised to have only one pursuer to shake off. As we have seen, the true reasons lay elsewhere, in the realms of lacklustre leadership, while the *Gloucester*'s efforts to pass on information were entirely successful, despite Howard Kelly's early, consciously double-meaning complaint: 'I am deliberately being interfered with!'

In his first discussion with General Liman von Sanders, the German Military Mission leader, Souchon got agreement for a plan to strengthen immediately the obviously decrepit fortifications at the entrance to the Dardanelles, which he had observed with alarm. More mines, guns, communications and men were needed, and German officers ought to supervise the work. The admiral also asked Berlin to send him two more admirals, ten seaman officers and as many junior officers and men with suitable technical qualifications as could be spared, as reinforcements for the Mediterranean Division. The energy with which Souchon set about his work in Turkey is in noteworthy contrast to the dilatory conduct of his French and British counterparts. 'I intend to move forward against the Black Sea as soon as possible,' he told Berlin. After his talks with German diplomats and Turkish officials, Souchon sent this signal back to his ships:

To reassure public opinion, Turkish goverment declaring, with knowledge of German government, that *Goeben* and *Breslau* have been sold to Turkey. For political reasons it is necessary not to counter these rumours. *Ships of course remain German* [author's italics].

He also asked the *Goeben* to report the state of her machinery and boilers as a move into the Black Sea was 'imminent'. But the combative, thrusting admiral was to find that life was not quite as straightforward as that in the mysterious East.

The battlecruiser had once again been coaling all day from German colliers called to her sides. In the early evening there was a pause when the body of Stoker Hans Heller, who had died that day from the scalding he received when a boiler tube broke during the race east, was ceremonially taken ashore for burial with honours. The fourth and last fatal casualty of the escape, Machinist's Mate Passmann, was similarly honoured the next day. By mid-morning of the 13th all bunkers were at last full with 3,000 tonnes of good quality coal. Captain Ackermann reported that fifty boilermakers and 8,000 new tubes would be needed to restore the ship's boilers to proper working order. All of them leaked so badly that three or four would have to be out of action at all times for running repairs, leaving the ship with a maximum sustainable speed of 18 knots, two-thirds of her design performance. In a few months, the captain warned, she might not be able to put to sea at all.

In Constantinople, Souchon moved on from one round of talks to the next. He had a long meeting with Enver, the Minister of War and stoutest proponent of the German alliance, who told him that Turkey would move against Russia as soon as political clarification had been achieved, with luck in a few days (it was still Bulgaria and Rumania that worried the Turks). Enver explained that Jemal, the Navy Minister, was being difficult about

the continued and now acutely embarrassing presence of
the British Naval Mission, whose members were still
aboard Turkish ships and in the naval dockyards in
positions of command. Souchon also met Jemal and
demanded from both ministers the removal of all British
personnel from the fleet and its installations. After some
hesitation his request was accepted. It was now understood that Souchon was to be C-in-C of the Turkish fleet
while remaining chief of the German Mediterranean
Division.

There was clearly some tension between Souchon and
Wangenheim over the admiral's burning desire to take an
active role at once in which was still thought likely to be
a short war – especially since Germany was now in a
position, thanks to the arrival of the Mediterranean
Division, to sever the lifeline between Russia and her
allies. There was, after all, an enemy fleet in the Black
Sea and enemy coastal regions bordering on it which
were now open to attack. Such operations, especially if
combined with Turkish land assaults, would force the
Russians to retain considerable forces in the area instead
of sending them south and west against Austria and
Germany, which must provide relief in Central Europe.
The Ambassador, however, sympathized to some extent
with the Turks' desire to secure their flank by means of
an understanding with Bulgaria in particular, better still
an active commitment by her to fight alongside the
Central Powers. Bulgaria and Rumania were likely to
wait as long as they could before committing themselves,
to see how the war in Europe progressed, and there need
be no doubt that the Entente Powers were using every
means to win them over to their side or to neutralize
them. Both German officials were agreed, however, on
the principle that Germany's advantageous position in
Turkey, achieved by diplomacy and bolstered by the

arrival of the navy, must be maintained and exploited to the maximum. German officers were now at the head of both the army and the navy in Turkey, and the German warships could make a demonstration before Constantinople at any time it seemed appropriate. On the 14th, the Admiralty in Berlin underwrote Souchon's plan to campaign in the Black Sea:

Concur proposal undertake operation Black Sea, [with] agreement *or against the will* of Turkey [author's italics].

The message, however, instructed Souchon to work closely with Wangenheim, and advised him to delay for a while to allow Turkish mobilization to advance further.

Certainly the condition of the Turkish fleet and the defences of the Dardanelles and the Bosporus gave Souchon much food for thought, to say nothing of the difficulties the more experienced Liman von Sanders was having with the army. The admiral had learned from his own brief observations and reports from Humann and other officers of a daunting list of deficiencies. There were no torpedoes; the minefields were old and neglected and had many large gaps and the mines available were of poor quality; the guns in the forts were old and decrepit too, as was much of the fabric of the buildings; the watchkeeping was appallingly slapdash and unskilled. There was not even a signalling network worthy of the name. The state of the ships of the Turkish fleet beggared description. He therefore added to his request for reinforcements from Germany a call for gun captains, mine technicians, signallers, guard-boat commanders and rangefinder operators. To stiffen and train the Turkish fleet he asked for a further ten seaman officers, ten engineer officers, sixty torpedo mechanics and also staff officers to replace those of the British Naval Mission who were about to be relieved of their posts.

On August 15, Souchon proposed to Jemal, the Navy
Minister, that the British officers should be expelled from
the fleet and its dockyards forthwith and that the *Goeben*
and the *Breslau* should appear off Constantinople under
the Turkish flag on the following day. This was agreed
without demur, in the early hours, whereupon Souchon
had a signal sent to the *Goeben* to hoist the Turkish flag
at once (but to retain the German command pennant),
the same instructions to apply to the *Breslau*. At the
other end of the Sea of Marmara, feverish preparations
were in hand. The name *Sultan Yavuz Selim* (a sixteenth-
century Turkish ruler of renown) was attached to the
Goeben; the *Breslau* was renamed the *Midilli* (after
Mitylene, a town on the island of Lesbos, then Turkish).
The German sailors were now wearing two hats as members of the Mediterranean Division and of the newly
reviving Turkish Navy. This was literal as well as meta-
phorical: the red fez of Turkey was issued to all ranks,
from Souchon downwards, a fact which caused some
amusement among the German sailors (at least until a
new item of 'bull' was added to their routine – pressing
the soft maroon headgear on a special brass mould). The
Germans had been busy making the first practical addition
to naval strength from their own resources, converting
the *General* to an armed merchant or auxiliary cruiser by
the addition of light guns and the strengthening of her
deck to take them; and six German steamers were
adapted to form a minesweeping division, all in a matter
of days. An ad hoc but efficient communications network,
manned twenty-four hours a day, was set up to link
the *Goeben/Yavuz* as fleet flagship, the Dardanelles and
Bosporus forts, the coal depots (now under German
armed guard), the Turkish ships, lookout and signalling
stations and the army headquarters, as well as the German
Embassy and Turkish headquarters.

Souchon returned to the *Goeben* on the steamer *Corcovado* on the late evening of August 15 and ordered Ackermann and Kettner to have steam up for 12 knots for the following (Sunday) morning. The ships were now moored only a few hours' sailing time from the Ottoman capital.

The German ships in line ahead, the *Goeben* leading, across the Sea of Marmara to the waterway between Constantinople and Scutari at the southern end of the Bosporus, where they dropped anchor in the late morning. On the flagship there now took place a smart ceremony, watched by large crowds onshore. The Turkish Navy Minister, Jemal Pasha, was piped aboard and his personal ensign hoisted. The ship's band played the national anthems as Souchon was officially appointed Director and Commander-in-Chief of the Turkish fleet and no less officially 'handed over' the *Yavuz* and the *Midilli* to the service of Turkey. As far as Souchon was concerned, this was a politically necessary pantomime which made no difference to the realities of the situation: Germany had taken command of the Turkish Navy and intended to put it to use against her enemies as soon as it could be made ready. The sailors stood to attention as their new nominal chief, Jemal, was piped back over the side, whereupon his ensign was hauled down and replaced by Souchon's admiral's flag. He took the salute from the deck of the *Goeben* as a line of Turkish warships sailed past for ceremonial inspection. After all this, Admiral Souchon was conveyed ashore for an audience with the Sultan whose supreme naval commission he now bore.

The latest and finest additions to the royal fleet, the *Yavuz* and the *Midilli*, sailed back without him to their new anchorage at Tuzla Bay in the Sea of Marmara, where they were joined by the most serviceable of the Turkish Navy's ships: the old battleships *Torgud Reis* (formerly SMS *Weissenburg* of the Imperial German Navy, built in 1891) and the *Messudieh* (built 1874 and reconstructed in 1902 in Genoa), escorted by eight destroyers, all under the command of Commodore Arif Bey, the most senior Turkish naval officer afloat. When the new C-in-C returned from Constantinople, he inspected these units of his new command. He was less than delighted by what he saw and realized, if he had not guessed it already, that a long and arduous uphill task lay in front of him. But he had at last executed his order from Berlin of less than two weeks earlier, to proceed to Constantinople, despite all the vicissitudes, mechanical, nautical, naval and above all political, that he had encountered. He was now aching to turn his success to the best possible strategic account of Germany.

In the meantime the laggard British Mediterranean Fleet had assembled in strength outside the Dardanelles. The *Weymouth* had been joined by the other light cruisers *Dublin, Chatham* and the gallant *Gloucester*, and the three battlecruisers, *Indomitable, Indefatigable* and *Inflexible*, the fleet flagship with Admiral Sir Berkeley Milne aboard. Just after midnight on the morning of August 13, Milne was told, without error this time, that Britain and Austria were at war and he was to return to Malta where he would lay down his command and return to England. Eventually the *Indomitable, Indefatigable* and *Gloucester* were left to guard the stable door of the Dardanelles, which had been closed in the face of the Royal Navy. It was to be a long wait; and for all Souchon's impatience to have at the Russian enemy, it was to be a long wait for the Germans too before they could exploit the terrible opportunity their escape had given them. Well before that moment arrived, the angry naval authorities in Britain had begun an investigation. The French were much slower in this respect; but as their failure preceded that of the British, we may reasonably examine their prolonged inquiry first.

PART THREE
The Inquest

He who hesitates is sometimes saved.

James Thurber,
The Thurber Carnival

Admirals, extoll'd for standing still
Or doing nothing with a deal of skill.

William Cowper,
Table Talk

In war one does not improvise.

Victor Augagneur,
French Minister of Marine, 1914–15

7

The French parliamentary investigation

One of the main reasons why the considerable French contribution to the escape of Souchon's ships has been almost completely overlooked is the very fact that the French official inquiry into the circumstances started late, took a long time and never produced a report. The British investigation by contrast, as the next two chapters will show, was swift, thorough and dramatic, even if the findings seem mild; the inquiries effectively took place behind closed doors but it was public knowledge that they were taking place and their results were made known while the relevant events were still quite fresh in people's minds. The fact that an admiral was put on trial for the first time in some forty years, in wartime and against a background of almost unrelieved gloom in the war at sea, speaks for itself. Besides, British attention in those early days of the war was naturally focused on the nation's pride and joy, the Royal Navy; the army's contribution on the Western Front was as yet small, at least in numbers, compared with what was to come. It was completely different from France, where attention was understandably fixed on the great battles in the north. The national territory had been violated by German armies for the second time in forty-four years, the capital was threatened and all hope of salvation rested with the French Army. France had at least been spared a war on two fronts by Italy's neutrality, which released 80,000 men for the north. Another 80,000 men had arrived safely from North Africa (XIX Corps plus troops from Morocco and Tunisia) to take their place in the line. The navy was very much secondary in any case, and events in the Mediterranean in the early days were soon overshadowed by the desperate struggle on land. By the middle of August, Austria-Hungary was at war with all three members of the Triple Entente but this had no direct effect on the French position because the whole Austrian fleet was bottled up in its Adriatic cul-de-sac. It was only later when the German invasion had been halted and the war of attrition in the trenches began that people had the time to wonder, *Que fait donc l'armée navale?*

Further, before the Western Front became bogged down in the mud, the German threat to encircle Paris persuaded the French government to evacuate to Bordeaux early in September 1914. The administration was in chaos, parliament was not sitting, the press found it inordinately difficult to get information about anything, few people seemed to know much about what was going on and the great silence from the navy passed unnoticed. It was only at the turn of the year that parliamentary deputies were in a position to start asking M. Augagneur, the Minister of Marine, what the navy was up to. Apart from all that, the real significance of the escape of the German ships did not become clear until the very end of October, when they irrupted into the Black Sea to attack the Russians. Even so, the real pressure on the French government about the inertia of the navy began to build up only towards the end of 1915. By that time Italy had entered the war on the side of the Entente (May), and it was the Italians and the British who seemed to be doing most in the Adriatic against the Austrian fleet; what is more, the disastrous adventure of Gallipoli, a British initiative, though it was to drag on into 1916, had already gone sadly awry, a fact at least in part attributable to the less than enthusiastic contribution of the French fleet, whose commander, Admiral Boué de Lapeyrère, was still allied C-in-C in the Mediterranean.

Things came to a head in October 1915. The French government had become increasingly concerned about shipping losses in the Central Powers' very successful submarine campaign in the Mediterranean. At the same time Lapeyrère's requests for more small vessels and for the arming of merchant ships against the underwater menace were repeatedly turned down. The simmering dispute came to the boil at the beginning of the month, when the government directly attacked Lapeyrère's poor record against the submarines in a telegram to him on the 9th. The next day the admiral, who had never made a serious attempt to assert French leadership in the Mediterranean, replied with a brief message from his base at Malta:

My state of health not permitting me to assume the responsibilities which fall upon me in the present circumstances, I have the honour to request the Minister [of Marine] to agree to relieve me of the command of the fleet.

The request was accepted with alacrity and was swiftly followed by the resignation of the minister, Augagneur. It remains only to record that the ensuing change of leadership of the French Navy made little positive difference to the conduct of the rest of the war in the Mediterranean; the nation's energies remained almost wholly committed to the bloody struggle in the north. Lapeyrère died in 1924.

On 3 March 1916, then, the French parliament ordered an investigation into the entire conduct of the war at sea in the Mediterranean thus far. By then the Gallipoli campaign had been completely abandoned and it must have been clear to all what a disaster the failure to catch the German ships in August 1914 had really been; most of the ensuing inquiries were thus concerned with that. Although the French inquiry started long after the British one had been completed and forgotten, was pursued in a desultory manner throughout the rest of the war and produced no startling results (those responsible having resigned before it began), it deserves recording because of its findings.

The man chosen to lead it by the Marine Committee of the Chamber of Deputies was both a deputy himself and a retired senior admiral, Amadée Bienaimé, a man of vast experience in naval administration and of an independent turn of mind. He had served as Director of the Naval Division at the Ecole supérieure de Marine, the French naval academy, and later as naval chief-of-staff. Both these posts required him to devote rather more time to naval strategy than was given to most admirals. He drew up a naval modernization programme in 1901 but resigned soon afterwards when the period of naval neglect mentioned in chapter 2 began. Frustrated in his chosen profession, he got himself elected to parliament to pursue the best interests of the navy, as he saw them, in the public domain. But there was also to be a great deal of frustration for the grizzled admiral as he probed deeply into his country's poor naval record, which he found shaming. Not the least of his difficulties was the presence of the Marine Committee of that most interested of parties, Victor Augagneur, who was to give evidence but whom Bienaimé openly accused of suppression of information, destruction of relevant documents and helping to prevent publication of a report on the investigation. Bienaimé's inquiries were supplemented by separate investigations conducted into the *Goeben* affair by M. Chaumet, then Minister of Marine, in October 1917, and by M. Abel, a deputy, who produced a report of his own to add to the dossier in May 1918. Finally, angered by the absence of a report from the Marine Committee, seventy-three deputies of all parties in the chamber signed a motion on 9 April 1919 demanding publication. On June 24 the dossier was made available in parliament, but no report or findings were ever issued, nor was the matter debated. This was too much for Bienaimé, who immediately decided to write a book analysing the contents of the dossier. It was published in Paris by Jules Tallandier in 1920 and was not put together without further frustrations: in a note referring to M. Abel's report, for instance, Bienaimé remarks: 'At the time of going to press, we learn that this file has disappeared from the Ministry of Marine!' No matter – Bienaimé knew its contents. Even though his book is laced throughout with open hostility, even contempt, towards those he regarded as responsible for the poor showing of his beloved navy, it is invaluable as the principal, and on many details the only, source of information on the inquiry (after due allowance is made for the indignation factor). The *Goeben* fiasco dominates it. The central question which Bienaimé set out to answer was formulated as follows:

If the fleet, in executing the orders of the government, had set sail without delay and had proceeded with the best units at the appropriate speed, would it have arrived in time to bar the route to the German cruisers, throw them back upon the British ships which were offering it their collaboration and, in consequence, blockade the enemy, if not destroy him?

The answer, it is no surprise to discover, was: '*Oui.*'

The terms of reference of the inquiry were to establish whether there was something other than mere bad luck involved in the escape of the *Goeben* and the *Breslau*. One of the first exhibits examined was Lapeyrère's report to his ministry of 7 August 1914, written in Toulon. It describes how, after learning that the German ships were then heading westwards, he finally set sail in the early hours of August 3, and what ships were involved. The troops in North Africa were very much on his mind:

I have said how much importance I attached to the immediate problem of the transports, independent of cover at a distance, and I decided to employ all my forces for this, while reserving [the possibility of] concentrating the first-line squadrons in the east if the expected attitude of Italy were modified.

After describing how he divided the fleet into three groups, the admiral wrote that he heard of the bombardments by the Germans of Bône and Philippeville in the early hours of August 4. 'Hoping' that they would continue to demonstrate along the Algerian coast in a westerly direction, he put on speed to stop them at Algiers, leaving the slower ships behind, and diverting Group A, the largest, away from Philippeville towards Algiers. During the night of the 4th to the 5th the combined forces off Algiers cruised in search of the enemy, but 'he did not appear'. So the C-in-C, from the 5th onwards, bent his attention to the troop transports, rediverting Group A to Philippeville and leaving Group B at Algiers to this end while taking his flagship and two other battleships for an offensive sweep – to the west, despite messages saying the Germans were now going east.

In his evidence to the Marine Committee, Admiral de Lapeyrère explained that the French fleet had been engaged in extensive manoeuvres before the outbreak of war. Hulls were befouled with marine growth and virtually all capital ships, always subject to boiler trouble, had lost up to three knots from their design speeds. The destroyers were fine, but not to be allowed out alone when the *Goeben* was at sea. The German flagship with her ten 11-inch guns of a range of 15,000 metres (understated) and her speed of 28 knots (overstated) 'was the mistress of the sea.' But why had he not charged at the foe?

. . . I was very surprised by the expression which was used: 'Why not have charged at the foe?' If I did not charge at the foe, it is because I could not do it. How miserable a hunter would have been who, running after a hare, tired himself out after four days of pursuit – and you [can] see how far away he would have been from what he was chasing.

If he appeared to have disobeyed orders, the former C-in-C said, it was under the pressure of events. He had indeed favoured covering the troopships at a distance while taking the offensive at the start of hostilities. But when he was told on the evening of August 2 that the *Goeben* was off Bizerta, he took the elementary and obvious precaution of forbidding the transports to sail without escort. It was only in the very early hours of the 4th that he got a clear reply to his messages to Paris about forming convoys. (Only a few hours after that, he learned of the coastal bombardments.)

Why had the admiral been so slow in starting? He told the committee that he had initially been uncertain of the posture Italy would adopt in the coming conflict; that he (obviously) had no knowledge of the Germans' intentions but had assumed they would interfere with the transports; and that he would in any event have found it impossible to block the channel between Sardinia and Tunisia in time on the basis of learning, less than three hours before leaving Toulon, that the Germans were at Messina.

Also, soon after he left Toulon, the admiral went on, an Italian steamer had been heard signalling in 'clear' (uncoded) that the whole French fleet was heading south 'at top speed'. He knew that a German collier was positioned in the Balearics, a likely place for the Germans to wait for a chance to raid the transports. He therefore decided deliberately to go slow in order to confuse the enemy as to his intentions and keep his options open, he solemnly explained.

Lapeyrère could not recall having seen a series of messages in the last days of peace strongly indicating the likely neutrality of Italy, even when these were read out to him at the committee hearing. (By the evening of August 3, it was official and he had been told.) The admiral also said he had been confused by the series of messages about the sightings of the Germans from the North African coast. He flatly denied having seen a message reporting that the British had sighted the *Goeben* and the *Breslau* on the morning of August 4, only about two hours after Group A so narrowly missed sighting them. But the separate investigation by M. Abel, a deputy on the committee acting on its behalf, had unearthed the fact, not only that it had been transmitted to the flagship *Courbet*, but that the vessel had acknowledged the call to it just before transmission began, at 8.35 P.M. on August 4. Yet no record could be found of any such message in the ship's signal or cipher logs. The log of the *Diderot*, by then in company off Algiers, had, however, recorded this signal at 8.50 P.M. (Was this sheer inefficiency, coincidence, bad luck or something more sinister? M. Abel never found out and concluded, bitterly but not altogether unjustifiably, that even if the admiral had seen it, he would on the basis of much other evidence have done nothing anyway! Besides, had he got it, it would have been nearly twelve hours out of date.)

Vice-Admiral Pivet, who had been naval chief-of-staff at the relevant time, confirmed that many ships had boiler trouble at the beginning of the war. He also accused Augagneur, his minister, of refusing to lend his name and authority to orders to the fleet commander prepared by the staff; his view had apparently been that the C-in-C was responsible to the government as a whole and it was not for the minister or the chief-of-staff to give him orders or to interfere in instructions given in advance: their execution was purely a matter for the commander. M. Augagneur had been heard to deliver himself of the extraordinary dictum that 'in war one does not improvise'! The minister had also destroyed papers.

Initially the former minister had not been able to understand what all the fuss was about: 'As the transports were made without accident, as our fleet was intact and as the same result was arrived at as [would have been] by combat, everything was for the best.'

In his evidence to the committee, he dismissed the allegations of Pivet as only to be expected from a man whom he, Augagneur, had dismissed in December 1914 because he was not up to the job, intellectually or physically. Still a member of the committee throughout the inquiry, Augagneur struck his colleagues as of lively intelligence but impulsive, superficial and a bit of a sophist in argument. His approach was to give close support to Lapeyrère's position, most probably on the grounds that he could hardly disassociate himself from the admiral's actions. Pressed on the subject of the missing papers, Augagneur waxed indignant: 'Do I have to keep an account of what my subordinates propose to me? Some subordinate gives me a letter, I don't accept it, I accept neither its construction nor its form, I tear it up; for me the letter never existed!' It has to be admitted that there are many contexts in which this cavalier approach to filing would be most refreshing, but it does seem out of place in this one. Augagneur went on to claim that the order of his predecessor, the unfortunate Gauthier, to the C-in-C to let the troopships sail independently and singly actually ran *counter* to earlier general instructions given to Lapeyrère. Cheerfully putting words into the admiral's mouth and putting himself in his place for the benefit of the committee, he said: 'That's all very well [to let them sail alone]; that does not alter the fact that if the German ships fall upon the transports, it is I [Lapeyrère] who will be responsible. As I have nothing to do in the western Mediterranean, I am going to go on escorting the troop-transports.' The admiral's role had simply been to cover the western basin of the Mediterranean while the British covered the eastern; in fact the naval agreement between the two countries *forbade* the French C-in-C to enter the eastern basin. Augagneur went even further out on his limb: the C-in-C did not have orders to seek or pursue the German ships. The ex-minister seemed to be going out of his way to exonerate the ex-commander (who could not, however, according to Bienaimé, be accused of trying to hide behind Augagneur).

Lapeyrère cited a message he had received on August 4, the minister's first day in office and sent in the late morning: 'Government expresses full confidence and would be pleased to receive your reports regularly. Victor Augagneur.' The former minister told the committee that Lapeyrère had every reason to regard this clearly personal and introductory message of generalized goodwill as approval for the actions the admiral had taken before the minister took office and of which he knew almost nothing. The committee unearthed two other messages from Augagneur to Lapeyrère which helped the case of neither. One, dated August 6, said: 'It is important that the destruction of the *Goeben* and the *Breslau* should be effected as soon as possible in collaboration with the British forces and all your efforts should be directed

towards that end.' The other was dated the 8th and is
quoted in full in chapter 3: it ordered the admiral to stop
escorting troopships and join the British to prevent the
Austrians from getting into the Dardanelles. The latter
part of the order was both premature (Austria had not
yet declared war on the Entente) and irrelevant (its fleet
never went near the Dardanelles), but the first part was
yet another repetition of the order to forget about convoys
and go east. Come to that, the committee wanted to
know, why had the admiral not joined up with Milne or
at least concerted his movements with him in those vital
early days? In a note to the committee Lapeyrère replied
that he had made no offer to assist the British C-in-C
'because he did not need it as he was offering [me] his'!

As marshalled by Bienaimé, who made liberal use of
large quantities of fact, the evidence gathered by the
committee and analysed by him in the absence of any
official report or conclusions is a woeful recital of incompetence, hesitation, incomprehension and delay. The separate inquiry in October 1917 by M. Chaumet, then
Minister of Marine, had concluded that Admiral
Lapeyrère failed to understand his role once war broke
out and had disobeyed his orders. To this finding Bienaimé added ministerial weakness, general dereliction of
duty and a misplaced obsession with keeping the fleet
intact: 'It is, however, not to service such timidities that
warships are made! In war, fear of blows is the opposite
of wisdom.' Over-caution (and over-estimation of the
German ships as opponents) undoubtedly played a role;
at this distance it is possible to add the psychological
factor of morale. The confidence based on primacy and a
long tradition of success which saw the British Navy
through its early setbacks in the war had largely been
built on the no less lengthy series of defeats suffered by
France's second service. The morale of the French Navy,

especially at the top, was unable to overcome the long periods of inactivity into which it was soon allowed to sink.

There is no more fitting *envoi* than the poignant dedication Admiral Bienaimé set down at the beginning of his angry book:

To my former comrades of the navy, who would have been so happy to play at sea the decisive role to which their valour and the might of their weaponry entitled them to aspire.

8

The British court of inquiry

The British Admiralty's investigation of the circumstances surrounding the escape of the German ships into Turkish waters got under way with remarkable speed, within a week of the end of the abortive chase. Before considering the swift action of the authorities, we should remind ourselves that the Admiralty's concern was focused on the fact that an opportunity had been missed of inflicting an early blow on the Germans by means of a quick victory at sea, which, with the forces available, should have been obtainable at an acceptable price in losses. Even though Souchon had reached his destination, it was still not clear at this stage, in the middle of August 1914, what his escape signified or that he had intended all the time to go to Turkey. To London, unaware of the secret Turco-German treaty, it looked as though the Germans had simply fled through the only bolt-hole left to them and that they should have been caught; but their escape meant that the *Goeben* had removed herself from the Mediterranean board, leaving the Austrians as the only enemy there; a net, if inglorious, *gain* for the Entente. Turkey, after all, was still proclaiming her neutrality. Indeed the Admiralty investigation, the court of inquiry, its report and the decision to court-martial Troubridge all took place before Souchon broke out into the Black Sea at the very end of October 1914, and even the trial itself was completed within a fortnight of that portentous event. In short, London's reaction to the failure of the British Mediterranean Fleet was in no sense prompted by the shocking results of Souchon's mission, which still lay in the future, but only by shame and anger that the Royal Navy had missed its first chance in a century to win an important sea battle at a significant psychological moment – in the opening days of the biggest conflict in Europe since Napoleon's time. The rest is hindsight. The reaction of the navy is admirably summed up by Admiral Beatty's remark in a letter to his wife at the time (he was then commanding the battlecruisers of the Grand Fleet and was to become the most dashing allied naval leader): 'To think that it is to the navy to provide the first and only instance of failure. God, it makes me sick.'

Admiral Sir Berkeley Milne was due to be transferred from the Meditrereanean command to that of the Nore, in home waters, but the state of tension immediately preceding the outbreak of war and then the war itself put paid to that. On August 12 he was ordered to sail back to Malta in his flagship, the *Inflexible*, and on the following day he received instructions to return home:

The following agreement has been made with the French government. The German cruisers in the Mediterranean being disposed of [sic] and Austria being the only enemy, our armoured ships [i.e. heavy cruisers] except *Defence* to be withdrawn from Mediterranean. The supreme command of the French and remaining British forces in the Mediterranean to be vested in the French naval C-in-C. As you are senior to the French C-in-C you will have to return home with the armoured ships, leaving Troubridge and [Vice-Admiral] Carden [Admiral Superintendent, Malta] under French orders.

Milne reached Malta on August 14; three days later, after handing over the Mediterranean Fleet's papers and orders to Carden, he sailed for Plymouth in the *Inflexible*. On the way, he wrote his letter of proceedings of August 20 in which he gave his account of the *Goeben* affair, quoted in chapter 5 and sent to the Admiralty when he docked.

The Admiralty asked Milne to clear up two points, in a letter marked 'secret and personal' and dated August 25:

About the time when *Goeben* and *Breslau* sailed from Messina, *Indomitable* sailed from Bizerta after completing with coal. She was thus in a position to go in pursuit at once, while *Gloucester*, being throughout in touch with the chase, would have guided *Indomitable*'s movements. It is, therefore, not understood why you took *Indomitable* with you to Malta, when you went there to coal the other two battlecruisers.

When *Goeben* and *Breslau* reached Cape Matapan, you recalled *Gloucester* on the ground of her being short of coal, with the result that the enemy was never seen again. What was the state of her bunkers at that moment; was her recall due to a report from the ship; and, if her recall was imperative, why was not *Dublin* who appears to have been not very distant, sent to replace *Gloucester* in her all-important duty of keeping touch with the enemy?

Milne dealt with these queries in a letter of August 26. He said that when *Indomitable* left Bizerta she was 365 miles away from the *Goeben* which then appeared to be making for the Adriatic, where Troubridge was in place to attack. When the Germans turned away, Milne wrote, his concern was to bar their escape to the west and to block a renewed approach to the Adriatic. So he thought it best to keep the three British battlecruisers together, to resume the chase as soon as all were fully coaled or to be ready to tackle the Germans should Troubridge drive them westwards. Had *Indomitable* been sent in pursuit at once, she would still have been fifteen hours behind the *Goeben* if the latter had been sailing at a mere, steady 15 knots when Milne got his false alarm about war with Austria. On the basis of that, he argued, he would have had to recall *Indomitable* in keeping with his War Orders about concentrating his forces in such an event. The battlecruiser would then have been short of coal on rejoining his flag without having got near the *Goeben*. It was a neat answer.

On the recall of the *Gloucester* and the failure to replace her as shadow, Milne said the light cruiser had told him she had 700 tonnes of coal left at midnight on the night of August 7 and was burning fuel at the rate of 350 tonnes a day in the pursuit. He therefore knew she was low on coal off Cape Matapan, and she would have trouble in maintaining top speed because fuel would by then have to be brought from distant reserve bunkers. The Germans' higher speed left them able to round on her and catch her at any time, and she had no help within reach, if sunk, she would send no more information and the Germans would still have got away. He could not deprive Troubridge of the *Dublin*, the one light cruiser left to him, because of her speed and the order to keep a tight watch on the Adriatic, repeated in a number of telegrams.

His strong sense of self-preservation now thoroughly engaged, Milne went on to a general defence of his actions (for which he had not been asked). Having made the telling point about the alarms and excursions over Austria not once but twice (correct Italian press reports saying the Austrian fleet was to put out – briefly as it happened – from Pola, destination unknown but probably to meet the *Goeben*, were also passed to him by Malta very late on August 6), he began this unsolicited second section with a list of the orders he had been given. Apart from his general standing War Orders No. 2, he had been instructed: to stop the Germans interfering with French troop movements; stop them leaving the Mediterranean via Gibraltar; stop them entering the Adriatic and watch the Austrians; protect commerce in the eastern Mediterranean; be prepared for Italy joining the Central Powers; 'rigidly' respect Italian neutrality by staying six miles offshore (thereby excluding a run through the Strait of Messina). The whole of his effort had therefore been bent to stopping the Germans coming west. 'The idea that belligerent ships would proceed into a neutral port and there be sold did not enter my calculations and, I submit, could not reasonably have been guarded against; (although he admitted he had thought they might attack Salonika to disrupt the delivery of supplies to Serbia through that port).

He had, he added, also been worried about coal supplies which had taken some days to secure:

In conclusion I submit that the main objects set before me . . . were completely attained, although the greatly superior speed of the *Goeben* and *Breslau* prevented their being brought to action in the six days between the declaration of war and the German vessels entering the Dardanelles.

We have already seen, in chapter 5, that Troubridge had reported to Milne on August 16 on his movements. The rear-admiral was also ordered by the Admiralty to explain his conduct and replied from the *Indefatigable*, still on watch off Tenedos, on August 26.

In summary, his case opened with a reminder that Milne had passed on to him the order to husband forces and to avoid being brought to action against superior force. He had asked Milne whether he thought one enemy battlecruiser fell into this category (and been told that the question did not arise because two British battlecruisers would be attached to his squadron of heavy cruisers). He had given much thought to the question ever since assuming command of his squadron, and was convinced that a heavy cruiser could not take on a battlecruiser unless in narrow waters and limited visibility, where superior speed and guns would be offset. 'The multiplication of cruisers had no bearing on this question when the meeting was in the open sea.'

His ships were slow, with a squadron speed of 18 to 19 knots; HMS *Warrior* had difficulty in keeping up with the rest, and on the crucial night of the 7th he had reduced to 18 knots to be able to keep his ships together. 'The squadron's guns cannot be said to be effective at over 8,000 yards. No hits have been registered above that range.' The crews were good, but at longer range the guns had a large spread of shot when fired together. The *Goeben*'s speed was reported to have reached 27 knots and the effective range of her guns was 16,000 yards. Captain Wray (his flag captain) had witnessed German 11-inch guns on trial and found their shooting to be perfect at 14,000 yards.

The two battlecruisers had been detached on August 3 from his command to dash west to close the Strait of Gibraltar to the Germans:

As the French fleet was guarding the approaches to the western Mediterranean, *I confidently anticipated the return of the battle-cruisers*, and having in mind my dual mission to watch for the exit from the Adriatic of the Austrian fleet and to prevent the German ships from entering the Adriatic, I took up a good position on the Greek coast on interior lines that would enable me to cut *Goeben* off from the north or south, and *there I awaited the battlecruisers, whose presence I felt was necessary for our purpose*, of which opinion of mine the C-in-C was fully cognisant [author's italics].

Troubridge had been certain that the Germans were bound for the Adriatic and prepared to fight them in a night action, preferably also in narrow waters. When *Gloucester* reported the *Goeben*'s change of course, Troubridge thought it was a feint and continued north, convinced that the Germans must head for the Adriatic.

'When I realized she was bound for Matapan and east-ward I turned and steamed full speed to cut her off, hoping to do so at daylight, when I could perhaps get to my range. I was however too late and found that I could not come across her until 6 A.M. Daylight was at 4 A.M., and in the fine clear weather prevailing in the Mediterranean at 6 A.M. each day the visibility was from twenty-five to thirty miles.' He now faced the problem he had raised hypothetically with Milne. He foresaw two possibilities: the *Goeben* could circle round the squadron and pass on, or she could save time by passing it within her own but outside its gun range and do what damage she liked. In these conditions the only thing he and his squadron could hope to gain was a reputation for boldness and attacking an enemy with all the advantages on his side, and against orders to boot.

I felt if I followed the course I was then following I should have, in the earliest stage of the war, engaged a superior force of the enemy under circumstances of the greatest advantage to her [sic] and giving her and German arms all the prestige that attaches to early success.

On the other hand I felt it was for myself personally a most grave decision to make, to avoid action. My motives might be misinterpreted. Blame might be attributed to me that I could not support. The fact that my force was not composed as originally intended might be lost sight of in the disappointment at the *Goeben* passing east.

Their Lordships will, I am sure, realize that it was a very great decision that was called for at this moment. To risk in war the whole of one's fortune with the half of one's force is contrary to the whole teaching of all great masters of the art of war.

To act for one's own immediate interests, instead of keeping in mind the greater interests of the country and the objects at stake during a long and arduous war; these and many other considerations influenced me in my decision, and I gave up the chase.

His squadron, he concluded, had shown a great understanding of his motives and decision. He had obeyed orders and eschewed the chances of personal glory, and asked for understanding.

Admiral Prince Louis of Battenberg, cousin of the King and First Sea Lord, friendly with Milne after years of contact at court, minuted both admirals' explanations in his own hand, concluding that Troubridge was gravely at fault whereas Milne had generally behaved correctly with one or two exceptions. On Milne's report he noted that the C-in-C had made the correct dispositions in the circumstances as perceived at the time. He had successfully prevented the Germans from disrupting the French troop movement. The Germans had not entered the Adriatic as expected – 'why they went east after a while is beside the point' – but Troubridge had been placed to block either move.

Admiral Troubridge signally failed in carrying out the task assigned to him by his C-in-C. The road to the east was open to the enemy and he took it, closely shadowed by a determined light cruiser . . .

As soon as Milne received Troubridge's 'amazing telegram' he recalled the *Gloucester* for inadequate reasons, but the Germans then entered the Aegean, 'where their presence was of less consequence to us,' so the recall of the *Gloucester* could be passed over. Everything Milne had done once he knew where the Germans had gone was correct, so that he would have found them in the end if they had not entered the Dardanelles. 'The outstanding feature of this interesting operation, in which the enemy played the part of a harmless fugitive' (!), was the superiority in speed of the German ships over their British equivalents, Battenberg wrote, an advantage which only superior numbers and manoeuvring could counter. 'It was thus quite correct for Admiral Milne to keep the enemy between two groups of ships, each superior in numbers, and had his second-in-command done his duty, the enemy was bound to be brought to action,' he concluded.

Under all that is a much shorter, positively pithy comment by Churchill, the First Lord: 'The explanation is satisfactory, the result unsatisfactory.' The Admiralty proceeded swiftly to let Milne off the hook in a letter dated August 27, which said:

1. Your general dispositions and the measures taken by you from July 27 until you handed over the command in the Mediterranean to the French admiralissimo are fully approved by Their Lordships.
2. That the two German cruisers were not brought to action and disposed of is of course to be regretted, but Their Lordships note that this was primarily due to the failure of Rear-Admiral Troubridge to carry out your instructions. Their Lordships intend dealing with this matter independently.
3. Their Lordships request that you will now strike your flag and report yourself at the Admiralty on the termination of your command.

This exoneration was relayed to the British public in a statement issued by the Admiralty press bureau three days later:

The admiralissimo of the French fleet, Vice-Admiral Boué de Lapeyrère, has assumed command of the combined Anglo-French fleet in the Mediterranean. As a consequence, Admiral Sir Berkeley Milne, Bt, who is senior to that officer, has given over the command of the Mediterranean Fleet and returned home.

The conduct and dispositions of Admiral Sir Berkeley Milne in regard to the German vessels *Goeben* and *Breslau* have been the subject of the careful examination of the Board of Admiralty, with the result that Their Lordships have approved the measures taken by him in all respects.

If Battenberg's assessment of Milne's conduct seems lenient in isolation, it looks positively laudatory when compared with his savage commentary on Troubridge. In his minute of September 7, the First Sea Lord wrote:

He . . . failed to carry out his clear duty, both tactically in declining to attack the enemy, and strategically in not heading off the enemy (for which he was very favourably placed) and driving him back into the arms of the superior force under the C-in-C . . . Not one of the excuses which Admiral Troubridge gives can be accepted for one moment.

Battenberg dismissed the argument about the relative ranges of the *Goeben*'s guns and those of British heavy cruisers as exaggerated: the difference was not so great and the German ship would have been a much larger target. The argument on speed was weakened by the fact that tactical disposition of four ships could offset it.

The escape of the *Goeben* must ever remain a shameful episode in this war. The flag officer who is responsible for this failure cannot be entrusted with any further command afloat and his continuance in such command constitutes a danger to the state.

Battenberg therefore recommended the immediate recall of Troubridge to England and the establishment of a court of inquiry to investigate his conduct, while Milne should attend as a witness. Churchill concurred.

The scapegoat had been elected unanimously, and his name was Troubridge. Milne's excuses for having been so slow on the uptake, which was his major contribution to the escape of the German ships, were so intimately bound up with the errors of judgment, sloppy drafting of orders and general confusion on the part of the Admiralty (to say nothing of their mistake, clearly seen and signalled by Lord Fisher, in appointing Milne in the first place) that they could hardly be separated from each other. Rather than face up to its own shortcomings, from which a competent counsel for the defence could have been expected to make much capital, the Admiralty singled out and seized upon the apparently simple fact that the junior admiral had avoided battle in questionable circumstances. The contrasting manner in which the two admirals dealt with the queries from the Admiralty is quite revealing: Milne's cool exercise in damage-limitation and understated buck-passing; Troubridge's untidy and emotional plea for understanding which obviously had the opposite of the desired effect. One senses that his real crime in the eye of his accusers was that he *changed his mind* and then blurted out the fact. The whole story of the escape of the *Goeben* and the *Breslau* is a catalogue of missed opportunities, in which context a simple failure by Troubridge to make a move in time to catch the Germans after their surprise change of course would probably have been just one more regrettable misfortune. That he made the correct move and for a while put himself in the right position to give the Royal Navy its only serious opportunity of 'winging' the *Goeben* (whereupon she could have been destroyed by the big ships almost at their leisure), and only then threw away the chance by sheering off, is the nub of the charge against him. His semi-public battle with his own conscience, his attack of doubt and his very honesty – none of them intrinsically bad qualities, surely – compounded his difficulties and lend the story of the fateful night in August the aspect of a classic tragedy for a most likeable man whose personal courage, as shown by his earlier and subsequent career, was never called into question. A smart, legalistic response to the Admiralty's criticism might just have prevented the coming ordeal, but that was not Ernest Troubridge's manner.

There is one other matter which may be dealt with here precisely because it played no significant role at either the inquiry or the trial. It was clear from the outset and should be clear from the foregoing that the case against Troubridge would turn on the question of whether or not one battlecruiser was a 'superior force' to four armoured cruisers: hence the interest in the *Goeben*'s reputed higher speed and the performance of her heavier guns. But there is a strange omission in all the main arguments, an extraordinarily underplayed factor which even hindsight permits us to say should have been seen as at least as curious as the 'incident of the dog in the night-time' in the Sherlock Holmes story. The value of the capital ships of the day was computed on the basis of three principal attributes: guns, speed *and armour*. The protection built into the German battlecruisers was markedly superior to that of their British counterparts and almost equal to that of a battleship. Except at an unlikely close range, therefore, a 9.2-inch shell, the heaviest available to Troubridge, might well have bounced off a ship built to cope with direct hits from 12-inch guns: a shell from the latter weighed well over a third of a tonne whereas a 9.2-inch shell weighed 380 pounds, just half as much. It was indeed a curious incident that almost nothing was said about this added advantage of the *Goeben*, which was compounded by the relatively thin armour of Troubridge's ships.

On 9 September 1914 the Admiralty instructed Admiral Sir Hedworth Meux, the C-in-C Portsmouth, to preside over a court of inquiry on which Admiral Sir George Callaghan would also sit, together with any other officers thought appropriate (in the event the two admirals sat alone). The inquiry was held at the Navigation School in Portsmouth on September 22, Troubridge having been summoned there from the Mediterranean on September 8, and lasted just the one day. Its purpose was to establish whether there was a case to answer at a court-martial.

The hearing began with a reading aloud of the pertinent documents, including extracts from Milne's report, telegrams, Troubridge's two reports and various orders. The court adjourned after that for lunch and to give Milne the chance to read some of the papers which he had not seen before. In the afternoon, Milne was seated in the witness chair and questioned by the president, Admiral Meux, who warned him that anything he said might be used against him and he was therefore not obliged to answer incriminating questions. The former C-in-C, Mediterranean, began by disposing of Troubridge's point about expecting to have two battlecruisers with him:

The impression of the rear-admiral seemed to be that the two battlecruisers were permanently attached to him. Of course this could only be an impossibility.

They had been attached as a temporary precaution: 'The rear-admiral could not expect me to remain alone with my flagship during the war.'

Milne confirmed that Troubridge had spoken to him about the problems he saw for his squadron in engaging the *Goeben*. He remembered agreeing that 6-inch guns would not be much use but that the 9.2-inch would be 'very serviceable' despite the Germans' range advantage.

I agreed with him that . . . under certain circumstances, if he were caught unawares, it might be difficult to fight a successful action, although it would be difficult for the *Goeben* to engage four ships at once, knowing that one ship finds [it] as much as she can do with her [gunnery] control to engage more than two ships [at once].

This was an extremely damaging point against Troubridge, who, Milne added, 'did not leave me with the impression that he would not engage.' He had said it would be difficult and he would try to fight among the Greek Islands. Milne then went on to indulge in a little self-protective casuistry which also damaged his former subordinate:

Before going into the question of the *Goeben* and the *Breslau* leaving Messina, perhaps I may put in a statement, that regarding the dispositions of ships I received the Admiralty['s] approval in all respects.
The president: I do not think it really affects the question.
Milne: The reason I say that is that the rear-admiral says he ought to have had the two battlecruisers.

Troubridge, Milne went on, had indeed done right both in trying to stop the Germans entering the Adriatic and in turning south to try to cut them off when they changed course. He got the impression that Troubridge would attack in daylight from his signals, and he could also call on two light cruisers and two destroyers to help him; the *Dublin* had the then new, 21-inch, long-range torpedo. 'But a change of opinion on his part took place.' Milne then complained that the telegram informing him of Troubridge's change of mind had taken so long to reach him that 'it was too late then for me to order him to go on . . . and it was consequent upon that signal he made that two or three hours afterwards I signalled to him . . . why he had not gone on.' It is not entirely clear from the records whether Troubridge's message took one hour ten minutes or two hours ten minutes to get through because there is generally much confusion between local time and

GMT; but it is clear that Milne took at least two hours six minutes to react to it. Milne then went on to say that he understood the term 'superior force' as used in the controversial telegram from the Admiralty of July 30 meant the Austrian fleet.

The rear-admiral, intending to cross the *Goeben* at six in the morning, showed me that he did not consider the *Goeben* too strong for him, and that anyhow he intended to bring her to action. Of course, having read the rear-admiral's report now, I know his grievance [about the battlecruisers] but I did not know . . . at the time.

This marked the end of Milne's statement, but there were some clarifying questions still to come from the court. The first asked whether Milne had had any idea before the 'change of opinion' that Troubridge had no intention of fighting in daylight.

No, because he started to do it, and said he was going to do it. If he had put the urgency call on that signal [i.e. marked it 'urgent'] I should have got it almost at once, and should have told him to continue the chase.

Did Milne agree with Troubridge's observation that the number of armoured cruisers at his disposal made no difference to the innate superiority of the *Goeben* on the open sea? 'No, not at all . . . For the reason that I consider it very difficult for one ship to engage four ships at once, for the purpose of [gunnery] control.' Milne also disagreed, despite his express disclaimer of gunnery expertise, with Troubridge's assessment of the relative ranges of the German and British guns, putting the *Goeben*'s range at 15,000 yards and those of the cruiser squadron at between 13,000 and 14,500 – an observation which is little short of outrageous distortion, as we shall see. He completed his evidence with this remark:

I should like to add one thing: that under any circumstances there cannot be anything against the personal gallantry of the rear-admiral, and I feel sure that in doing what he did in not heading off the *Goeben* he did what he considered right, and that this alone influenced his actions after having made up his mind to cut the *Goeben* off at six o'clock. One can only conjecture what would have happened, but as the little *Gloucester* had followed her for hours without her turning round to sink her, which she might have done at any time – one can only conjecture what the *Goeben* would have done if she found the squadron across her path.

It is pertinent to add at this point that Troubridge was not represented by a lawyer at this court, which clearly did not feel bound by the rules of evidence that govern the proceedings at trials.

Now came Troubridge's turn to give evidence. He began by asking for the production of the 'telegram' placing the two battlecruisers under his command, of which Milne then said (correctly unless there is a gap in the records) he had no knowledge. He could perhaps have added, had it occurred to him or had he remembered, that his sailing orders to Troubridge, written on August 2, told him he would be given the two capital ships ('under your orders') to back up his watch on the Adriatic – 'remaining such distance in rear as will enable them to concentrate and give support.' The same order contained the instruction to put the two big ships on the *Goeben*'s tail should she be sighted, into which it is surely no distortion to read that, if she were not and in the absence of any indication to the contrary, they would stay with him. When they were detached in keeping with the Admiralty's orders of August 3 to use them to close the Strait of Gibraltar to the Germans, Troubridge was not told that he would not get them back, for what that is worth. But the court did not have all this drawn to its attention. Instead Troubridge was given the same warning as Milne about his right not to make self-incriminating statements.

He started with an indirect attack on Milne, pointing out that his reports thus far had been governed by a determination not to criticize his superior officer.

When an officer commanding . . . any organization receives from a superior authority a direction that he is to avoid being brought into action by the enemy, it must follow inevitably that he risks his reputation for everything that an officer holds dear. The superior authority who gives such an order is therefore bound by every code of honour known to any fighting organization in the world to support, to sustain and to countenance before the world an officer who has acted in obedience to such an order.

He went on to argue that when an officer is told to avoid an engagement with a superior force, he alone should decide in the absence of a definition of 'superior force' what it meant. He would clearly have had to make such a judgment, he said, had some part of the Austrian fleet for which he was watching come out against him, and would have done so on the basis of what ships were actually approaching. He then cited the 1913 fleet manoeuvres in which his squadron had come within range of the 'enemy' *Lion* (a battlecruiser): 'She seemed to me to be almost out of sight, and in a moment half of my squadron was adjudged by the chief umpire to be out of action [due] to her fire.' In talks with his colleagues he had come to the conclusion that the invention of the battlecruiser had 'killed the armoured cruiser'; the former type could cope with a squadron 'quite easily at leisure.' (It may be noted with hindsight that the Battle of Jutland in 1916 seems to support this contention to some extent: no fewer than three out of four of his old squadron were sunk by German big guns, admittedly fired from several ships.) He had reported this as his principal lesson from the manoeuvres, and Milne had invited him to lecture the officers of his command, when he repeated his view. His main contention, however, was that it had been up to him alone to decide what was a superior force in the circumstances.

Troubridge then claimed that when Milne passed on the instruction not to fight a superior force he was not aware that he was to get the two battlecruisers. This is untrue: his sailing orders, referred to above, contained both points. He added: 'Obedience to such an order entails the gravest risk that it is possible for an officer to take.'

The contrary order, to attack at all costs, entails no risk at all, and is easy of fulfilment by anybody; but the greatest decisions that it is possible to leave to an individual officer are entailed by an order to avoid a battle.

It is quite clear from this that the risk Troubridge was referring to was one of honour, not mere death, destruction, damage or wounds. He said he had gone into the point of what 'superior force' meant at some length with Milne and he had always publicly adhered to the view that a battlecruiser was superior to a cruiser squadron: but when he learned he was to have two battlecruisers himself, he thought the question irrelevant. He insisted that when they were detached, he expected to get them back. He also knew that in the event of war the British ships in the Mediterranean were to come under the command of the French C-in-C; the evidence is confused at this point but it does imply that Troubridge believed, when the bulk of the British forces was put under his command at the outset, that this was connected with the impending assumption of supreme command by a French

The Anglo-French fleet at the entrance to the Dardanelles,
February/March 1915

British troops at Gallipoli

The Kaiser speaking to Enver Pasha on the *Goeben*,
October 1917

admiral junior in rank to the British C-in-C. He might well have made a lot more of this order. He added that Milne had shown him the fleet War Orders but he had never carried out the prewar instruction from the Admiralty to inform relevant subordinates of his views on war and battle.

Casting aside a little later his inhibition against criticizing a superior, Troubridge stated bluntly that when the *Goeben* went to Messina the second time he thought Milne should have sealed her up there by a proper blockade. The French were perfectly capable of stopping the Germans escaping westwards; all the British had to do was to back up the *Gloucester* with first the armoured cruisers and then the battlecruisers.

That was my opinion, and that is the reason why I hoped that others at the Admiralty or the C-in-C himself would see that also, and in the expectation that every moment this particular disposition, which seemed to me the only possible one, would be decided upon, I myself took up with my squadron a position on strictly interior lines.

But it was really a court of inquiry into Troubridge's conduct, not Milne's, and this devastating comment on his tactics was never put to the erstwhile C-in-C. It must be added that Troubridge at no time took up his idea with his chief during the hunt. Yet ultimately the point was not lost on the Admiralty which, as will be shown, responded in the hallowed tradition of the 'Silent Service' – in silence, but effectively.

Had the *Goeben* come out to him during the night while he was without the battlecruisers, Troubridge said, he would have tried to lure her into an engagement among the Greek Islands and hoped that his low-lying cruisers would initially be mistaken for destroyers worthy only of her secondary armament. He would then fire back with all his 9.2-inch guns and also torpedoes. But the next day Milne ordered him to leave night work to the destroyers. When she began her run east Troubridge was aware of the move to sea of the Austrian fleet and suspected an attempt at a junction might be in progress, despite the *Goeben*'s alteration of course which he felt might mean anything or nothing. Then, however, it became clear to him that he could not now hope to meet her under the conditions in which he would be able to neutralize her inherent superiority (darkness and narrow waters). He then claimed that before his decision to attack, he had decided *not* to attack, for this reason (in other words he was now saying that he changed his mind not once but twice). Then he felt he could not obey the order to avoid battle with a superior force; he became 'bloody-minded' about it: 'I felt I would fight her.'

About half an hour after that my flag captain and the navigating commander came into my chart-house. I need hardly say that all the responsibility is mine.

Troubridge now permitted himself a complaint about the repeated general assumption by Milne that he could not fail to cut across the *Goeben*'s course had he sailed on. 'But as a matter of fact the instant the *Goeben* sighted me her course would be precisely what she wished it to be.' Unfortunately this was not the point; the complaint against him was that he had not tried. After describing the conversation with Wray and the navigator, Troubridge went into the now familiar gunnery argument as he saw it and the risk to his squadron:

I regretted that I had had a moment of weakness, and I cancelled my orders for battle, and I reported the fact to my C-in-C.

Later in his evidence the rear-admiral claimed that the conditions in which he would have met the *Goeben* had he persisted would have left her free to dispatch his ships one at a time from beyond their range; he would never have been able to drive her back on to Milne as had been suggested, on the open sea, especially as the C-in-C was 300 miles away. His duty was to obey his orders, which overrode the alleged duty to engage the enemy in the circumstances. 'I considered that it was my clear duty to avoid being brought to battle and I have done it.'

Troubridge completed his evidence-in-chief, which took the form of a long, uninterrupted statement, with a reluctant allusion to his own feelings:

Sir Berkeley Milne has spoken very handsomely about me here. Frequently, sir, in my life I have been asked to risk it . . . my ancestors have done it for generations; my only son is doing it now in the fleet; it is absolutely nothing. But here, sir, on the first day of the greatest war in history my country has asked me to risk my honour; they have asked much more than my life; in telling me to avoid a battle they have asked me to risk my honour, the honour of the great name I bear. I leave it in your hands, sir.

The supplementary questions from the court once again went into the vexed issue of relative gun performance, and probed, sometimes sharply, the circumstances in which he would have met the *Goeben* had he not changed his mind. Troubridge insisted that his true moment of weakness had been his impulse to attack, not his decision to refrain, and that Milne had been fully made aware of his reservations about a fight with the *Goeben*. Meux, the president, now turned to Milne and put this point to him again: had he been aware that Troubridge would not fight in the open or in daylight? Not if he were to be taken unawares, said Milne. So what would the C-in-C have done had he known Troubridge would not attack at the material time?

I should have ordered him to do it, more especially on this occasion, and when I say this occasion I mean when he had two light cruisers with him, one with long-range torpedoes. I remember perfectly well the conversation with the rear-admiral upon this point, and I know that he did feel there would be a difficulty in successfully engaging the *Goeben* owing to the long-range guns and what he considered his shorter-range guns, but he never left with me the impression that he would not engage her if necessity arose.

One does not necessarily expect admirals to know the finer points of the rules of evidence, but the question was disgracefully hypothetical and the answer terribly prejudicial. It will be noted that not a shred of evidence was brought to show that an attack was *necessary*, however *desirable* it might have appeared after the opportunity was abandoned by Troubridge. Nor was any expert evidence on offer about the gun ranges. Troubridge understandably waxed indignant, pointing out that Milne had given him no specific instruction.

If the C-in-C had signalled to me: 'You are to fight the *Goeben* under every circumstance,' nothing in the world would have taken such a load off my mind . . . [after] signal after signal explaining that I could not effect anything against her except under most extraordinarily fortunate circumstances, surely, sir, the whole air would have been cleared if I had had a decision . . . A clear issue, sir, was all that was wanted: I never got it.
The president: I cannot help thinking that, according to your argument, whenever you sighted the *Goeben* you and your squadron ought to have run away.
Troubridge: No, sir. I tried to fight him at night. I tried to fight him at dawn.
Q: I mean if you had met him in the daytime.
A: Well, sir, if you will tell me what is to be done with a 19-knot ship against a 28-knot ship! I had decided she was a superior force . . .

Troubridge concluded his evidence, and with it the proceedings, with a last appeal on the point of honour:

If after giving an officer orders that he must avoid action with a superior force for some ulterior political reason, at the moment of which I know nothing, and he judges it is a superior force, such orders can never be given if he is not supported. It would be impossible to say to an officer: 'You must risk your honour, and if you do it we will down [sic] you, we will see that you lose it.' The *Goeben* to me was a much greater force than . . . two Austrian cruisers and two battleships because of her speed and guns.

The court of inquiry pronounced the next day in a letter to the Admiralty. It expressly avoided discussing the general disposition of the Mediterranean Fleet to concentrate exclusively on the question of whether Troubridge should have tried to engage the *Goeben*. The two admirals on the court rejected the 'superior force' argument on the ground that the combined weight of the broadsides of the four armoured cruisers at least matched the weight of the *Goeben*'s. The not altogether irrelevant factor of comparative range was dealt with by ignoring it. The court conceded that the German ship 'had undoubtedly much greater speed and thicker armour,' but doubted whether Germans guns were more accurate than British at long range for lack of evidence. Troubridge had been right when he signalled his intention to attack, but his reversal of that decision was 'deplorable and contrary to the tradition of the British Navy.'

We are of opinion that although the *Goeben* might through superior speed have declined action, yet if she had accepted battle the four cruisers, possibly assisted by *Gloucester* and *Dublin* (with long-range torpedoes), and her two torpedoboat destroyers *Beagle* and *Bulldog*, had a very fair chance of at least delaying *Goeben* by materially damaging her.

Troubridge's failure to explain to his C-in-C in advance that he would not attack in open water in daylight unless he had a battlecruiser was regrettable. It should have been clear to the rear-admiral that the order to avoid action with a superior force in the crucial signal of July 30 referred to the (slow) Austrian battleships, as shown by the sentence, 'The speed of your squadron is sufficient to enable you to choose your moment.'

On October 1, therefore, the Admiralty officially notified Troubridge by letter that he was to be tried by court-martial on a charge under section three of the Naval Discipline Act, covering failure to chase an enemy beaten or in flight for reasons of treason, cowardice or negligence, the first two motives carrying the death penalty. To allow both sides to assemble witnesses, some of whom had to be recalled from abroad, the court-martial was eventually convened at Portland on Thursday, 5 November 1914.

9

The trial of Admiral Troubridge

For that he, Rear-Admiral Ernest Charles Thomas Troubridge, Royal Navy, Companion of the Most Honourable Order of the Bath, Companion of the Most Distinguished Order of St Michael and St George, Member of the Royal Victorian Order, having command of His Majesty's First Cruiser Squadron, then being a person subject to the Naval Discipline Act, did, on the seventh day of August, 1914, from negligence or through other default, forbear to pursue the chase of His Imperial German Majesty's ship *Goeben*, being an enemy then flying.

Thus read the charge sheet for the court-martial convened aboard the flagship of Admiral Sir George Le Clerc Egerton, C-in-C Plymouth and president of the court – HMS *Bulwark*, a pre-dreadnought battleship of 15,000 tons (which was to blow up mysteriously before the end of the month). With him on the court were Vice-Admiral Sir Cecil Burney, commanding the Channel Fleet, three rear-admirals, four captains and Paymaster-in-Chief F. J. Krabbé in his capacity as Deputy Judge-Advocate of the Fleet (his job was to advise the court on points of law and procedure). The prosecutor was another rear-admiral, Sydney Fremantle, who had resisted pressure from within the Admiralty to bring the more serious, potentially capital, charge of cowardice and adhered to the allegation of negligence. For the defence ('the Accused's Friend') there appeared Mr Leslie Scott, King's Counsel and Member of Parliament, one of the leading advocates of the day, who was instructed by the prominent solicitor, Sir Henry Johnson. The press had not been barred but did not even apply to attend.

The warrant convening the court and the charge sheet were read out, followed by Fremantle's 'Circumstantial Letter', a document amounting to an indictment and setting out a summary of the prosecution's case. Its contents are familiar to us now and need not detain us, consisting as they do mainly of extracts from the orders and signals already quoted. It was decided that the court would sit in open session except when state secrets might be revealed. Captain Fawcet Wray, Troubridge's flag captain, made a brief appearance to produce the logbook of HMS *Defence*, flagship of the First Cruiser Squadron, and stepped down. He was followed by Commander G. M. Marston, an Admiralty navigation expert, who had correlated the movements of the German ships, Troubridge, *Gloucester* and *Dublin* on to a single chart of the eastern Mediterranean in various colours of ink, on the basis of logs and position signals made at the time. Once again there was much confusion about times, as between GMT, Central European, local and ship's times, but it was established that the squadron would have been twenty-five miles ahead of the *Goeben* and across her path at 5 A.M. GMT had both continued on their respective courses as at 2 A.M.. It would have been 5.25 A.M. had Troubridge not reduced speed when he altered course, and somewhat further ahead of the Germans, about forty miles.

The third witness was Milne, who soon earned a rebuke from the judge-advocate for mentioning the fact that there had been a court of inquiry before the court-martial, which was detrimental to the accused: the prosecution should prevent any of its other witnesses from repeating the lapse. This was followed by a three-cornered dispute involving Scott, Fremantle and the court, about access to the logbooks of Milne's flagship, *Inflexible*, and Troubridge's, *Defence*, which contained discrepancies. Scott demanded access to them if they were to be used by the prosecution and the president at first refused on security grounds; Scott eventually won the right to be shown relevant entries in their context with mimimum censorship.

The court was cleared for the whole of the time Milne gave evidence, armed with the Admiralty signal-book put together for the trial, from which he read extracts in support of his description of ship movements in the first week of the war. He said he had been convinced, until he got the message about the abandonment of the chase, that Troubridge would cut the *Goeben* off at 5 A.M. GMT: he had been told twice that she was his objective; he had not signalled he was too weak or wanted help. He had detached the two battlecruisers from his subordinate's flag because he believed the Germans were westward bound and because the Admiralty ordered them to Gibraltar. He had not given Troubridge any reason to assume he would get them back. Nor, in eve-of-war discussions, had he gained the impression that Troubridge would not attack the *Goeben* because she was too strong. Milne had said then that he did not think the range of the German guns was that much greater, and that it would have been difficult for the *Goeben* to engage more than two ships at once. Troubridge had said he would lose some ships and Milne had agreed this was 'very likely'. The rear-admiral had said his best chance was in a fight among the Ionian Islands. 'I think, myself, that the First Cruiser Squadron could engage the *Goeben*,' said Milne, 'but there is no doubt, I think, she [sic] would lose some ships.'

Rising to cross-examine, Leslie Scott quickly brought up the question of the British battlecruisers and pressed Milne to agree that the battlecruisers were the appropriate ships to send against the *Goeben*. The Admiralty had said as much and it would be safer to have two for the task. But it was only grudgingly that Milne admitted that the battlecruisers were better suited than the heavy cruisers, that two were better than one, and that the Admiralty's belief in this could reasonably be inferred from the August 2 telegram saying, '*Goeben* must be shadowed by two battlecruisers.' Milne conceded: 'It may have meant that.' Scott experienced similar difficulty in persuading Milne to admit that he would have left the two capital ships with Troubridge, or at any rate had no intention to withdraw them from him when he gave the rear-admiral his sailing orders, on August 2. But he could not recall Troubridge asking him for his views about the relative strength, *vis-à-vis* the *Goeben*, of the battle-cruisers and the heavy cruisers in the context of 'superior force'. Milne took the phrase to refer to the Austrians, and could not recollect saying that the question would not arise with regard to the *Goeben* as Troubridge would have two battlecruisers. On that he would not budge.

Having previously refused to let the defence see Milne's secret War Orders, the court ruled that the whereabouts and dispositions of the French fleet were not relevant and could not be gone into. Scott, who had realized the subject as pertinent to the likelihood of the return of the battlecruisers to Troubridge, decided not to make an issue of this curious ruling. Instead he went back to the central issue of 'superior force'. Milne then agreed that the orders on the matter necessarily left the man on the spot discretion to decide what it meant; and that a force inferior in one set of circumstances might be superior in another. Asked to list the elements to be considered in assessing comparative force, Milne mentioned three: 'Gunpower, weather and speed. I do not know anything else.' The omission, little less than astounding in the context, of any mention of armour was, astonishingly, not picked up by Scott or the court.

Milne refused to be pinned down on the relative performance of various types of naval gun on the grounds that he was not an expert and was not informed about the very latest developments. He said he did not know whether the *Goeben*'s guns had a maximum elevation of thirty degrees rather than the customary British fifteen, and might therefore carry to a range of between 25,000 and 30,000 yards, far more than Troubridge had given them credit for. But when Leslie Scott sought to introduce as evidence a letter from his unrelated namesake, Admiral Sir Percy Scott, long recognized as unsurpassed in the world as a gunnery expert, the court refused, even though Sir Percy had been prevented from appearing in person by his war duties. Mr Scott bowed to the court's ruling that an Admiralty gunnery expert was available and he would have to suffice. For the record, Sir Percy's letter confirmed the extreme range of the German 11-inch gun. He also wrote that the maximum range of the *Defence*'s guns was 16,000 yards at their maximum elevation of thirteen and a half degrees.

Superior speed of course gives the choice of range, and if the ship with superior speed has also guns superior in range to those of her adversary, she will take up a position outside the range of her adversary's guns, and keep herself at that range, her adversary becomes a target only she is powerless to resist.

The punctuation is eccentric but the meaning is absolutely clear: Troubridge may have severely understated the gun range of both types of ship (perhaps he was estimating effective rather than maximum range) but his overall contention that the *Goeben* could shoot about twice as far as the *Defence* and her sister-ships was entirely vindicated. Sir Percy's opinion would obviously have been of great value to Troubridge's case, but the court made it academic.

It also protected Milne from close questioning on what he would have done in Troubridge's place, when Scott disingenuously invited him to demonstrate with the aid of the correlated chart of ships' courses introduced as evidence. The president, Egerton, took the view that it was unfair to ask Milne to work out the problem on the spot without warning and in front of an audience. Scott offered time but was overruled. Undeterred, he moved on to give a demonstration of his forensic skill by drawing out Milne's hostility to Troubridge.

Q: You understand, blame the rear-admiral – is that right?
A: Yes.
Q: You blame him, not because he failed to sight the *Goeben* that night, but because he let the *Goeben* escape. Is that right or not?
A: In a way, yes; and in a way, no.
Q: Let us have it in the way Yes and then in the way No. If the *Goeben* put on extreme speed he could not catch her, is it not? Obvious – common ground?
A: The admiral did not try.
Q: That is another question. The point is, as I understand, the charge which the admiral is meeting, and which you are supporting, was that the admiral let the *Goeben* escape; putting it into simple English . . . what he did was to miss the chance of sinking her. That is what it comes to?
A: Missed the chance of engaging her.
Q: He had orders at that time to avoid engaging with superior force?
A: Yes.
Q: You told me he could not engage the *Goeben* if she did not want to be engaged?
A: Yes.
Q: If the *Goeben* did not want to be engaged, she would not be engaged?
A: Yes.
Q: Now, whether it was prudent or not to go into the neighbourhood of the *Goeben* and, in effect, say to *Goeben*, if you would

like to engage us, we should like to engage you, depends, does it not, [on] whether as a compensation for the obvious risk involved to our ships, there was any reasonable possibility of doing any damage at all to the *Goeben*. That is what it must have depended upon?

A: The admiral had two signals made to him that the *Goeben* was the primary consideration, and one also from the Admiralty that the *Goeben* was the objective.

Q: *Were not both those signals made to him when he had the battlecruisers?*

A: *Quite true* [author's italics].

Had this been a boxing match before an impartial referee, Scott would now have been accumulating points at great speed. A little later, having got Milne to admit that the situation would have been entirely different had Troubridge had the battlecruisers with him, as he had done when he got his orders about the *Goeben* ('It would have made a certain success [sic]: no doubt about that'), Scott risked a wounding shaft:

If the battlecruisers had been watching at each end of the Strait of Messina, that success would no doubt have been pretty near certain; but even these battlecruisers had two or three knots inferiority of speed to the *Goeben*? [author's italics].

A: Three and a half.

. . .

Q: But do you agree with me that if he was wrong in deciding, as he did, to go south to attack her in daylight, that does not prevent his being right when he stopped?

A: I think the admiral could have made up his mind before, instead of saying he was going to do it.

Q: I can say he might be justly blamed in sending the signals, but that does not decide the question that he was not to follow?

A: I think he should.

It was getting late, and Scott did not bother to point out that, once again, Milne's answer bore little relation to the question. He could be well satisfied with his afternoon's work. He had with Milne's very reluctant and unintended assistance brought out the *Goeben*'s advantages and that she would almost certainly have had the initiative; that Milne, whose own dispositions had been less than perfect, effectively blamed Troubridge for everything; and that the proposition that the *Goeben* had been a superior force in the circumstances was at least worthy of serious consideration. The court adjourned for the night.

On the second day of the trial, November 6, Scott continued to grapple for a firm hold on Milne, which was beginning to look like attempting to straighten a snake against its will. It took dozens of convoluted questions to get him to concede that on the night in question the *Goeben* seemed to be capable of her full speed, a good seven knots faster than the squadron's. But by taking the former C-in-C through Troubridge's signal replying to Milne's question as to why he had abandoned the chase (see chapter 5), line by line, Scott got his unequivocal agreement that he had understood the whole of the explanation it contained. So much the better for Milne, for Scott now produced a note he had written to Troubridge from Malta on August 17 in his own hand:

My dear Troubridge,
    Just time for a few disjointed lines.
    Under new regime. I leave for home tomorrow. I am glad you are going to Dardanelles – am not sure now about *G* and *B*. I quite understand your reply about not engaging them, but still wished you had and knocked three or four knots speed off them: all this 'to do' would not now have happened – but there it is – I have wired you to send *me* in a full report to the Admiralty regarding the events of those nights, and the night when *Goeben* left Messina . . . [Milne's emphasis].

Did 'I am not sure about *G* and *B*' mean Milne had changed his mind? Scott asked. 'No,' said Milne. 'That referred to the *Goeben* and the *Breslau* in the Dardanelles.'

Scott was surprised. 'Oh!' he exclaimed, 'but it goes straight on: "I quite understand your reply about not engaging them." What was the point [on] which you were not sure about them in relation to the Dardanelles?' Milne said: 'What they were going to do . . .' In other words he insisted that his remark in the letter referred to the future rather than the past, although the context permits the opposite conclusion to be drawn. And so it went on. Milne denied that any message from Troubridge before he changed his mind gave any indication that the rear-admiral had any misgivings, not even the one about drawing the *Goeben* into the islands 'where we can engage her at our range.' He persisted in denying that there was any significant difference in range; he denied that his own message about using destroyers for night attack could be read as meaning not to use the cruisers. Scott now proceeded to press Milne hard about his own dispositions, including the failure to bottle up the *Goeben* in the Strait of Messina by placing a battlecruiser at each end. As Milne twisted and turned, Scott's questions were such that they had the effect of statements which spoke for themselves. The warning to Milne from the judge-advocate, that he was not obliged to answer questions that might incriminate him, in the midst of all this also speaks for itself even louder. The skilled defending barrister did not fall into the trap of exploiting Milne's evasiveness in a theatrical manner, as he might have been tempted to do in front of a jury. With admirable restraint he seems from the record to have relied on a steady, understated, erosive drip-effect, perhaps taking the view that something more histrionic might be counter-productive in grilling, as a civilian, a full admiral before a court made up of naval officers junior to him. Only once, with the sceptical monosyllable 'Oh!' when dealing with the letter to Troubridge, did he permit himself the luxury of a tiny display of emotion. Small wonder that on the resumption of the hearing after lunch on the second day the prosecutor, Fremantle, sought to repair the damage by eliciting from Milne a coherent explanation that it was his orders to respect Italian neutrality by rigidly staying outside a six-mile limit off her coast which had led him not to seal off the Strait of Messina. But Scott had established beyond reasonable doubt that even under such restrictions the *Goeben* would have been forced to come under the guns of at least one British battlecruiser had they been correctly placed. That this struck home is shown by the fact that the court itself put a series of questions to Milne about his dispositions which helped him to recover some lost ground. But the question, 'Were you satisfied in your own mind that the rear-admiral understood he was to attack the *Goeben* if he met her?' drew an immediate objection from Scott, of the kind that would have been most helpful to Troubridge at the earlier court of inquiry: 'The question as to whether the rear-admiral was right or wrong . . . must depend on the orders he received from his C-in-C, not what was inside the mind of the C-in-C and not communicated to him.' The question was withdrawn.

The next witness was Troubridge's flag captain, Fawcet Wray, summoned by the prosecution. He described the various courses and speed of the squadron during the night in question, his answers crisp and to the point. He then made it clear that he at least was fully aware of Troubridge's reservations about a fight with the *Goeben* without the British battlecruisers, of which he had made no secret from the outset. It was the prosecutor who elicited from Wray the opinion that Troubridge's messages about his plan to attack in daylight were incompatible with the admiral's stated policy of accepting battle only under conditions which helped to offset the *Goeben*'s advantages. Wray went on to describe the conversations he had with Troubridge during the night run south (fully reported in chapter 5), admitting freely that he had advised his chief not to attack. With considerable moral courage, Wray told the court:

I understand that the admiral is charged with failing to pursue the chase of the enemy. There was nothing for him to fall back upon. There was nothing for him to do . . . I do not think the admiral was justified in attacking or attempting to attack the *Goeben* at all, unless the battlecruisers were within easy reach . . . within visual touch . . .

Mr Scott asked the captain in his capacity as a gunnery specialist to confirm the abnormal capacity for elevation of the German 11-inch gun, which he did, quoting from his own observations of the *Goeben* in port before the war and from textbook references. This would give her guns a greatly increased range, almost double that of the *Defence*'s, and a high degree of accuracy up to 24,000 yards, or twelve sea-miles. Wray then argued that so long as the *Goeben* was outside the cruiser squadron's gun range but within her own, she constituted an *infinitely* superior force: the result was in accordance with the mathematical formula that $^1\!/_0 = $ infinity. Before the exchange became too philosophical, Scott won an important point by persuading the prosecution to state that it did not dispute the high elevation of the *Goeben*'s guns (and implicitly the ship's consequent great advantage in range). Yet even now the difference in armour which would compound that advantage was not raised. But Scott was able to profit from the recent engagement between the Austrians and the French at the mouth of the Adriatic, which Wray had seen: the Austrian light cruiser *Zenta* had been sunk by two hits from the French heavy guns at a range of 16,000 yards. Wray showed no fear of contradicting Milne's evidence, in which he supposed that the *Goeben* would somehow have come within range of the squadron in daylight despite the latter's inferior range and speed: 'She would be foolish if she did; there was absolutely no reason to suppose that she would.' Scott also used Wray to bring out Troubridge's acute distress over the conflict between his instinct to fight the enemy and his perceived duty not to do so at the time. 'His one object in life was to fight,' said Troubridge's flag captain. Wray confirmed that he was the writer of a letter to Troubridge, unaddressed, unsigned and cryptic only out of fear that it might fall into the wrong hands, and sent after the rear-admiral had been recalled home. It pointed out that Troubridge had understated the *Goeben*'s range advantage in his answer to the Admiralty's queries (his 'second letter'):

My dear Admiral, – The day after you left I went on board and saw the [admiral's] secretary, and he showed me your second letter. I am afraid you rather missed the point that I impressed upon you at the time which was not to do with comparative effective range, but that her *effective was probably greater than our maximum*, hence the suicidal effect . . . it is an important point and unanswerable by critics . . . Good luck to you, dear Admiral, and a speedy return to us [author's italics].

In other words Wray believed, and he stuck to it in court, that the *Goeben*'s guns were so superior that she could have hit the heavy cruisers with much effect before they could hope to hit her at all.

The evidence now given by Commander W. F. French, the Admiralty's gunnery expert, was highly technical, but Scott drew from him the opinion that in the perfect weather prevailing at the time of the chase, 'I think probably in an hour's time you [*Goeben*] would have hit them all [the heavy cruisers] comparatively frequently, at the time keeping out of range yourself.'

Scott: Under the circumstances you in command of the *Goeben* would be superior to them?
French: Yes.
Q: You have no doubt that the *Goeben* could do that at 17,000 yards?
A: I have no doubt.
Scott: I have no further questions.

With the gunnery witnesses, at least, he had struck gold, especially as both of them had been called by the prosecution. French added on re-examination by the prosecutor that he thought the difference in *effective* range between the German and British guns concerned was at least 4,000 yards, or two miles. More gold, as the court adjourned at the end of the third day and of the case for the prosecution.

The whole of the proceedings on the fourth and last day of the trial were taken up by the defence case. It opened with Troubridge himself reading out a statement (unsworn) which took him about an hour to deliver. The court adjourned for an hour to consider it, and on the resumption, Troubridge was sworn and subjected to cross-examination by Fremantle, the prosecutor, and questions from the court, which together took more than two hours, with a one-hour break for lunch about halfway through. The court then adjourned for the last time to consider its findings, which took precisely four hours to reach. Troubridge began his long declaration and apologia with two general points:

When an officer in command of a . . . force is ordered . . . to avoid being brought to action . . . it is clear that in his obedience he may risk . . . his reputation for all that an officer holds dear. The superior officer who has issued such an order is, therefore, bound in all honour to support in his action the officer who acts in obedience to such order – the most difficult and unwelcome that it is possible for an officer to receive . . .

And secondly:

Where an officer commanding a . . . force receives . . . orders . . . to avoid being brought to action *by a superior force of the enemy*, then in the absence of any precise instructions for his guidance, it is clear that he may at any moment be called upon to decide what, in his judgment, constitutes a superior force [Troubridge's emphasis].

The accused admiral argued that those in authority should back 'the honest, reasonable and considered judgment' of the subordinate, even if they did not fully agree with his assessment and even if '*the after consequences of his decision, unforeseen at the moment, prove vexatious to the superior authority or adversely affect the general policy of the country*' [author's italics]. Here is Troubridge's plea for immunity from hindsight, just eleven days after the *Goeben* entered the Black Sea and shelled Sevastopol. It was asking a lot. The admiral, blamed by superior authority for the escape of the Germans (as shown by the charge against him), sought to shift the blame to those above him. It was also an appeal to the principle of loyalty verging on the unconditional, and as such very risky. He cited two examples. One was the consistent refusal of Admiral Togo to commit his forces in the early stages of the Russo-Japanese war (which Troubridge had witnessed as an observer) because he had secret orders to husband his forces for the later fleet actions which destroyed the Russian Navy: Togo's colleagues and subordinates had been furious with him and there had even been rumours of an assassination plot, but his superiors publicly supported him throughout (and he had not even been faced with a superior force when he hung back). The other instance concerned a British tragedy in the early weeks of the war, when three older cruisers, *Aboukir, Cressy* and *Hogue*, had been sunk by the superior force of a German submarine attack. When the *Aboukir* went down, the others went to her crew's rescue and were promptly sunk in turn for their gallantry. The Admiralty called this an error of judgment by the would-be rescuers and forbade the fleet to repeat the mistake. Clearly here the error identified was that the officers concerned had failed to take evasive action.

Troubridge then summarized his orders and movements at the start of the war and the forces of the enemy he might encounter. He deployed the now familiar arguments about the importance of the battlecruisers on both sides, British and German. He and his officers, he said, would have taken on the Germans without battlecruiser support 'with great pleasure', but for the order about superior force. It had been his considered and publicly stated consistent opinion that in the open sea a battlecruiser was superior to a cruiser squadron in the conditions prevailing on August 7. But Milne had told him at the outset that he would give Troubridge two battlecruisers. It all seemed admirably clear. The two capital ships were there to deal with the *Goeben*, the cruiser squadron to cover the Adriatic. Had things been left that way, the Germans must have been brought to action. When the two battlecruisers were ordered west they sighted the *Goeben* and were told to 'hold her' as war was imminent. The German ship got away but was soon traced to Messina, from which the British battlecruisers were only a few hours distant. 'I took it for granted they would at once proceed to shadow her and to hold her. It was with feelings of dismay that I found this was not done.' Milne was now directing operations and Troubridge had no idea of what was going on, but assumed the French were blocking the western exit from the Mediterranean. (This argument overlooks the fact that the French and the British were not yet in touch, another lamentable failure.) When the run east began, Troubridge moved to the attack against his better judgment because 'my own deep conviction was that the *Goeben* had no right to be escaping at all and that if she had been sealed up in the Strait of Messina by the battlecruisers, as I thought she ought to have been, she never would have escaped.' So he remarked to Wray, 'The Mediterranean [Fleet?] will stink if we don't attack her.' He added:

Gradually, however, it forced itself more and more upon my mind that though my decision might be natural, might be heroic, it was certainly wrong and certainly in the teeth of my orders. The result was that after a mental struggle between my natural desire to fight and my sense of duty in view of my orders I came to the conclusion that I was not justified in allowing her to bring me to battle under the conditions in which we should sight one another.

The way the French fleet had dispatched the Austrian *Zenta* at eight miles had shown that Troubridge's light cruisers would have been useless against the *Goeben* and could not be seen as significant reinforcement in such an action, in the circumstances of August 7. Milne's argument about the lack of significant differences in range had been demolished by the gunnery witnesses. It was the fundamental issue in the case (as the principal prop to the 'superior force' argument). Because Troubridge was not free to divulge the orders under which he had acted, he had been obliged to endure their unpleasant consequences since returning home. He concluded:

In our service we all risk our lives for our country every day and give no thought to it . . . But here, in the first days of this great war much more is asked of me. In obedience to orders to avoid being brought to battle I am asked to risk my honour and the honour of the great name I bear. There was a moment – I have said it – when I felt too much was asked of me: I could not do it. Then I reflected. I felt that was unworthy of me. If my country asked it of me then even my honour I would imperil. And so, sir, I leave it in your hands.

Before the cross-examination began Scott made a slip of the tongue which may fairly be held to speak for itself: 'I wish to save the time of the court as much as possible by not having to repeat on oath practically the whole of *my* long statement'! [author's emphasis]

The cross-examination of Troubridge and the ensuing questions from the court unearthed more detail on such matters as coal, signals and movements but no new sensation. But Troubridge was questioned as to whether he could not have asked Milne if he was expected to attack in daylight and in the open sea:

Physically, yes; but morally, sir, I think no. At that time I had so vividly in my mind the fact that he knew I considered her a superior force, that I did not think it proper to make such a signal as that to the C-in-C. I confess I had it sometimes in my mind to make lots of signals to him, but you will all understand there are things you cannot very well do. You might with one individual, and not with another. I had been a long time under the C-in-C's command, and I knew he did not like suggestions, and that sort of thing. I did not think I could do so with propriety.

Even though Troubridge was defending himself against a serious charge and therefore was anxious to present himself in the best possible light, this remains an interesting comment on Milne's style of command, when added to the fact that he did not discuss his war plans with his subordinates as he had been told to do by the Admiralty.

Had Troubridge considered going further east to the narrow waters near Cape Matapan to wait for the *Goeben*? He had, he said: he decided not to because, 'not being able to conceive any mission for the *Goeben* in the east unless it was Egypt,' he feared he might be lured right away from the Adriatic whereupon the Germans could have turned round, dashed back and linked up with the Austrians. 'That was what I was precisely ordered to prevent.' Why had he changed his mind about the daylight attack after signalling his intention to make one?

Because I went down and got out my orders and studied them. I had for a year been thinking how to get at that ship in daylight. I knew I could not get near her, and I knew I had told my C-in-C I considered her in broad daylight to be a superior force, but I knew I would be faithless to my trust, and I knew what it is difficult to realize now. I have been in the Admiralty and I have conducted the negotiations with the French, and nobody knew better than I the enormous importance they attached to the Austrian fleet coming out, because they would send their troops back at once. I knew we should betray them and be faithless to them. The whole thing they asked us to do in the Mediterranean was that. I realized it was unworthy of me from my own personal gratification or ambitions, or whatever you may call it, to disobey these orders and risk the whole thing, to lose perhaps – whether we would or not I do not know – and to have let the *Goeben* divide the Mediterranean Fleet into two halves, one strong and one weak, and let him fall on the weaker, and my C-in-C with a few battlecruisers only a few hours off. I realized I was doing it for myself only; that was the truth, the desire to do something, that was what governed me, instead of my orders and the interests of the country as a whole.

After putting a few more questions, including one which showed that Troubridge fully understood the German tactics in the evasion and the run east and that he had been able to work out Souchon's thinking correctly after the event, the court adjourned when Mr Scott announced that the defence proposed to call no other witness. He also asked to be excused because he had a pressing engagement, which seems a little eccentric at this distance.

The court reassembled at 7.25 in the evening for the finding, which, even more curiously, was read out with the public excluded. The first nine paragraphs summarized the facts established before the court. The document concluded:

10. In view of the instructions received, the accused was justified in considering that he must not abandon his watch on the Adriatic, having regard to the transportation of the French troops then taking place between Algeria and France, and the possibility of the Austrian fleet coming out.
11. In view of the instructions received from the Admiralty by the C-in-C and repeated by him in his sailing orders to the accused, and also the signal made on August 4, *viz*, 'First Cruiser Squadron and *Gloucester* are not to get seriously engaged with superior force,' the court are of opinion that, under the particular circumstances of weather, time and position, the accused was justified in considering the *Goeben* was a superior force to the First Cruiser Squadron at the time they would have met, *viz*, 6 A.M. on August 7, in full daylight in the open sea.
12. Although it might have been possible to bring the *Goeben* to action off Cape Malea, or in the Cervi Channel, the court considers that, in view of the accused's orders to keep a close watch on the Adriatic, he was justified in abandoning the chase at the time he did, as he had no news or prospect of any force being sent to his assistance.
13. The court therefore finds that the charge against the accused is not proved, and fully and honourably acquits him of the same.

Not Guilty. It only remained for the president of the court, Admiral Sir George Egerton, to pick up the sword of Rear-Admiral Ernest Troubridge which had lain on the table in front of the court throughout the proceedings and solemnly hand it back.

The story of the trial of a flag officer in wartime for not engaging the enemy could hardly be expected to end there. Nor did it. The transcript made its way round the Admiralty for comment by senior officers. By this time Lord Fisher was back from retirement in his old job as First Sea Lord, in succession to the disgracefully ditched Battenberg who had fallen victim to his German name. Fisher was the first to attach a minute commenting on the case, and predictably he criticized his old *bête noire*, Milne. 'This most disastrous event of the escape of the *Goeben* and lamentable blow to British naval prestige would never have occurred had Sir B. Milne [sic] been off Messina with the three battlecruisers . . . – even if short of coal – at the time *Goeben* was in Messina harbour, for then *Goeben* could not possibly have escaped . . .' But Milne had been right in deciding (belatedly) to ignore the question of Italian territorial waters if necessary.

The next comment was made by the Fourth Sea Lord: 'It is probable that there is not much difference of opinion as to the incorrectness of the finding . . . a great blunder has been committed.' But Troubridge had been acquitted, and to avoid further controversy, it would be best to let things lie, Captain Cecil Lambert concluded. The Third Sea Lord was Rear-Admiral Frederick Tudor, who was also critical:

The finding of the court-martial appears to be correct on the evidence educed, but I am of opinion that its conclusions are wrong, both from the commonsense point of view and technically.

Tudor took the view that the order about superior force and the two orders about the *Goeben* being his objective should together have led Troubridge to conclude that his squadron was not regarded as an inferior force and that he was expected to attack. If he disagreed, he should have told Milne instead of misleading him about his intentions. 'The whole action of the rear-admiral contrasts most strangely with that of the captain of *Gloucester* who, in spite of inferior speed and of vastly inferior power, clung tenaciously to the *Goeben* until twice ordered back.' (One may reasonably intrude here to speculate as to what Their Lordships would have said had Kelly lost his ship between the first withdrawal order and the second . . .) Tudor found Wray's gunnery evidence exaggerated and, on imputed German accuracy at long range, 'farcical'. He went on to conclude with a point which verges on the unanswerable and which the prosecutor would have done well to bring out:

That the ships of the First Cruiser Squadron stood a chance of being severely punished during an engagement with the *Goeben* can be accepted, but that they could have been destroyed, or nearly destroyed, before the *Goeben* had *expended all her 11-inch ammunition* appears to me to be out of the question [author's italics].

The Second Sea Lord, Vice-Admiral Sir Frederick Hamilton, was blunt: 'The court has been entirely led off the track by a clever lawyer.' It was a simple charge of not fighting the enemy, and all one had to show was that the cruisers had been in a position to attack but did not. If Troubridge had based his defence on the argument that a move further south would have helped the *Goeben* to evade him and get into the Adriatic at high speed, that would have been 'a good strategical excuse'. But he had given his case away by offering the defence that he had been an inferior force. Wray's comments on the superior force issue and the argument about infinite superiority deriving from greater gun range was 'an answer which I never expected to hear from a naval officer.' The court had been diverted into trying Milne for his dispositions, 'and so admitted a cloud of irrelevance to obscure the issue.' Milne was not the accused and it was unfair to judge him 'without letting him have an opportunity to defend himself' (a curious comment in the light of his performance as a witness, we may think). If Milne had put his battlecruisers at both ends of the Strait of Messina, 'the *Goeben* could very possibly have come out at full speed and been away before the ship outside could have worked up to full speed.' (But this objection could have been met by having the blockading ships under half an hour's notice of full steam; a thumbnail calculation suggests that the *Goeben* would have had to run the gauntlet of eight 12-inch guns for at least half an hour if the ships had been well placed . . .) Hamilton, however, did criticize Milne for not ordering Troubridge to engage when he got his subordinate's 'abandoning' telegram. If Troubridge saw a conflict between his orders to regard the *Goeben* as his objective and to guard the Adriatic, he should have said so. Hamilton concluded: 'I am of opinion that nothing more should now be done in the matter, except that Captain Wray should also remain unemployed, as it is decidedly dangerous to have an officer of his opinions in a responsible position.'

The most considered and penetrating comment was made by Admiral of the Fleet Sir Arthur Wilson, a highly regarded and vastly experienced officer and holder of the Victoria Cross, who was working at the Admiralty as an adviser to help out in the war (Admirals of the Fleet 'never retire'). He pointed out that if the *Goeben* had been chasing the cruiser squadron outside its range but within her own, the light cruisers would have had an excellent chance of a torpedo attack. The court had concluded that the *Goeben* was a superior force under the circumstances:

The *Goeben* could no doubt choose her own range but unless the German gunnery is very much better than ours she would have to expend all her ammunition before she could put the four ships out of action keeping outside 15,400 yards [sic].

The decision of the court-martial has very little bearing on the escape of the ships as nothing Admiral Troubridge could do after the ships were once clear of the Strait of Messina could prevent their escaping if they wished to do so without fighting and our battlecruisers were too far away to take any part in the pursuit.

No one had foreseen at the time the effect of the ships making for the Dardanelles. The two other contingencies, their making for the Adriatic or the Strait of Gibraltar, were provided for.

Wilson delivers no judgment on whether Troubridge should have attacked, nor does he condemn him for not doing so. He avoids all emotive language and does not attack Wray for going to Troubridge and persuading him that an attack would be the suicide of the squadron (which is how Wilson saw the flag captain's role). His analysis is calm and factual and makes no recommendations: not for him the rush to judgment, and in his place of honour and fulfilled ambition he was free to take a detached view from a position of unassailable independence. It would have been good had Wilson been invited to comment on the reports which led to the court of inquiry. It would also have been fascinating to be a fly on the wall when the court-martial reached its finding!

There, officially, the matter rested. Unofficially the repercussions continued for some time, and it was not only to be Troubridge, the acquitted admiral, who never forgot 'the *Goeben* affair'. Curiously enough, in the circumstances, of the three naval officers who came under fire for their role in it – Troubridge, Wray and Milne – it was the first-named whose career suffered least after the trial, whatever private purgatory he inhabited for the rest of his life and whatever bitterness accumulated in his soul (the evidence for which is cited below). Obviously the Admiralty could not be seen to be punishing a man who had been 'fully and honourably' acquitted, but it refused to appoint Troubridge, who was fifty-two in 1914, to another seagoing command. Instead, he was appointed head of the British Naval Mission to Serbia at the beginning of 1915, and in this obscure job on the fringes of the war he proceeded to distinguish himself. In the country which had been the epicentre of the events which led to the war he won the respect of the Serbians for his tireless efforts in organizing the rescue of troops and civilians from the war-zone. In 1916 he took charge of local naval forces which saved Belgrade from a bombardment. He was promoted vice-admiral in 1916, received the knighthood that normally goes with such rank (and for his services in the Balkans), became full admiral in 1919 and retired from the navy in 1921. He then spent three years on the International Danube Commission and died in 1926. A year or two before that he put down on paper his considered thoughts on the first week of the war in the Mediterranean, his *Rough Account of Goeben and Breslau*, which surfaced for the first time in 1970, in E. W. R. Lumby's book for the Navy Records Society.

In it he criticizes Milne for not demanding a court-martial the moment he himself was acquitted, as Admiral Keppel had done in 1780 after his second-in-command was tried and acquitted in connection with 'errors of judgment in his conduct in contact with the enemy'. Of Churchill, on whose staff he once served, Troubridge wrote: 'How often Mr Churchill has said to me, "In politics one can never afford to admit that one has made a mistake." And so he remains true to principle in his book.' The work referred to is *The World Crisis*, which had just begun to appear. Although he admired Churchill, he thought he knew his cruisers better than a First Lord with so many other things to think about. He goes on to say that his decision to avoid battle was not particularly connected with his orders about superior force. 'It was a principle I should in any case have followed,' in the circumstances of open sea and high visibility. He added that Milne had spent an embarrassing ten minutes in court trying to work out how the slower squadron could catch up with the faster *Goeben* before he was rescued by the president; and Fremantle, the prosecutor, had told him later that he and navigation officers had 'sat up till two in the morning endeavouring to solve this insoluable problem' and gave up.

Churchill's question as to why Troubridge had 'changed his mind' was the observation of a civilian who had never seen service at sea. One chance for getting within the cruisers' range of the *Goeben* would have been poor visibility, so it had been his duty to steam south to see what the weather was like in the probable area of contact; but it had been a perfect morning everywhere. So he had to be sure he was not sighted by the Germans, which was what actually led him to alter 'the course of the squadron to one parallel with the course of the *Goeben* but some forty miles distant, and at the same time well ahead of her.' He then reported to Milne, 'conceiving that this would give him an opportunity did he desire it to order a battle at all costs.' But he got no reply for six hours, 'a fact of which no real explanation was ever given.' (In that case, why did Troubridge use the phrase 'abandoned the chase' in the message referred to?)

His account of the eve-of-war conversation with Milne about the orders and the meaning of 'superior force' adds nothing to what Troubridge said in court. It was a case of Milne's word against his and there was no way of resolving that problem when no witnesses had been present to attest to what had been said. He claims that he had originally been told by the Admiralty that the court of inquiry was to be a general one as distinct from an investigation specifically concerned with his own conduct. He was therefore unprepared, and although it had been open to him, when he was told the truth about the inquiry's terms of reference, to say nothing, he had decided to make a statement anyway (arguably one of Troubridge's greatest tactical errors). He then found out that Milne 'slowly and with great deliberation' denied his own version of the conversation. He realized that he had to 'fight my own battles with him hostile, instead of with him shouldering some of the responsibility as I had expected.' He added: 'It was necessary that someone should suffer for the escape of the *Goeben*.' Churchill would not accept any blame, nor would Battenberg, nor now would Milne. 'There only remained myself.'

He claimed that the court-martial had been held 'in secret' although we have seen that it was not, except for certain sensitive evidence related to security and the reading of the finding, and that the record had never been published 'to this day'. In fact until very recently court-martial records were not released for seventy-five years, which would have meant waiting until 1989 to see them but for the special concession made to Lumby. Troubridge said many individuals and newspapers had offered to take up his case but he refused for the sake of not causing controversy in the navy, which had suffered grievously from it in the past. He went on in his account to make an observation which might well have caused him agony:

I was informed by an officer of high rank [unnamed] that [in] the last letter he received from my old friend Admiral Cradock he said, alluding to the fact that I was to be tried by court-martial for not having engaged the *Goeben*, 'I will take care I do not suffer the fate of poor Troubridge.'

On 8 November 1914, the Sunday when Troubridge's court was in recess, Cradock engaged the crack German Cruiser Squadron under Graf Spee off Coronel in Chile, with his own squadron of unquestionably inferior ships, and was annihilated, with the loss of his own life and most of his ships and men. It was the first British naval defeat in battle for a century and it shocked the country. Fisher wrote to his most brilliant subordinate, Beatty, at the end of that awful month for the Royal Navy: 'Steer midway between Troubridge and Cradock and all will be well, Cradock preferred.' Troubridge's feelings when he first heard about Cradock's letter can only be guessed at now. He wrote:

Had I done as poor Cradock did at Coronel and the British Navy, as it inevitably would have, had suffered a defeat in the first days of the war and the loss of a squadron and four thousand men, can one not imagine the whole posse who fell upon me for not courting such a disaster, falling upon me for incurring it?

Churchill would have cited the order about superior force; Milne would have said he passed it on and that Troubridge himself had said he regarded the *Goeben* as superior and had demanded the matter be left to his own judgment. (All this is highly probable but of course it remains purely hypothetical.)

Troubridge concludes his brief account with the claim

that he had been told by a British arms company representative that the man had told the British Embassy in Constantinople before war was declared that the *Goeben* would sail there, and his source was the Turkish Minister of Marine, Jemal Pasha. 'He was told to go about his business. The whole course of the affair would have been changed had the Embassy communicated this important item of news to England.'

All in all, the *Rough Account* adds little to the record except for the intriguing story about the prewar tip from the arms salesman, a Captain Vere of Armstrong and Vickers, who was probably involved in the sale of the two dreadnoughts to Turkey, and of course the sad anecdote about Cradock. The tone is bitter and we may be sure Troubridge never got over the night of 7 August 1914. There is no trace of *esprit de l'escalier*, the perfect answer which comes too late, and the passage about the alteration of course, the 'abandoning' message and giving Milne the chance to order him into attack regardless is simply a distortion which the facts cannot be made to fit.

In the case of Captain Fawcet Wray, the vengeful suggestion of the Second Sea Lord that he should 'remain unemployed' was accepted by the Admiralty. He was punished without trial, having been refused any chance to clear his honour both at the court-martial of Troubridge and afterwards, by not being found a post until 15 February 1915, when he was given command of the old light cruiser HMS *Talbot*. In her he won the Distinguished Service Order at Gallipoli, and although he eventually reached the rank of vice-admiral on the retired list after ending his active service in 1922, there can be no doubt that his career was blighted by his being passed over. The move from flag captain of a heavy cruiser squadron to command of a twenty-year-old light cruiser can only be seen as a demotion. On 3 August 1917 Wray made a statutory declaration before a City of London commissioner for oaths, in an attempt to clear his name.

Wray declared that his personal honour and his character as an officer had been 'impugned by allegations of cowardice and default,' and he had been denied the chance of clearing himself or restoring his reputation. After narrating the now familiar events of August 2–7, Wray said that Troubridge had stated on a number of occasions that he abandoned the chase 'in consequence of the advice I gave him in my capacity of flag captain.'

My advice as described by Admiral Troubridge implied cowardice on my part and from statements that have been made to me it would appear that this was the impression that was received by Mr Churchill and other high officials at the Admiralty who had the privilege of studying Admiral Troubridge's evidence at the court of inquiry. The same impression has been received by my brother officers. Mr Churchill, I have been informed, stated that 'poor Troubridge was wrangled with by his flag captain for two hours and eventually was persuaded by him not to fight.'

Churchill had refused to see him. But, Wray went on to claim: 'The advice I tendered was not given with the intention of dissuading him from continuing the chase of the *Goeben* . . . on the contrary, I actually remonstrated with him when I realized that he had decided to abandon the chase.'

He had suggested on August 6 that the squadron should position itself in the middle of the Strait of Otranto, the mouth of the Adriatic, so that it would be placed to drive the *Goeben* towards either shore and engage her within the range of its lighter guns. Troubridge had turned this down, said Wray, because it implied an action in the open sea. During the fateful night Wray had been pleased when Troubridge told him he was going to attack by lying across the *Goeben*'s bows 'and more or less going bald-headed for her.' But then the captain had realized that such tactics would not prevent the *Goeben* with her speed and range of fire from circumventing the squadron and damaging it at the same time. His claims at the court-martial about her shooting capacity at extreme range had been vindicated by subsequent events in the war, and she would have had few problems when being chased by ships seven knots slower.

Having been a party to the proposed plan of 'cutting off' the *Goeben* and having after full consideration come to the definite conclusion that the plan was utterly impracticable I conceived it to be my clear duty to go to the rear-admiral and tell him what I thought of my previous advice as to *our method of preventing the name of the Mediterranean stinking*. I did not go to him to advise him to abandon the chase [Wray's emphasis].

In short it was the proposed tactic that implied the suicide of the squadron because of the circumstances attending an attack, not the idea of attack *per se*. 'When the rear-admiral gave orders to alter course . . . I thought that he was merely hauling off to gain time while he asked the C-in-C for instructions and also to reconsider the problem. I frankly admit I was astounded when he announced his intention to the squadron of abandoning the chase.' (Can this be what prompted Troubridge, who must have seen Wray's affidavit, to make a remarkably similar explanation in his *Rough Account* for the first time? We can only speculate.) When Troubridge altered course a second time, Wray went on, he actually went to remonstrate with him (presumably because this made it clear he was turning away altogether), and suggested the squadron proceed to follow the still pursuing *Gloucester*, to give her something to fall back on. He had not been given the opportunity to add this to his evidence at the court-martial, which had been interested only in the conversations prior to 4 A.M. on the 7th. Troubridge had replied that the decision now lay with Milne, who decided three hours later to pull back the *Gloucester*. Wray claimed that Troubridge had distorted and even invented much of what he attributed to him about the gunnery question. During his evidence at the court-martial, Troubridge had effectively cleared Wray, 'but I regret to say that owing to his attitude towards me since the court-martial the effect of it has been nullified.'

Wray claimed that Troubridge had repeatedly urged him not to act to clear his honour, and promised to intercede for him with Churchill. When he left for Serbia Wray asked him whether he had done so and he 'stated that he had had no opportunity and didn't see why he should do anything because after all if it had not been for me he would have fought the *Goeben*. I then asked him if that was the case how could he reconcile that statement with his evidence at the court-martial. He replied: "My dear Wray, by the time you are an admiral and have a staff of your own you will realize that you must be loyal to your staff. *I did that to save you*"' [Wray's emphasis]. Wray concluded by complaining that the Admiralty had ignored all his pleas for help to clear his name, whereas Milne had been exonerated publicly and Troubridge acquitted by his peers.

But there had been nothing to stop Wray slipping in the occasional sentence during his evidence to the effect that his advice had been against the method of attack rather than the attack itself, except perhaps loyalty to his chief. To judge by his unsigned letter to Troubridge this loyalty was very strong and may be said to do him credit. But it seems odd that in that note the only misunderstanding he mentioned to the admiral had to do with gun ranges: one would think that if Wray felt his commander had wrongly taken his advice as a general counsel against attack, this would have been a rather more fundamental matter to point out. If this wider misreading by Troubridge only became apparent to Wray when he heard the admiral's evidence, why did Wray say to the court that he did not think the admiral was justified in attacking the *Goeben at all* without battlecruiser support, without adding the qualification 'in the circumstances'? In the end, of course, as Troubridge said at the court of inquiry, the responsibility for his actions was his alone, regardless of whatever advice he had received from juniors. Wray was entirely within his rights to give his advice; it was his job and his duty to point out the difficulties, and his advice on gunnery had been accurate. Finally we may wonder at Wray's claim that his highly charged, emotional comment to Troubridge, 'Admiral, that was the bravest thing you have ever done in your life,' referred only to a change of tactic rather than a change of heart about attacking. If Wray was hard done by, as he was for being punished without being heard, he must be seen to have contributed to his own fate.

Admiral Sir Berkeley Milne was also prompted to defend his role in the *Goeben* affair, by the publication in 1920 of the first volume of Sir Julian Corbett's official history of the war at sea. This is a worthy work, considering how soon after the war it was written, although subsequent revelations indicate that Corbett had not seen all the records. But he did criticize, though not harshly, Milne's dispositions and his tardiness during the chase, making the point that the battlecruisers should have been used to seal the Strait of Messina. Milne was driven into writing a short book in 1921 to defend his name, a purpose this curious volume entirely failed to achieve. It is a querulous and quibbling effort which reveals no new facts and is full of logic-chopping. Milne complains, for example, that Corbett had written in a letter to a magazine that he had consulted senior officers engaged in the chase before writing his account; but he had not approached Milne himself. 'I regard it as extremely unfortunate (at least) that Sir Julian Corbett should permit himself to assert, or to imply, that his narrative was submitted to me before publication.' Corbett asserted or implied no such thing at any time. Milne says he went to see Corbett about his account but got no satisfaction: 'Upon my discussing the matter with Sir Julian Corbett, he was unable to afford me any explanation or to suggest any redress.' This is a most peculiar way of reporting such an encounter: one may ask whether Corbett was dumbstruck or, if he said anything, what it was, but Milne does not say. He does claim that Corbett implied a charge had been brought against him whereas in fact he had been publicly exonerated, as Corbett stated. To read such an implication into Corbett's text is quite plainly a distortion, one of many indications that Milne was the kind of person who could not take any criticism from any source about anything, and also that his grasp of semantics was alarmingly poor. Corbett's assessment will strike any fair-minded reader as balanced, moderate and even sympathetic on such matters as the faults in his orders and the Admiralty's delays and mistakes. Milne, on the other hand, tends to treat the reader of his little opus as an idiot: 'For the benefit of the lay reader it should here be explained that it is useless to try to overtake a ship which is faster than her pursuer . . . Therefore . . . it is necessary that the faster ship should be intercepted by crossing her course . . . That the pursuing ships must be so disposed as to cut off the faster ship pursued, is an elementary maxim in tactics which the author of the "Official History" strangely ignores.' Corbett doubtless took this amazing fact as read just as, in a different context, he might not have bothered to point out that one cannot catch a fast car from behind with a fleet of milk-floats. This has nothing to do with tactics but rather with the basic laws of logic and physics, and it still does not explain why Milne did not make sure of an interception by blockading Messina.

The story of Milne's prolonged declining years (he died in 1938 at the age of eighty-three) is pathetic. He was not allowed to take up the Nore command but was put on half-pay and never got another post. As the years wore on he fired off letters to all and sundry complaining about his treatment and became something of a resident club bore to the British Establishment. Even his request in 1919 for a court-martial had been ignored, which is hardly surprising in view of his public exoneration. It was a plea which would have sounded better if made in 1914, but the refusal became one of a growing accumulation of grievances. He preserved all the correspondence on what clearly became a grand obsession, the final legacy of a small-minded man. Milne, one of nature's truly petty officers, is surely an outstanding example of the adverse workings of the British class system insofar as it is built on unearthed privilege. Fisher, a man who rose to the top on merit (which the British system also permits), was absolutely right about Milne from the very beginning, long before he was put to the test and found wanting.

The other party to the *Goeben* affair was the Admiralty itself, specifically the man in charge, Winston Churchill. It need hardly be said that the episode did not ruin his career (not even the Gallipoli disaster did that in the end). His account of the affair is referred to in chapter 4, but there is a superbly written coda to it:

–

In all this story of the escape of the *Goeben* one seems to see the influence of that sinister fatality which at a later stage and on a far larger scale was to dog the enterprise against the Dardanelles. The terrible 'Ifs' accumulate. If my first thoughts on July 27 of sending the [battlecruiser] *New Zealand* to the Mediterranean had materialized; if we could have opened fire on the *Goeben* during the afternoon of August 4; if we had been less solicitous for Italian neutrality; if Sir Berkeley Milne had sent the *Indomitable* to coal at Malta instead of Bizerta; if the Admiralty had sent him direct instructions when on the night of the 5th they learned where the *Goeben* was; if Rear-Admiral Troubridge in the small hours of August 7 had not changed his mind; if the *Dublin* and her two destroyers had intercepted the enemy during the night of the 6th to 7th – the story of the *Goeben* would have ended here.

The terrible 'Ifs' accumulate. A resonant, justly famous phrase from a great man and a great writer, which subtly avoids greater blame by accepting lesser. The catalogue of 'Ifs' is far from complete. If the Admiralty had given proper priority to immediate coordination with the French at staff level; if the French had attacked when they sighted the Germans; if the alarm about Austria had not been falsely sounded; if the British and French governments had not arrogantly and blindly dismissed Turkey (and Germany's manifest interest in it) from their strategic calculations . . . and so on. The failure to catch the *Goeben* is a failure of leadership: the higher the level at which the various mistakes were made, the greater was the responsibility. At Churchill, the buck stops. As Arthur Marder points out, the escape of the Germans caused the first allegation of 'bungling in high places', which was to become with much justice one of the recurrent themes of the First World War, and was first levelled at Churchill as early as October 1914. 'The "ifs" will explain, but they cannot excuse,' Marder wrote. 'Instead of a smashing success which was easily within the British grasp and which would have been of inestimable psychological, political and strategic value at the beginning of the war, a bitter disappointment was the result. The escape of the *Goeben* was a blow to British naval prestige and naval morale.' The verdict of the grand master of British naval history of the period is: 'The responsibilities for the escape of the *Goeben* must be shared by Troubridge and the Admiralty equally, with Milne in third place.'

How differently events might have gone in the Mediterranean in 1914 was demonstrated by a spectacular clash twenty-five years later. On 13 December 1939 one of eight groups of ships formed to deal with the German surface raiders in the Atlantic sighted the pocket battleship *Graf Spee*. The German ship, equipped with a modernized version of the tried and tested 11-inch gun, had been built to comply with the terms of the Treaty of Versailles of 1919, which limited the tonnage of German war vessels to 10,000. She was a masterpiece of shipbuilding for she could outgun almost anything fast enough to catch her and outrun almost anything large enough to sink her. Commodore Henry Harwood, RN, had three cruisers under his command in Force G – the *Ajax*, his flagship, the *Exeter* and the Royal New Zealand Navy's *Achilles*. Lighter and faster than the *Defence* type, they were also less well-armed, two of them with 6-inch guns. In daylight, on the open sea and in good visibility off the eastern coast of South America, Harwood sent his ships into the attack at top speed, the *Exeter* with her 8-inch guns on one side, the *Ajax* and *Achilles* on the other. After ninety minutes the *Exeter* was almost as badly damaged as it is possible for a still floating ship to be and was ordered to limp to safety in the Falkland Islands, while the other two retired out of range to shadow. All they had done to the *Graf Spee* was to wing her by causing limited damage. She put into the neutral harbour of Montevideo in Uruguay while Harwood, soon reinforced by the cruiser *Cumberland*, waited offshore. On the 17th the *Graf Spee* disembarked a large part of her crew and put to sea accompanied by a German merchantman. In the afternoon the steamer took off the rest of the sailors and at sunset the battleship succumbed to a series of shattering and spectacular explosions. Although Captain Hans Langsdorff, by all acounts an outstanding officer, did have orders to scuttle if cornered, he shot himself two days later. It was a famous victory for Harwood and an immense boost for British morale, and he was most deservedly and instantaneously promoted to rear-admiral and knighted. But his victory was won by German default as much as the courage and spirit of his men. The lesson of the Battle of the River Plate, which offers many analogies to the fight Troubridge never fought, is that victory and defeat do not depend on the balance of forces alone but also on unfathomable factors. The *Graf Spee* was undoubtedly a 'superior force', but you never know your luck.

Having been able to examine the story of the escape of the *Goeben* and the *Breslau* from both sides, we know, unlike Milne and Troubridge, that the first-named ship was by no means as superior as she looked or as the manuals suggested. One detects on the British side a certain defeatism, expressed in the attribution to the Germans of immunity to Murphy's Law, which decrees that everything which can go wrong will go wrong. The *Goeben*'s boilers were dangerously defective. She had a coal problem. Souchon was let down by his allies. He got an order which could easily have been read as cancelling his instructions to go to Constantinople. He had no refuge. His men came periously close to complete exhaustion. He had prepared his ships for scuttling. The terrible 'buts' accumulate.

Several of these difficulties were known to the Royal Navy, which nevertheless based its calculations on the assumption that the Imperial Navy, for all the excellence of its ships untried and untested, would perform flawlessly. The thought that the new, unused and highly complex naval technology might be giving the Germans at least some of the same problems as the British experienced never occurred. Neither Milne nor (especially) Troubridge can be called a coward, yet they were both manifestly afraid of risking their ships in action. Churchill's 'Fate' played a much smaller role in the *Goeben* affair than human error.

We may legitimately conclude that Milne was in fact as much to blame as Troubridge and the Admiralty. But when all is said and done there is no escape from the judgment that Rear-Admiral Ernest Troubridge should have had a go.

PART FOUR
The Consequences

Do your utmost – the future of Turkey is at stake.

Admiral Wilhelm Souchon,
Signal to all ships, 29 October 1914

If blood be the price of Admiralty,
Lord God, we ha' paid it in full!

Rudyard Kipling,
The Song of the Dead

10

The Black Sea campaign

The Kaiser and his aides were delighted with the first fruits of Admiral Souchon's arrival in the Straits. Intelligence reports probably exaggerated the degree of panic along the Russian Black Sea coast which, insofar as it existed, was most likely due to the Turkish mobilization in support of the Ottoman Empire's posture of armed neutrality rather than to the presence of the German ships. But Russian army units which were to have gone to face the Germans or the Austrians had to be kept in, or even diverted to, the coastal region. With German officers in command and in key posts in the Turkish Army and Navy and German ships in the Straits, the Central Powers held a trump card for the peace negotiations, to end what everyone still believed would be a short war, whether or not Turkey actually joined the fighting; if hostilities spread and endured, Germany and Austria had a most important new springboard for attacking Russia, the main enemy of both. For the moment they could afford to wait until Turkish uncertainty about the intentions of Bulgaria on the northern flank was resolved. Souchon took the opportunity to start working up his enthusiastic but formidably feeble new command while the newly arrived Admiral Guido von Usedom took charge of the no less decrepit fortifications of the Straits and General Liman von Sanders pressed on with the stiffening of the Turkish Army.

The Entente Powers meanwhile had begun to rue their shortsighted neglect of Turkey, which had given the dapper Enver Pasha and his principal cabinet ally, the shambling but shrewd giant Talaat Bey, their chance to commit the country to the German cause. The Russians offered Enver a defensive military alliance on August 16 ten days after the War Minister had himself suggested something similar in a moment of unease about the implications of the secret treaty with Germany. But the *Goeben* and the *Breslau* had dispelled his doubts and he brushed aside the Russian arguments about their limitless military strength and their request that the German sailors at least be sent home. On August 18 Rear-Admiral Arthur Limpus, head of the British Naval Mission which was still in place though no longer allowed to board Turkish ships, called on Enver with a conciliatory message from his chief, Winston Churchill, First Lord of the Admiralty. Limpus assured his host of Britain's abiding goodwill towards Turkey and expressed regret for the seizure of the two Turkish dreadnoughts, to which London had been unable to see any alternative in the circumstances. The money paid for them would be returned in full and the ships would be given to Turkey after the war. The admiral reminded Enver that the combined and allied fleets of Britain, France, Russia and Japan were in a position to dominate the world and urged him to send all the Germans in Turkish service home before they brought disaster upon his country, whose only realistic policy was strict neutrality. On the other hand Britain could graciously condescend to take a tolerant view in the circumstances of the 'purchase' of the two German ships, and no doubt if the German sailors remained aboard much might be learned from them; Britain would be happy to replace them after the war. This too fell on deaf ears; Enver was not now to be diverted from his conviction that he had picked the winning side, and that the sooner Turkey took an active role in the war, the more she would stand to gain from the spoils of victory when peace came. But he was constrained by the divisions in the cabinet and the poor state of readiness of the armed forces.

Souchon, who was later to describe the period between his entry into the Dardanelles and his breakout from the Bosporus into the Black Sea nearly twelve weeks later as the worst time of the war for him, was also obliged to play a waiting game. On August 18 he signalled to the Admiralty in Berlin:

Think it possible break out of Bosporus if Turkish government can be successfully deceived beforehand. Ambassador thinks operation in Black Sea premature at present. Ambassador lays great weight on presence *Goeben, Breslau* inside Narrows for now until Turkish mobilization further progressed and political situation clarified. Hold this view correct in light of general war purpose . . .

The admiral's first inspection of his new command threw up some astonishing and daunting difficulties. The Turkish Navy then consisted of 10,000 men – and no less than 8,000 officers. There was, however, a severe shortage of warrant and petty officers. The most proficient men had gone to England to collect the two now confiscated dreadnoughts, and had not yet returned. Most of the ratings were of inland peasant stock and had virtually no seagoing experience. Only a small proportion was actually living aboard ship, the rest being in barracks ashore. The ships themselves were in an appalling state of neglect and their crews had little or no knowledge of signalling, navigation, shooting, torpedoes or damage control, and coal and ammunition were in short supply. The officers were looked down upon as an inferior breed to their army colleagues (something to which German naval officers were also accustomed at home, where the army remained much the senior service). Despite all this,

Ambassador von Wangenheim reported to Berlin as early as August 21 that a German naval officer had been favourably impressed by the morale and discipline of the Turkish sailors as the Germans began to train them up. By the end of the month hundreds of German reinforcements had arrived by train through neutral Rumania and Bulgaria. They wore civilian clothes and, if asked, pretended to be engineering workers on their way to constructions jobs and the like in Turkey; some brazenly wore their naval uniforms, however, and drew protests from the Russians and the French about breaches of neutrality. The Germans also took the risk of sending ammunition and other vitally necessary supplies by the same route, as well as by barge along the River Danube. One of Souchon's first acts was to scour Constantinople for coal and oil and have all available stocks concentrated in guarded stores, including 8,000 tonnes of Welsh coal, the world's best for ships' furnaces, which had been delivered before the war. German officers were put in charge of arrangements to ensure regular supplies of coal from the mines of north-western Anatolia via the Black Sea and the Bosporus. Others soon stopped shaking their heads over the condition of the Turkish warships and started supervising repairs. The ancient battleship *Messudieh*, her main armament of two 9.2-inch guns still missing and represented by wooden dummies, was assigned the role of floating artillery battery in the Dardanelles; her seaward-facing 6-inch guns were left in place but the landward ones were removed and sited ashore. For her, at least, the war would be over by Christmas. At this point the Turkish ships under Souchon's command that were capable of immediate deployment amounted to ten: the old battleship *Torgud Reis*, the torpedo-gunboat *Berk-i-Satvet* and eight destroyers. Another elderly battleship, two armoured cruisers and several smaller vessels needed urgent repairs, and were detained in shipyards.

Just as Souchon was beginning to get to grips with the formidable problems of his new command, General Liman von Sanders was undergoing a bout of despair about his own task of making the Turkish Army ready for war. In the middle of August 1914 he asked the Kaiser to recall him to Germany, together with his military mission. On the 19th, Souchon tried very hard to persuade the general, who was senior to him, to take a more optimistic view but seemed to make no impression; Liman's request was, however, turned down firmly by Berlin. By the end of the month Souchon had deduced that the British, despite the arrival of French warships to reinforce them off the Dandanelles, were anxious to avoid war with Turkey (the Germans were kept fully informed of all Entente diplomatic moves in Constantinople). Bullishly the admiral reported to Berlin on September 5 that the Turkish fleet would be ready for action in eight days. The next morning Souchon pressed Enver for permission for a naval demonstration off the coasts of Bulgaria and Rumania, with which the Turks still hoped to conclude a military agreement, as a gesture to concentrate their minds. Enver was at first favourably inclined but changed his mind when he realized that such a move might also have the opposite effect from that intended. In mid-month, as the British repaid the last instalment of the Turkish dreadnought money, the Germans in Constantinople and the war party in the Turkish Cabinet failed to agree on how, when and even whether to make some kind of move against the Entente Powers from Turkish territory: Egypt and Suez, the Crimea and the Caucasus were considered as objectives, but there was as much disagreement between the German generals and admirals as between the Germans and the Turks as to the best target. The war party was firmly opposed, because of the divisions in cabinet, to Souchon's demand for permission to deploy his ships in the Black Sea, for which Berlin was now pressing. Souchon diverted some naval funds to the purpose of bribing the Turkish press to show more favour to the German cause, and on September 18 he obtained an interview with the Grand Vizier, Said Halim, at which he accused the Turks of bad faith and repeated his demand for permission to exercise in the Black Sea. The next day he received a message from Enver permitting a strictly limited reconnaissance manoeuvre by two ships. Souchon promptly sent three, but he heeded the plea from Ambassador von Wangenheim not to dispatch the *Goeben* or the *Breslau*, to avoid undue alarm in Bulgaria and Rumania. Having extracted from the reluctant Turks permission for Black Sea exercises for small numbers of ships on a regular basis, Souchon organized a naval parade off Constantinople on September 21, to try to influence political and general opinion in his favour, although most of the Turkish ships were still in miserable condition and the *Goeben*'s boiler repairs were far from complete.

Events really began to move in Souchon's direction when the Dardanelles entrance was closed in the last days of September after a British destroyer had stopped a Turkish one (see chapter 11). By October 3 Souchon was able to send the *Goeben* and two Turkish battleships into the Black Sea for gunnery exercises. His policy now was to lull the Turks into accepting such manoeuvres as routine while he worked up the ships to a pitch at which an 'incident' with the Russians could be engineered. On October 7 Souchon was invited to regularize his position as Turkish fleet commander by becoming an admiral in the Turkish Navy, directly answerable to Turkish General

Headquarters, which came under Enver as War Minister. He politely declined. The next day the *Breslau* entered the Black Sea to try to locate the Russian Black Sea Fleet, which, however, was confined to its main base at Sevastopol to avoid provoking the Turks. On October 12, Souchon chanced his arm by sending out the whole of the Turkish fleet that was serviceable for an exercise and was duly if unharshly rebuked by Enver. The War Minister, encouraged no doubt by a German offer of a 'soft loan' of two million Turkish pounds (in effect a bribe to Turkey to enter the war), was steeling himself to unleash the frustrated Souchon against the Russians. The energetic admiral was busy with his staff drawing up a detailed operational plan in consultation with both Enver and the German General Staff in Berlin. Although both the cabinet and the 'Young Turks' of the ruling Committee for Union and Progress were divided on the issue of entering the war, Enver's commitment was underpinned by the fact that both bodies had a majority in favour of the German alliance. Further, some of those who favoured neutrality made no secret of their view that going to war later could become a good idea if there was manifest profit in it, and that they would have changed their ignoble posture already had the Central Powers been able to produce a few more of the spectacular victories of the opening weeks of the war. The British Naval Mission under Admiral Limpus finally left for home on September 16, by which time the Turks had reason to believe that Bulgaria would join the Central Powers and act against Serbia. The Turks felt confident enough to press the Central and Entente Powers alike for an end to the humiliating 'capitulations' whereby foreigners in Turkey enjoyed immunity from the authorities there, a point eagerly conceded by both alliances. The Turks also supported the anti-British Khedive of Egypt in his rejection of a demand from London that he go into exile in Italy at the end of September; he stayed on in Constantinople. But the Germans recognized that the neutralists, though a slowly dwindling minority, would recover lost ground if much more time passed without either an irreversible Turkish involvement in hostilities or new evidence of progress towards victory from the Central Powers; and even the war party seemed determined to hold out for more and more concessions.

Once again it was the Germanophile Enver who made the decisive and fateful move. On October 22 he drew up a set of proposals for Turkish intervention in the war and had them sent to the German General Staff for comment. These included fleet action to seize naval supremacy in the Black Sea without prior declaration of war on Russia, Turkish Army attacks on Russian territory and moves against the British in Egypt as well as various initiatives in the Balkans, depending on the eventual attitudes of Bulgaria, Rumania and Greece. The General Staff in Berlin signalled its approval the next day, politely pressing for early naval action and an expedition against Egypt as soon as possible (it never really got near to success and was eventually a complete failure). On the 24th, Enver gave Souchon a set of sealed orders to Turkish captains to follow the German admiral's instructions, accompanied by an order to Souchon himself to enter the Black Sea with the whole fleet, attack the Russians there and seize maritime supremacy, in his own good time.

Admiral Souchon, by now wise in the ways of the Turkish leadership, was determined to execute Enver's secret order before there was yet another change of mind in Constantinople. Aware that Enver was acting largely on his own initiative and also that Wangenheim had at last swung round to the view that immediate action was essential for Germany's interests, Souchon was determined not to let his hard-won opportunity slip out of his hands, as he made clear to the German Admiralty on the 26th:

Entering Black Sea with fleet under guise of fleet exercise, with intent to attack . . .

The next day the Turkish fleet with its two German reinforcements filed out of the Bosporus into the Black Sea for the first time in almost four decades. Later the same day Souchon called a captains' conference aboard the *Goeben* and revealed to them the nature of the operation upon which they had embarked under the impression that it was just a large exercise. He unfolded a detailed plan for a series of closely coordinated and carefully timed attacks on Russian Black Sea ports, including Odessa, Feodosia, Novorossiysk and the main naval base at Sevastopol, accompanied by minelaying. The operational order ended with the Nelsonian words:

Do your utmost: the future of Turkey is at stake.

Seldom can a commander have been more correct in his advance assessment of the importance of an action: Souchon was more right than he could possibly know in his *envoi* to the Turkish and German sailors, also hoisted as a flag-signal on the *Goeben*, as they carried their cargo of war in the general direction of the Crimea and the Caucasus. He allowed the whole of the 28th and the ensuing night for getting his mostly unfit ships with their untried crews and uncertain machinery to their respective starting lines. For all that the little destroyers assigned to Odessa started their bombardment early, giving the Russians the chance to alert all their coastal stations, the operation described at the beginning of this book was a complete success: the Turco-German fleet, at a cost of only minor damage and no losses, achieved its momentous objective of provoking Russia into declaring war on Turkey, with all that this entailed. In his first message to Constantinople Souchon made a formal attempt to dissimulate, to assist Enver when the dread news reached his vacillating colleagues:

Russian fleet observed all movements Turkish fleet October 27 and 28 and disturbed all exercises in a planned way. Russian fleet opened hostilities today. Fleet commander.

As lies go this was pretty outrageous, even if the fleet did see a single Russian steamer off the mouth of the Bosporus as the procession of warships emerged from the narrow waterway (it was waiting for another to join it after the master gave up hope in the nick of time of getting through to the Mediterranean one month after the Dardanelles were closed). In Constantinople the news of the raids on the Russian coast swept round the city very quickly and was received with a mixture of exultation and fear. On the next day, the 30th, the Russian, British and French Ambassadors asked the Turkish government for their passports, and Sir Louis Mallet for Britain presented an ultimatum. The Turks were given twelve hours to promise to send home all German officers and the crews of the *Goeben* and the *Breslau* and to demobilize. When this was ignored, Russia declared war on November 2. The next day the British ships off the Dardanelles shelled the entrance forts (see chapter 11); when this apparently failed to move the Turks, Britain and France finally declared war on the Ottoman Empire, on November 5.

While Admiral Souchon punctiliously observed Turkish protocol on the day after the raid, sending a flowery message of respectful congratulation to the Sultan on the occasion of the Muslim festival of Lesser *Bairam* which began on the 30th and lasted three days, the news of the casting of the die predictably threw the cabinet into confusion and crisis. The Grand Vizier, even after the ultimatum, wanted to apologize to the Russians and offer compensation. He refused to accept responsibility for the aggressive act which had precipitated Turkey into war, an understandable if unrealistic reaction given that he had not been told in advance; he too had thought the ships were going on exercise. Prince Said Halim therefore ordered Enver to recall the ships immediately; Enver agreed, provided hostilities could be broken off without damage to Turkey and her coastline remained protected, and a message was sent to Souchon. It was followed by another from Commander Humann in the German naval bureau in Constantinople, advising his chief to ignore it on Enver's instructions. The triumphant admiral took this latest manifestation of double-dealing in his now practised stride: 'That fulfils what I expected,' he noted in his war diary. 'War Minister and Navy Minister express their congratulations on my successes. They will get their way, which meets our political needs, because they have the majority on the Committee [of Union and Progress].' With varying degrees of enthusiasm the cabinet did nothing more, which amounted to accepting the *fait accompli* presented by Enver Pasha. But the handful of Russian steamers still in the Straits were allowed to go home, and Souchon had to send a special message asking for the Black Sea lighthouses to be extinguished and for their largely French crews to be ordered out. After a quiet patrol off the mouth of the Bosporus, the *Goeben* brought him back to shore on the afternoon of October 31, his task accomplished.

The German admiral had no intention, however, of sitting out the rest of the war which he had just done so much to spread and lengthen. Despite the enthusiasm and high morale of the Turkish sailors in their first action, he was profoundly dissatisfied with their standard of training and the mechanical performance of their ships, and the signalling during the multiple attack on Russia had generally been abysmal. Repairs and training were resumed with renewed energy. There was now an enemy fleet at each end of the Straits, and Souchon had to plan for defensive action against the inevitable attack from the Mediterranean, and for aggressive operations against the Russians bottled up in the Black Sea.

The main strength of the Russian Black Sea Fleet lay in a squadron of five pre-dreadnought battleships. Three, *Ievstafi*, *Ioann Zlatoust* and *Pantelimon* (formerly the *Potemkin* which almost started a revolution in 1905), each displaced 12,800 tons and had four 12-inch guns and a design speed of only 16 knots. The older *Rostislav* (9,000 tons) had four 10-inch guns, while the doyenne of the squadron, the *Tri Sviatitelia* (1893 and 12,500 tons) had four elderly 12-inch guns. Also under the flag of Vice-Admiral Eberhard, a thoroughly competent commander, were two very old reserve battleships, two middle-aged cruisers, twenty-six destroyers (nine capable of 33 knots), two gunboats, four small torpedoboats and eleven submarines. The *Goeben* was much superior to the squadron in speed, armour and armament and was thus capable of seizing the initiative in the Black Sea, Souchon's next task. But the Russians were close to completing three super-dreadnought battleships in their Black Sea yards: the *Imperatriza Maria* and *Ekaterina II* were due to be commissioned in autumn 1915 (the third, *Alexander III*, was ready for battle in November 1917, by which time the Revolution had put an end to Russian naval activity –

she was promptly renamed the *Volya*). These each had ten modern 12-inch guns, 12-inch armour and a design speed of 24 knots. Though somewhat slower than the *Goeben* (her chronic boiler troubles permitting), they were a menacing proposition, quite capable of wresting supremacy from Souchon. He had the fastest capital ship but only the one; a single mine, torpedo or lucky shot could give the Russians the upper hand. An attack by two or more of the nine latest enemy destroyers could also account for the *Breslau*, his fastest ship. In these circumstances, dreadnoughts or no, the Turkish vessels could be used only in secondary roles.

The first clash was not long in coming. The Russians bombarded the northern coast of Anatolia, where the Turkish coal mines were, sinking three unescorted troopships, to the fury of Souchon and the horror of the Turks. Also in the first week of November, the *Breslau* counterattacked Poti on the Georgian coast at the eastern end of the Black Sea. On the 17th of the month the bulk of the Russian fleet shelled Trebizond, and the *Goeben* and *Breslau*, accompanied by a Turkish cruiser and destroyers, put out to sea to try to intercept them. Just after noon on the 18th two Russian cruisers were sighted in patchy fog off Balaclava (Crimea). As Souchon turned towards them, his ships suddenly came under a hail of shot from the Russian battle squadron at a range of less than 5,000 yards. The five battleships formed a line behind and between the two cruisers and had been hidden in fog while Souchon's vessels were not. Behaving as if he were at the head of a line of battleships himself, Souchon tried to execute the classic manoeuvre of 'crossing the enemy's T' – sailing across the bow of the leading ship so as to be able to concentrate all his fire upon her. The Russian countered with the equally classic sideways turn on to a parallel course. The shooting on both sides was of a high standard with the *Goeben* scoring hits on the leading Russian, the flagship *Ievstafi*, and having to take one 12-inch shell on her port side in return. This very nearly proved to be the 'lucky shot' which would have meant the end of Turkish seapower: the Russian shell struck the *Goeben*'s third casemate (fortified cell) and blew it and its 5.9-inch guns into the sea with the loss of twelve sailors. A fire started, releasing noxious fumes and setting off the ready ammunition; only the quick action of a petty officer below in flooding the adjacent magazine prevented flash from setting that off as well. Aboard the Russian flagship thirty-three men were killed and thirty-five wounded, although damage to the heavily armoured hull was minor. The ten-minute exchange ended when Souchon withdrew after having fired just nineteen rounds of 11-inch; the rest of his ships had already retired, careful to keep the embattled *Goeben* between themselves and the Russian line which their lighter guns were not capable of damaging significantly.

On the way back to the Bosporus, Souchon's force stopped two Russian schooners and, after ordering the evacuation of their crews, sent them to the bottom. From the prisoners Souchon had the satisfaction of learning that his October 29 action had achieved almost total surprise and caused considerable damage as well as panic along the Russian coast, with many people fleeing inland. The fantastic rumour had circulated that German ships were also at large in the Caspian, a completely landlocked sea. The ethnic German community in southern Russia had come under suspicion of spying for the German Navy. Before the end of the year other prisoners taken by the *Breslau* during cruiser-warfare forays revealed that the *Goeben* had become the subject of a legend akin to that of the *Flying Dutchman*. Wild stories of the battle-cruiser having a *Doppelgänger*, probably resulting from untrained eyes confusing her and the *Breslau* at a distance when they were sailing together, were going the rounds; the *Goeben* had acquired the reputation of a 'devil-ship' and some captives claimed that an order had gone out to the Russian fleet that, in the event of the sinking of either German ship, those responsible were to remain at the spot for twenty-four hours – in case she came to the surface again! These amazing myths showed the Germans that they had at least won the psychological advantage in their Black Sea campaign at the outset.

But, as the first engagement had shown, they were not to have it all their own way. On December 21 the *Goeben* and the *Breslau* set sail with some Turkish escorts across the southern shore of the Black Sea. Field Marshal von der Goltz, the German Army commander assigned to the Middle East, was aboard the flagship as a guest. On Christmas Eve the *Breslau*, patrolling separately, signalled after dark that she was in contact with the main body of the Russian fleet. In the early hours of Christmas morning she became involved in a brief and ineffectual exchange of fire before fleeing back to the *Goeben*. As Souchon's ships approached the entrance to the Bosporus in the early afternoon, the *Goeben* struck a mine which blew a hole under her starboard side and caused an alarming list; this was corrected two minutes later when a second mine damaged her port side below the waterline. One man was killed and the battlecruiser shipped 600 tonnes of water. Her exceptionally strong construction saved her from fatal damage from mines which had been anchored in 600 feet of water during a Russian minelaying operation – a record achievement. She had settled somewhat in the water but her bulkheads held and she was still afloat and under her own power. The Field Marshal's tunic was scorched by escaping steam: he kept it as a souvenir of an interesting outing.

This was a serious crisis for Souchon. His flagship, the only vessel in his command capable of deterring the Russians, was badly holed and the Turks had no drydock anything like large enough to take her. The admiral fell back on bluff and improvisation. Coffer dams were ordered for each hole, to be sealed against the hull with their tops above water, providing with the aid of constant pumping a pair of dry chambers in which the repairers could work on the holes, each larger than a double-decker bus. A month later the Turkish cruiser *Hamidieh* was reported in trouble off the mouth of the Bosporus, where she was being chased by two Russian cruisers. With his customary resourcefulness and mindful of the ubiquitous enemy spies in Constantinople, some of whom had wireless transmitters, Souchon had a message sent to the Turkish ship saying the *Goeben* was coming to the rescue and ordered steam up in all boilers. Soon a massive cloud of black smoke arose from the crippled giant's two funnels; not long after that, the Russian cruisers turned tail and the *Hamidieh* returned unharmed. Early in February 1915 the *Goeben*, her holes still unrepaired, was slowly moved out of the Bosporus in distant and purely psychological support of a sweep by Turkish ships trying to track down some small Russian vessels whose presence had been reported in the south-western Black Sea. No contact was made and the *Goeben* returned to her anchorage to await the arrival of the coffer dams and the replacement plates for her hull. She was unable to intervene when the British and French bombarded the mouth of the Dardanelles in February (see chapter 11); but the massive bombardment in mid-March coincided with the arrival at last of her coffer dams. No sooner had these been put in place than they were cast off as Souchon ordered the *Goeben* to raise steam, in case she were needed for a last-ditch stand. The Anglo-French fleet, however, withdrew on the brink of a breakthrough after the loss of several ships. By March 19 the *Goeben* was back at her anchorage in Stenia, the coffer dams were reattached and the repairs completed successfully in a few days without further interruption. Some of her smaller guns and machine gun teams were detached for the defence of the Dardanelles and to resist the Allied landings at Gallipoli.

From the end of March to the beginning of May the *Goeben* was used to cover troop and coal transports and for patrols and cruiser warfare. Early in April the Turkish cruiser *Medjidieh* hit a mine and sank but her crew were all rescued; on the same operation there was a brief brush between the Turco-German and Russian fleets but an exchange of fire produced no damage to either side. The repairs to the *Goeben* proved entirely satisfactory and Souchon looked forward to regaining the initiative. He may even have succumbed to the old German weakness of under-estimating the enemy; if he did, he was soon disabused by the Russians, who set a great trap for him on May 9.

Late that afternoon the alarm was sounded in Constantinople when a wireless message came in from a Turkish military post at the town of Eregli, about 100 miles east of the Bosporus on the north-west Anatolian coast. The signal reported that the Russian cruiser *Kagoul* had landed troops in the area after shooting up the town. By the time the *Goeben* had got up steam on Souchon's orders and rushed to investigate with a small escort of Turkish destroyers, the *Kagoul* had re-embarked the troops, whose landing had been a feint to cause alarm, and withdrawn northwards, where one or two other warships could be intermittently made out in the misty gloom. Aboard the *Goeben*, Captain Ackermann ordered a return to harbour because his bunkers were only half full. As the mist faded in the early hours of the 10th, two submarine periscopes were sighted. When the battle-cruiser turned towards them they dived. The *Goeben* continued westwards towards the mouth of the Bosporus and just after dawn Ackermann suddenly found himself in a desperate situation. The bulk of the Russian fleet, a total of seventeen ships including the squadron of five battleships in line ahead, lay across his path, sailing slowly northwards, the capital ships well screened by their escorts. The range was extreme at about 17,500 yards, but both sides opened fire at 6.50 A.M. GMT, the *Goeben* concentrating on the flagship *Ievstafi* and the second in line, the *Tri Sviatitelia* (Admiral Troubridge would have found it interesting to learn that Ackermann felt unable to tackle more than two targets at a time with his main armament). As the range closed with the Russians and the Germans on a converging course, the Russian shooting proved very good and the Germans had to take violent evading measures, dodging also at least two sighted torpedo tracks. Ackermann hoped to shepherd the Russians close enough to the Bosporus to get supporting fire from the shore batteries. When this had patently failed, he opened the range and pushed on northwards, hoping to draw the Russians away so that he could use his much superior speed to swing round behind them and race to safety. Three apparent hits on the *Ievstafi* did not affect her movements, but the *Tri Sviatitelia* pulled out of the Russian line with flames showing above her hull. Flames were also briefly discerned on the *Ioann Zlatoust* but she stayed in line. The Germans had time to note with professional approval the tight manoeuvring of the enemy and the disciplined shooting. The Russians began to swing eastwards and Ackermann followed suit, planning to circle at top speed behind the Russians when the time seemed ripe. The *Goeben* took two direct hits from 12-inch shells; one went through the deck forward and jammed the foremost 11-inch gun turret, the other hit the port side close to amidships, knocking out one 5.9-inch gun. When the Russians divined Ackermann's intention they turned a couple of points southwards so that their slower ships fell in behind him, to cut off his retreat. Ackermann now determined to fall back on his greatest advantage, the speed of the *Goeben*, whose boilers seemed to be in unusually compliant mood. He swung the ship hard to starboard and, ordering up every available ounce of steam, ran for home past the entire Russian line, taking care to keep at a distance of up to 22,000 yards from the enemy. Only a simultaneous reversal of course combined with closing the range would have enabled the Russians to interfere with this bold dash to safety, but they were able only to turn one by one from the head of their line; thus as the *Goeben* raced past, each Russian ship was caught facing the wrong way or only starting to turn. Neither side fired a shot; the Russians appeared stunned by the manoeuvre and their ships were too slow to counter it successfully. Georg Kopp, the wireless operator who wrote a book about his time on the *Goeben*, described the great ship behaving as if she were a speedboat, her bow rising out of the water and her aftermost turret almost awash as the stern dug into the water and, perhaps with slight exaggeration, exceeding 30 knots (which would have been the fastest she ever travelled). 'The *Goeben* driving past the enemy must have been a supernatural, indescribable apparition,' he recalled. The paint on the funnels was blistered and blackened by the heat and gave off a dull glow. Once past the much slower enemy she was able to cut her speed gradually until the Russians gave up the hopeless chase. As the scarred battlecruiser approached the safety of the Bosporus the *Breslau* came out with destroyers and minesweepers to escort her in. Cheering crowds lined both sides of the narrow waterway – the boom of the great naval guns had been heard all along the coast. The *Goeben* had fired 128 shells from her main armament, damaging three of the five Russian battleships and also a submarine which was bumped after failure to get out of the way when the German ship made a sudden turn. Ackermann lost just one man.

After this twenty-four-hour drama there was a lull in the Black Sea. In July 1915 the *Breslau* was badly holed by a mine while returning from a patrol and just managed to reach a floating dock in sinking condition, but she was soon made good again. Both sides were making increasing use of submarines after the Germans managed to get three boats into the Black Sea. Eventually they had eleven. The Russians used theirs to harass Turkish colliers and transports; both sides sank a significant tally of merchant ships with torpedoes during the campaign. But the Germans and Turks for the time being had the upper hand in this curious, detached struggle for mastery of an enclosed sea. The desultory Black Sea campaign seems all the more curious in its isolation when it is recalled that a tremendous struggle was going on at the Mediterranean end of the Straits for most of 1915, even if Souchon's operations were a major contribution to keeping open the lines of communication and supply for Turco-German land forces fighting Russia. Following the abandonment of the Anglo-French spring naval assault on the Dardanelles just as it appeared to be on the brink of victory, the Allies landed an invading army on the Gallipoli peninsula in April and, as described in chapter 11, withdrew only on 9 January 1916. Apart from a few changes of anchorage and preparations for a last stand in the event of a naval breakthrough, the *Goeben* and the rest of Souchon's command took little part in this dreadful campaign of attrition. The failure of the Russians to make a sustained attempt to help their embattled allies at one end of the Straits by applying pressure at the other starkly reflects the dominance the *Goeben* had been able to establish from the moment she intervened in the Black Sea. The Russians, of course, had taken terrible punishment on other fronts and also had the Turkish Army to contend with; and it is not as if they could be accused of lack of the will to fight at sea or even of incompetence. But there was only intermittent coordination between the Russians in the Black Sea and their allies in the Mediterranean. Yet on the eve of the final withdrawal from Gallipoli there came one last serious challenge to the *Goeben*'s supremacy.

It was a measure of how quiet things had become that on 8 January 1916 the *Goeben* emerged from the Bosporus once again to escort a single collier, the *Carmen*. On identifying two vessels on the horizon that clear winter's morning as Russian destroyers, the battle-cruiser began to give chase. Soon the as yet unidentifiable shape of a third ship came into sight at the limit of visibility. Kopp said it was at first identified as some kind of sailing ship, until a flash was seen to come from it, followed by a cloud of smoke. He remembered an interval of no less than sixty seconds before great columns of water rose into the air just 500 yards ahead of the *Goeben*. The next salvo struck only 200 yards ahead – first-rate shooting at a range of at least ten miles. The third salvo was a mere fifty yards short, as closely grouped as the others. The *Goeben* fired a total of twenty-two rounds of 11-inch shell in reply within four minutes but gave up when it became clear she could not reach the enemy ship. Captain Ackermann's only recourse was to turn tail and run: the new enemy was the *Imperatriza Maria*, the freshly commissioned first Russian dreadnought in the Black Sea, equipped with ten of the latest 12-inch guns which put up a brilliant first performance even if they did not strike home. It might have been a different story, the Germans recognized, had she not been firing into the sun, which probably explained why subsequent salvoes were further and further off target. She fired a total of about 150 shells at ranges of up to eleven and a half miles. Displacing 22,500 tons and with a main armour-belt of 12 inches, the *Imperatriza* proved herself capable of sustaining a speed touching 25 knots in the grim chase which followed; and two more of her type were known to be on the verge of completion. If a pair of these formidable new battleships ever got the *Goeben* between them, or between themselves and the coast, the battlecruiser's prospects of survival would be minimal. As it was, the *Goeben*, fortunate in having begun her flight with plenty of sea-room and at the limit of the Russian's superior gun range, still took three hours to open up a gap wide enough to convince her pursuer to abandon the chase. A vastly relieved Captain Ackermann reported to Souchon on his return the same evening, laconically: 'The *Imperatriza Maria* can run and shoot.' He recommended that some of the latest, larger German U-boats should be brought in to hunt the new Russian class. On the run home, Ackermann tried one last ruse in the hope of creating a chance for a counter-attack. He wirelessed for seaplane support with the idea that the aircraft might create sufficient distraction for him to put about and get close enough to his pursuer to be able to use his own guns. The one machine available was, however, forced to ditch in the sea with engine trouble so this bold scheme was not attempted. The *Goeben* found it eventually and was far enough ahead to be able to stop and use one of her guns as a derrick to salvage the aircraft. The final irony of the *Goeben*'s only clash with a ship that could match her was that the single collier she had so unnecessarily come out to escort was coolly captured and taken away by the new Russian battleship's destroyer escorts. These might have been better employed in a torpedo attack on the *Goeben* while she was preoccupied with the *Imperatriza*.

The latter was swept from the strategic board by an unexplained catastrophe only nine months later. On 20 October 1916 she blew up, apparently spontaneously, in the harbour at Sevastopol and was lost, one of a handful of warships around the world to be destroyed in such strange and tragic circumstances. Between the narrow escape from her guns in January and her untimely end, Souchon's ships never sighted her again. But in April 1916 the *Breslau* had an even more dangerous encounter with her sistership, the *Ekaterina II*. The German light cruiser on this occasion had been sent to Trebizond to escort supply and troopships and to bombard enemy positions and depots in north-eastern Anatolia in support of the Turkish forces fighting there. Having also sunk a Russian merchant ship and a sailing vessel, the *Breslau* had turned west for the run along the Anatolian coast for home when, early in the morning, the *Ekaterina*, escorted by the cruiser *Kagoul* and three destroyers of the latest Russian type (so faster than she), was sighted lying across her path. Lieutenant-Commander von Knorr, in command at this time, did not dare to attempt an evasion at full speed because there was as yet no indication that his ship had been seen and the huge smoke-cloud the *Breslau* would make would give her away. Instead he made north, towards the darkest horizon but also towards the Crimea with its Russian naval bases, at a judicious pace but with steam up for full speed at a moment's notice. Hardly daring to breathe, the men of the *Breslau* watched the Russians pass some five miles astern, still heading east and apparently unawares. But one of the destroyers began to turn towards her, followed shortly afterwards by the rest of the Russian group. The *Ekaterina*, obviously uncertain, challenged by searchlight, giving her recognition signal. Von Knorr turned to his signals officer, a promising sub-lieutenant of great efficiency and devotion to duty called Karl Dönitz, and ordered him to repeat the recognition signal in the hope that this would lull any suspicions. It did, and the Russian turned away again. When the gap had opened to ten miles, those on the bridge heaved a sigh of relief. Captain von Knorr then proceeded to overreach himself in a moment of unwonted and indefensible carelessness by ordering Dönitz to send an impertinent message wishing the Russians a safe voyage. Dönitz could not resist adding the German equivalent of 'Kiss my arse.' The reply was the unearthly roar of 12-inch shells passing overhead and hitting the water close enough to rock the *Breslau* with their explosions. Once again the Russians showed brilliance with their shooting from an untried ship and the third salvo actually straddled the hopelessly outgunned light cruiser with very near misses on either side. Von Knorr ordered maximum speed and a zig-zag course, but not before one Russian shell amputated her stem – fortunately sufficiently above the waterline not to affect her speed as she raced for the Bosporus with her well-deserved bloody nose. Only after the *Breslau* had opened the range to thirteen miles did the Russians cease fire; no destroyer attack was attempted.

That was the last time the Turco-German fleet came under fire from the Russian dreadnoughts, which do not appear to have been definitely sighted again before the Russians made their separate peace at the end of 1917 (by which time the *Ekaterina II* had been renamed the *Velikaya*). The Russians never seriously tried for the mastery of the Black Sea which these ships, properly handled by their demonstrably competent admiral and crews, could and should have enabled them to seize. Subsequently the Black Sea campaign, at any rate on the surface of the sea, became a matter of sporadic sightings with the occasional minor and inconclusive skirmish. The gathering storm-clouds of the Russian Revolution reduced naval activity on their side to a minimum.

The strain of war was telling in Turkey too as shortages mounted in Constantinople and elsewhere. In August 1916 a weak attempt at a coup against Enver's war party with a view to a separate peace with Britain and France alarmed Souchon sufficiently for him to make plans to use the fleet to suppress it, but the dominant political faction was able to deal with it without such aid, and many hangings followed.

The German sailors, despite their routine duties, had more and more spare time as the war made fewer demands on them, and bent their talent for organization and taste for order to ingenious regulation of their domestic circumstances. German crews did not live aboard their ships; as on the North Sea and Baltic stations, where they messed in barracks ashore except when going to sea, so in Turkey. In January 1916 they were able to obtain the use of two pieces of land on the European side of the Bosporus, north of Constantinople and only a couple of miles inland from their main anchorage at Stenia (now Istinye). On these the sailors, many of peasant stock, set up a farm and a vegetable garden. The second piece of land proved unsuitable but the first in what they came to call 'Steniatal' (Stenia Valley) was an enormous success, helping to ensure that they always had fresh fruit, vegetables and other luxuries when they went to sea. One of the Black Sea U-boats brought seed from Varna in Bulgaria (the new ally of the Central Powers), while the *Breslau* brought more from Trebizond. Buffaloes were used to pull the ploughs and soon a crop of maize was flourishing. A herd of pigs up to eighty strong provided regular access to the Germans' traditionally favourite Sunday lunch of roast pork. A temporary shortage of natural fertilizer was permanently solved by an arrangement with the nearest Turkish cavalry barracks to provide all the horse manure the green-fingered sailors could use. It remains only to record that eventually Steniatal began to show a small and steady profit. What Kaiser Wilhelm II thought of his sailors-turned-peasants when he paid his state visit to Constantinople and sailed and slept on the *Goeben* in the middle of October 1917 is not recorded, but as sailors he could not praise them highly enough. Nor did peace with revolutionary Russia at the end of the year mean that for them the war was over. They would soon be back in action, and the result was to be rather less than glorious.

In their Black Sea campaign, the *Goeben* steamed a total of almost 20,000 miles whereas the handier *Breslau* logged no less than 35,000, comparable with the average mileage of a modern car over a similar period.

We may also pause here to note what became of some of the principal figures in this history. Baron von Wangenheim, the forceful, Bismarckian Ambassador who concluded the fateful Turco-German secret treaty, died of overwork before the end of 1916. His partner in that enterprise, Enver Pasha, fled to Germany with Talaat just before the Armistice, their government having been overthrown in a peace-party coup. Talaat was perhaps appropriately (if brutally) shot dead in a Berlin street in 1921 by an Armenian student on a self-imposed vengeance mission. Enver, having been sentenced to death *in absentia* by the new government, soon tired of the life of an exile in gloomy postwar Berlin and made his way to Russia in 1919 to join the struggle for an independent Caucasus. He actually worked for the Soviet government in 1920–1 in the Asiatic section of the Foreign Ministry, simultaneously setting himself up as Communist leader of the Near East. He eventually disappeared into the convoluted post-revolutionary wars in southern Russia, turning against the Bolsheviks and dying in a cavalry charge against them in Soviet Turkestan in 1922; or he may have been assassinated – there are conflicting accounts and no definitive version of the end of this small man of insatiable ambition. Field Marshal Liman von Sanders fought a determined war until finally defeated by Allenby. He surrendered himself to the Allies when they entered Constantinople and was interned for a few months until he was allowed to return home, where he died in Munich in 1929 at the age of seventy-four, after writing his memoirs.

Wilhelm Souchon, arguably the most successful admiral in German history after Tirpitz and Dönitz (both of whom, however, were defeated in the end), lived to a ripe old age, weighed down with honours. He was promoted vice-admiral in 1915 and was awarded the Kaiser's highest decoration, the Order *pour le Mérite*, in 1916; three months before the end of the war he became the Kaiser's naval adviser in the rank of admiral. He was too senior for the residual postwar navy and retired in March 1919. He lived quietly thereafter to see Germany defeated a second time and died at eighty-one in Bremen in January 1946. He left two daughters.

11

Gallipoli and after – the legacy of SMS Goeben

By fulfilling his instructions to take the *Goeben* and the *Breslau* to the Dardanelles and then to attack Russia so as to force Turkey into the war on the side of the Central Powers, Admiral Souchon needed to do no more in order to justify the confidence placed in him by his superiors. We have seen how he thereafter did his utmost to take the war to Germany's main enemy, Russia, by seizing and retaining the initiative in the Black Sea, which was of great value to the Turkish and German land campaigns around its shores. The Black Sea campaign of the Imperial Navy's Mediterranean Division was of a piece and was therefore described to its conclusion in the preceding chapter, even though this entailed a departure from chronological order. But, apart from the detachment of some naval guns and machine gun teams and the occasional change of anchorage, Souchon's ships took no part in the defence of the Dardanelles against the naval and military campaigns launched by the Anglo-French forces in an ultimately disastrous attempt to undo the real damage he caused. While Souchon and his ships, and their Turkish allies at sea, turned their backs on the Mediterreanean to concentrate on the Black Sea and the lands bordering on it, their western enemies slowly and hesitantly gathered their strength for a series of attempts to reopen the route to Russia, culminating in that tragedy summarized by the singularly evocative name of Gallipoli.

The double triumph of Germany's diplomats and sailors in delivering within eight days both the Turkish alliance and the military means of activating it was a setback of such magnitude for the Triple Entente that an attempt to reverse it seemed inevitable to all concerned. But as the Germans galvanized and led their Turkish allies to strengthen the dilapidated forts of the Dardanelles, the British and the French vacillated about how best to reopen Russia's blocked artery. For their part, the Russians placed their ancient ambition of controlling the Straits above their immediate and truly desperate need, thereby complicating the strategic calculations. The final result was the Gallipoli campaign, a sound strategy which became a tragic failure because of bad planning, poor tactics and weak leadership. In all the campaigns of the First World War there is no story quite so poignant as that of the Dardanelles expedition. The failure of the invasion sealed Russia's fate; yet the invasion would in all probability not have been necessary but for the decisive shift in the balance of power at the junction of Europe and Asia caused by the arrival of the *Goeben*.

As we have seen, a considerable British naval force arrived off the Dardanelles to close the stable door behind the horse that had bolted inside. There was little activity until 26 September 1914, when the British stopped a Turkish torpedoboat which had come out into the Mediterranean. On finding German soldiers aboard, the British ordered the small ship back into the Straits. The reaction of the German general in command of the forts at the entrance to the Dardanelles, known as Weber Pasha, was swift, decisive and typical of the high-handedness of the German General Staff in that it was done without orders or consultation with the Turks. General Weber, acting on his own initiative, simply closed the Dardanelles. Enver backed him after the event. Mines were laid, large notice-boards were put up on shore, the lighthouses were doused and the ancient trade route through the Straits was severed, a blow from which it has never recovered to this day. The action was in breach of international convention and an act of war. It was also the first great dividend for the Germans from their still secret treaty with the Turks, most of whose cabinet were horrified. Hundreds of Russian grain ships piled up in one of the largest maritime traffic jams in history. The greatest material contribution Russia was in a position to make to her Entente partners, food for their populations in exchange for munitions, was suppressed. Eventually the ships returned piecemeal to their home ports in the Black Sea. They never came back.

After the *Goeben* led the Turkish fleet in the fateful bombardment of the Russian Black Sea coast at the end of October, the Entente Powers declared war on Turkey when a twelve-hour ultimatum went unanswered. Weber's economic death-blow to Tsarist Russia was driven home by Souchon's naval provocation. The first warlike response of the Entente came on the morning of November 4, when six of the British and French ships waiting in the Aegean for the *Goeben* shelled the twin forts at the mouth of the Dardanelles. But, like so many other acts on the Entente side in this new theatre of war, it was brief and ineffectual, no more than a gesture lasting twenty minutes. Outranged, Weber's gun emplacements stayed silent and kept their none too plentiful powder dry. The only effect of the little bombardment was to spur on the defenders to greater preparatory efforts for the real assault which, like reasonable men but wrongly, they assumed was quite imminent. But for forty days there was nothing, until on December 13, a Sunday, the elderly Turkish battleship *Messudieh*, forty years old and displacing barely 10,000 tons, was shattered by explosions. During the night the puny submarine *B11*, of about 300 tons and of a type going back to 1905, had boldly worked her way into the Straits, carrying a crew of just sixteen men under the command of Lieutenant Norman Holbrook, RN. He fired two torpedoes from a distance of 600 yards and got clean away by scraping along the bottom. For this display of individual daring, of a kind which was to be seen again and which contrasted so sharply with the curious ineffectiveness of senior commanders at the Dardanelles, Holbrook was given the Victoria Cross. Souchon moved the *Goeben* to a safer anchorage and ordered tighter watches throughout his fleet. But it was an isolated stroke.

Reopening the Dardanelles was understandably not at first uppermost in the minds of the British and French leaders, who were mesmerized by the unprecedented slaughter on the Western Front. The superiority of defensive over offensive weaponry had already imposed a pattern of immobile trench warfare from the Channel to the Alps, a line which was not so long that it could not be fully manned by the vast opposing forces, but neither could outflank the other. If there was to be a flanking movement it would have to be somewhere else altogether. Attention gradually and with many interruptions focused on Constantinople, the capture of which would help the Russians and expose the Central Powers to a new line of attack from the south-east across the Balkans and along the Danube. Kitchener, the Secretary of State for War, and Churchill, First Lord of the Admiralty, discussed the idea even before Turkey was propelled into the war. They considered persuading the Greeks to make a landing on the Gallipoli peninsula and silence the guns of the Turkish garrison, whereupon an Allied fleet could sail up the Straits, sink the *Goeben* and threaten Constantinople. The Royal Navy had successfully blasted its way through the Dardanelles in 1807, only to be frustrated by unhelpful winds which prevented it reaching Constantinople; Admiral Duckworth was stalled just eight miles short of his objective and withdrew after a week, but he had got through without army support, and he was even able to return to the Mediterrenean with minor casualties and all his ships still afloat. The Greeks, keen at first to attack their old enemy and former conqueror, changed their minds and the Anglo-French generals insisted that not a man could be spared from the Western Front.

If a problem defined is a problem half solved, then Lieutenant-Colonel Maurice Hankey, secretary of the War Council, performed this service by submitting a paper at the end of December 1914, incisively arguing the case for a Dardanelles campaign. This relatively junior officer in a key post showed a detailed grasp of grand strategy absent in too many of the powerful men he served. Correctly envisaging the tank as the answer to the deadlock in the trenches (a perception fully realized only a quarter of a century later), he urged meanwhile a blow against the Germans through an attack on their weakest ally, Turkey, by three corps of Kitchener's New Army, preferably supported by Greece and Bulgaria (both still neutral). It was an idea whose time had come. Grand Duke Nicholas, the Russian C-in-C, admitted to the British that he was in difficulties after the gigantic defeats inflicted by the Germans at the battles of Tannenberg and the Masurian Lakes and asked for a diversion against the Turks. This, he hoped, would draw Turkish forces out of the Caucasus, release Russian troops for his western front, and reopen the Black Sea route for exports of grain and imports of much needed arms and ammunition. Kitchener, originally sceptical about Hankey's proposal, was persuaded by the Russian plea at the turn of the year and suggested an attack on the Dardanelles to Churchill.

The First Sea Lord, Fisher, also supported Hankey – provided that the attack was 'immediate', and supported by troops. Kitchener, however, was still opposed to drawing troops from France and wanted a purely naval operation, and his word was law.

At the beginning of January 1915, therefore, Churchill telegraphed to Vice-Admiral Sackville Carden, the former Admiral Superintendent, Malta, who had succeeded Troubridge in command of the blockading squadron off the Dardanelles, to seek his views. Did he consider 'the forcing of the Dardanelles by ships alone a practical operation?' The ageing admiral's reply was cautious but not negative: 'I do not consider Dardanelles can be rushed. They might be forced by extended operations with large numbers of ships.' This judicious assessment showed no relish for action, which in retrospect makes it highly appropriate as the catalyst for subsequent events, but the implied approach seemed safe enough: a slow pass during which a large naval force would systematically hammer the forts one by one. On receipt of Carden's reply on January 5, Churchill consulted his advisers (with the notable exception of Fisher, which was to prove a mistake) and asked Carden to produce a detailed plan, which arrived six days later.

With a dozen battleships, three battlecruisers, four light cruisers, sixteen destroyers, six submarines, twelve minesweepers and some seaplanes and small auxiliary vessels, and vast quantities of ammunition, Carden believed he could do the job in about a month, weather permitting. The battleships at least were not much of a problem because there were more than enough second- and third-rate vessels in the British fleet awaiting replacement by dreadnoughts. The older ships had the big guns and the armour necessary and their slowness was not a disadvantage in the circumstances. The battlecruisers would be needed against the *Goeben*. The Admiralty accepted Carden's shopping list and even added to it a massive unrequested item: the latest battleship *Queen Elizabeth* with the awesome new 15-inch gun, just completed and about to go to the Mediterrenean for gunnery trials. She might just as well run in her firing systems by testing them against the Turkish forts, which her huge guns enormously outranged. Churchill's energies and powers of persuasion were totally committed to the naval assault plan, which he pressed at the War Council meeting in London on January 13. Kitchener, not required to divert any of his infantry, was in favour and saw little risk. The shelling could always be abandoned without significant loss if it did not work. So the War Council unanimously resolved:

that the Admiralty should prepare for a naval expedition in February to bombard and take the Gallipoli peninsula with Constantinople as its objective.

How ships were to capture the capital of the Ottoman Empire was not made clear. All they could do without troops was to reduce it to ruins; but insofar as any thought was given to the matter at the time of the decision, it may have been assumed that the threat from the great guns of the floating fortresses would prove enough. Liddell Hart, in his *History of the First World War*, regards such assumptions as 'delightfully naïve', but they were not altogether unrealistic. Even though the Admiralty fantastically forbore to give the command of the attack to the obvious man, Admiral Limpus of the recently withdrawn British Naval Mission to Turkey, for fear of unnecessarily provoking the Turks, it must have known from him how vulnerable the sprawling city was, and how a bombardment of it would cripple the Turkish war effort.

Turkey's two munitions arsenals were both on the shore; the entire creaking apparatus of government was within range of the guns from the water; a few shells could be expected to create large fires and general havoc in the narrow, combustible streets; the navy and its installations were hopelessly vulnerable; there was no realistic avenue of escape or alternative centre for the government, which might well have uncontrollable riots on its hands with an invincible enemy within the gates of the Golden Horn. Even without Limpus on the spot, a truly inexplicable omission based on an entirely misplaced forbearance which seems to have pervaded the whole sorry exercise of the abortive efforts to reopen the Straits, the approach of such a fleet in such a way at such a time must have forced the issue. After all, the arrival of one capital ship, the *Goeben*, had been enough to bring Turkey into the war; surely the arrival of a fleet would be enough to force her out.

As the ships began to gather and the ammunition supplies were assembled, Fisher, whose uncanny foresight we have already noted, turned against the idea of a purely naval assault. Grand old man and embodiment of the Royal Navy though he was, recalled to the colours as its chief for the war, Fisher at seventy-four did not carry the weight in the War Council borne by Field Marshal the Earl Kitchener of Khartoum, avenger of Gordon and architect of victory in the Anglo-Boer War. As dour and apocalyptic as Fisher was passionate and mercurial, he too showed flashes of foresight and was probably the first to realize that the war would be a prolonged slogging match of attrition rather than a swift campaign 'over by Christmas'. On him rested the ghastly burden of mobilizing the youth of a nation bred on victory at sea for the slow Armageddon in the trenches, as illustrated by the most famous recruiting poster of all time. It was for him

that his country felt a mystic need, a fact which gave him
an influence on the British war effort and its direction
unmatched by anyone and made of him a passive military
dictator, held back from tyranny only by his own character
and qualities rather than the resistance of others. Only 'K
of K' seemed to know the secret of victory; only hindsight
enables us to see that it was the navy Fisher built which
ultimately made it certain. Meanwhile, Churchill fell out
with Fisher over the Dardanelles as the Admiral of the
Fleet began to have second thoughts about the decision
with which the Admiralty as a whole had until then gone
along on the basis of full consultation. Fisher began to
worry, not about the possible losses of ships of no value
in the all-important North Sea, but of trained sailors
among their crews who would be needed for their replacements. Rightly seeing the containment of the German
High Seas Fleet as indispensable to the Allied cause,
Fisher finally set his face against any naval adventures
elsewhere. At the crucial War Council meeting of January
28 Fisher was in a minority of one and got up as if to
walk out. Kitchener took him aside to a corner of the
room at 10 Downing Street and persuaded him to return
to his seat. Afterwards, Churchill had a long talk with the
peppery First Sea Lord and the plan for the naval operation at last obtained his approval. Typically, having
been won over against his better judgment, Fisher threw
himself into the preparations. 'I went the whole hog,' he
said later, adding a translation into the dogwatch Latin of
the wardroom, '*totus porcus*'. He also added two more
pre-dreadnought battleships to the assault formation. The
French sent four battleships and supporting ships under
Vice-Admiral Guépratte, to complete by far the greatest
concentration of firepower ever assembled for action in
the Mediterranean.

The Dardanelles were defended, at their entrance and

along their length, by about a hundred cannon, distributed among eleven forts, which altogether housed seventy-two guns in fixed emplacements. Only a few of these were modern, but the Germans had added two dozen 5.9-inch (15-centimetre) howitzers which could be quickly redeployed and a handful of other modern pieces. The heaviest guns were in the two forts on either side of the entrance and the defences were reinforced by torpedo tubes, searchlights and minefields. For all the efforts of the Germans, the artillery was short of shells.

Using the *Queen Elizabeth* as his flagship, Admiral Carden began a deliberate, almost leisurely bombardment at long range on the morning of Friday, February 19. After about four hours of this, he closed the range to 6,000 yards, at which point some of the Turkish batteries began to fire back, but not seriously. Not much effect was discernible from the ships, which withdrew in the late afternoon. Then the weather closed in, forcing an interruption of six days. When the attack was resumed on February 25, the British second-in-command, Vice-Admiral John de Robeck, led his flagship, the *Vengeance*, into a fiercer bombardment at much closer range. The forts at the mouth were abandoned by the Turks and Germans, and Royal Marines and sailors went ashore to complete the destruction of the outer defences, meeting no real opposition. The minesweepers were brought up to clear the way for the intended violation of the Straits themselves, and found their most determined opposition in the strong current which flows unceasingly from the Black Sea through the Straits to the Mediterranean. The little ships came under fire but were hardly damaged, and at first they found no mines. On March 2 Carden signalled that he hoped to be off Constantinople in fourteen days unless the storms returned. The Allies were jubilant and world grain prices fell sharply. But too many chickens were being counted before they hatched. The Turks turned out to belong to that dangerous animal breed which, on being attacked, defends itself. Turkish troops arrived to oppose the landing parties and repossess the outer forts, and the mobile howitzer batteries began to lob shells on to the attacking vessels, something the heavily armoured battleships could all but ignore yet most unnerving for the smaller ships, especially the vital minesweepers. The shore batteries fell silent under bombardment but were able to resume firing with the mobile guns from new positions. By March 8, an impasse was reached: the minesweepers could not clear a path until the big ships annihilated the forts, and the battleships could not come forward until the mines were cleared. Then the weather once more halted operations. Captain (later Commodore) Roger Keyes, soon to become famous as head of the dashing Dover Patrol of destroyers, was Carden's chief-of-staff and he concluded that the merchant seamen and fishermen manning the minesweeping vessels were not up to their task under fire. For the sake of one more try he offered them a bonus and a stiffening of naval volunteers and got Carden's permission for a night sweep on the 10th, with six vessels. But once again the line broke under intense fire guided by searchlights and one minesweeper blew up and sank after hitting a mine. Despite the support of the battleship *Canopus* and her heavy guns, the flotilla turned tail under a hail of shot. But there were virtually no casualties apart from those aboard the sunken minesweeper. The next night Keyes tried again, but the sweepers retreated as soon as the Turks opened fire, despite his impotent rage. Nobody was hurt. Churchill was getting impatient and told Carden that caution was all very well, but the objective was such that losses could be tolerated if necessary to press home a decisive attack. On the night of March 13, Keyes made another sweep, this time with naval volunteers on the minesweepers (mostly adapted trawlers). They stuck to their task despite unprecedented fire from both shores, which put all but three out of action before Keyes ordered a disciplined withdrawal. In daylight a respectable collection of mines whose cables had been cut during the night came down on the current and were exploded by rifle fire from the ships, visible proof of progress at last. Minesweeping was stepped up and continued during daylight.

On March 14, after waiting for three days for a reply from Carden to his message urging the admiral on, Churchill sent him another signal in more specific terms. He told Carden to press on with the minesweeping regardless of reasonable casualties and passed on intelligence that the Turks were running out of shells, which the Germans were desperately trying to replace. He should hurry in case enemy submarines were sent to the Dardanelles. Carden acknowledged with a promise of full-scale attack on the 17th or as soon as possible. But Carden was beginning to crack under the stress of his first major action; despite his almost complete avoidance of losses he was apparently terrified of taking responsibility for the destruction of any of His Majesty's ships under any circumstances, a lack of resolution shared by many another admiral as we have seen. Medical advice was that he should go home, and Admiral de Robeck took his place for the planned grand attack, now retimed for the 18th. Churchill gave him the choice of postponement or going ahead without delay, and de Robeck promptly chose the latter.

Amid great excitement in the fleet, the new commander decided on a three-stage attack, each involving six capital ships, with the most powerful in the first line and the French battleships in the second, while the third waited with the minesweepers and destroyers off the entrance. On a fine spring morning the first line advanced, ignoring the shots from the shore, until it lay across the inner mouth of the Narrows with just enough engine revolutions to hold position against the current. Then, with deliberation and care, the *Queen Elizabeth* opened a cataclysmic bombardment of the shore, supported by the 12-inch guns of the others. De Robeck now ordered the French under Guépratte to pass through his line for a closer bombardment from half a mile ahead. The French admiral was straining at the leash (no hesitation in attack for him) and made his manoeuvre in style, leaving the British behind him with a clear field of fire and redoubling the shelling, which now reached such a pitch that nothing ashore seemed likely to survive it. But this was misleading. There were enough cool heads and steady hands and eyes ashore to use the defending artillery to some effect. Soon two ships in the British fleet line and one in the French suffered major hits but were able to continue firing because their armour had saved the crews. De Robeck now called up the third line of battleships to take the place of the French, whom he ordered to retire to the rear. As they sailed in line astern under the Asian shore, the second ship, the *Bouvet*, took a hit on one of her magazines, blew up and sank with the loss of 640 men, all in less then two minutes. The artillerymen ashore, whose fire had become ragged and intermittent under the intense naval barrage, were encouraged to step up their rate, although many shore installations had been reduced to rubble. But the ships carried on pounding both shores through the afternoon. De Robeck called up the minesweepers with a view to moving further forward, but once again the adapted trawlers fled as soon as they came under fire, a disastrous development which was followed by the crippling of the battlecruiser *Inflexible* when she ran on to a mine. Presence of mind and sheer heroism by the crew below decks saved the ship, which was able to limp away from the firing line. Five minutes later the 1898 battleship *Irresistible* was hit below the waterline, probably by a mine, and became the main focus of the defenders' fire. Apart from a handful of officers and men who stayed aboard voluntarily to prepare the helpless ship for towing away, the crew was taken off by a destroyer. De Robeck decided to withdraw for the night and ordered Keyes to stay in the Straits with the destroyers, and to organize the recovery of the *Irresistible* with the help of two other battleships, *Ocean* and *Swiftsure*. After wasting time by firing at the forts instead of concentrating on the salvage attempt, the *Ocean* was rocked by an explosion and began to list and also to sail in circles because her steering gear had been knocked out. Keyes ordered the *Swiftsure* to retire and took off the crew of the *Ocean*; then he went back to de Robeck on the *Queen Elizabeth* and got his permission to return after dark to sink the *Irresistible* by torpedo and find out whether the *Ocean* could be salvaged. As Keyes stole back on the destroyer *Jed*, a deafening silence lay upon the Straits which had been echoing all day to the sound of one of the most intense exchanges of artillery fire ever known. Mysteriously, neither hulk could be found; both had sunk but at least most of their crews had been saved. It was only after the war that it was learned that the three lost battleships had all been caught by a new and very small minefield laid along the Asian shore ten days before the assault, which the seaplane patrols had failed to spot. De Robeck was depressed by the losses and fully expected to be dismissed; Keyes and other senior officers, however, believed that the resistance could not last much longer and one more determined push by the fleet would be decisive. In fact, unbeknown to them, the shore batteries had used up half their ammunition stock in just one day and were down to a pittance of armour-piercing shell, their most important weapon. The Turks had also virtually run out of mines and had been driven to the desperate expedient of gingerly catching the mines sent down on the current against the *Goeben* by the Russians, who dropped them at the mouth of the Bosporus. The battle in the Straits had also generated panic in Constantinople, where there was a universal belief that the ships would arrive within days. But the Turks and the Germans gave real meaning to the concept of sticking to one's guns; so long as they could be fired and had ammunition, the gunners stuck to their task in spite of the infernal barrage from the ships. The Turks displayed a quasi-religious fervour while the Germans showed their formidable discipline. Sailors from the *Goeben* and the *Breslau* fought their unshipped naval guns alongside the German howitzer teams. They got little sleep after the ships withdrew because they were put to work to strengthen their emplacements for the next round which they were sure must follow daylight.

But it did not. A gale blew up, and the British and French were busy regrouping and repairing the damage to their ships, which was particularly heavy in the French squadron. The failure of the minesweepers led de Robeck to order the replacement of the last civilians by naval volunteers, of whom there was an immense number, reflecting the high morale of men scenting imminent victory. A message arrived from the Admiralty on the morning of the 19th, the day after the attack, regretting the lost ships but unequivocally ordering de Robeck to renew the assault. Four more British battleships and one French were promised as replacements and a squadron of land-based aircraft was already beginning to arrive, led by Air Commodore Samson. On March 20 de Robeck had sixty-two vessels ready to serve as minesweepers, all manned by British or French sailors, and he announced he would be ready to renew the fight in a few days. But on March 22, in circumstances which have never become clear, Admiral de Robeck changed his mind. To the initial incredulity and subsequent jubilation of the hard-pressed artillerymen on the shores of the Dardanelles, the great enemy fleet never returned to the attack. Four weeks of effort at a cost of 700 lives, three battleships sunk and two crippled, damage to several other vessels and untold quantities of ammunition were thrown away.

Whether de Robeck suggested or was persuaded to accept the abandonment of the naval campaign is not known, but is in the end irrelevant, because in faraway London the decision had been taken before the climactic bombardment of March 18 that the Dardanelles were really a job for the army after all. As the great enthusiast Churchill was egging on de Robeck, the thoughts of others, including Fisher and a newly converted Kitchener, were turning increasingly to a landing on the Gallipoli peninsula, shaped roughly like a pistol pointing at Constantinople. On March 1, Prime Minister Venizelos of Greece offered three divisions, but two days later the Russians firmly vetoed the idea: to have an Anglo-French force make a landing would at most lead to an occupation for the duration of the war, but a Greek success could permanently deprive Russia of a chance to reach the Mediterranean. The always incisive prose of Liddell Hart in his *History of the First World War* becomes positively savage as he deploys a harsh metaphor to describe the Tsar's attitude: 'Russia would not help even in helping to clear her own windpipe. She preferred to choke rather than disgorge a morsel of her ambition.'

On February 16 Kitchener released the crack 29th

British infantry division, but outrage among the Western Front generals caused him to substitute the raw but physically magnificent troops of the Australia and New Zealand Army Corps (Anzac) of two divisions, currently in Egypt. Then General Sir William Birdwood was sent to the area to assess the military situation, and after a few days, on March 5, he sent a dispatch to Kitchener saying he believed the navy could not succeed alone, three days after Carden had said it could. Kitchener's final, final decision fell on March 10: the 29th and Royal Naval divisions were to go and so would a French division he had requested, plus Anzac – a whole army of 75,000 men. General Sir Ian Hamilton was appointed C-in-C of the expedition, and was actually with the fleet when it undertook its great bombardment on March 18. Hamilton and de Robeck went into conclave on the *Queen Elizabeth* at Lemnos four days later. Exactly what was said at that meeting is not known or, more precisely, obscured by the markedly differing accounts from various participants, but it does seem clear beyond doubt that de Robeck went into it still thinking that the navy could finish the job and came out thinking it could not be done without the army. Keyes was outraged, but he was also outnumbered and outranked. To the end of his life, by which time he had proved himself to be one of the greatest admirals of his generation, he never changed his opinion. In London, Churchill felt the same but found himself virtually isolated in the same way at an acrimonious meeting of the War Council, which decided that the judgment of the naval and military commanders on the spot must prevail. In Constantinople the position of Enver, the War Minister, was considerably strengthened by the scarcely credible abandonment of the naval assault on the edge of victory, which he quite reasonably presented as a triumph of Turkish arms unmatched for many decades. And it was above all the British fleet, supreme in all the world, which had been driven off ignominiously. The first and most tragic victims of Turkey's resurgence of self-confidence towards a world full of infidels were the Armenians, who were now subjected to genocide on an unprecedented scale.

General Liman von Sanders, head of the German Military Mission and now also Inspector-General of the Turkish army, was assigned the task of preparing for the invasion which slack security on the Allied side soon revealed to be in preparation. He was given the Fifth Army of six divisions for the task, and his dispositions before and during the campaign are generally held to be entirely sound. The story of the Gallipoli fighting has been well and truly told more than once and may therefore be briefly summarized here.

A vast invasion fleet of 200 ships gathered off Mudros on the island of Lemnos and put the troops ashore on the peninsula at five different points on the morning of Sunday, 25 April 1915. Despite the ill-conceived and chaotic loading of the ships, the invaders established strong but confined beachheads at two places: Cape Helles, the extreme tip of the peninsula, and around what is still called Anzac Cove on its south-western edge. Fierce Turkish resistance in which Colonel (later General) Mustafa Kemal, Turkey's great postwar leader, was especially prominent combined with inept British generalship to limit the success of the invasion to these two toeholds. Volunteer machine-gun teams from the *Goeben* and *Breslau* were rushed to the front and stayed for the duration. Trench warfare on the Western Front pattern ensued, although the tortuous nature of the terrain and the fiercely hostile climate of summer gave it a peculiarly savage character; sometimes 'no man's land' was only a few yards wide. The courage and endurance of both sides soon produced stalemate. A new naval attack was abandoned in the middle of May after the Turks sank the battleship *Goliath*. On May 14, Fisher resigned after a petty quarrel with Churchill over reinforcements for the fleet, and within a fortnight Churchill himself was made to resign as First Lord. At the same time, submarines took a spectacular hand in the struggle for Constantinople: Lieutenant-Commander Boyle in *E14* got into the Sea of Marmara and sank a troopship with 6,000 men (half a division) aboard, all of whom were lost; then Lieutenant-Commander Nasmith in *E11* blew up an ammunition ship and many others. Both were awarded the VC. After that it was the Germans' turn: *Kapitänleutnant* Otto Hersing arrived in the *U21* and sank two old battleships, *Triumph* and *Majestic*, in quick succession. In the same month of May, the Lowland division was added to Hamilton's forces, which soon numbered eight divisions in all, more than the Turks had. The desultory war of attrition continued until August 6, when another landing with five more Allied divisions was made at Suvla Bay, north of the Anzac position. Abysmal leadership ensured that it achieved nothing beyond a new toehold, thanks largely, once again, to the super-human efforts of Mustafa Kemal, now a corps commander. In September the French offered a whole new army and the British found two more divisions for yet another invasion, which was postponed until November. Meanwhile Bulgaria, convinced by the Allied failure at the Dardanelles, entered the war on the Turco-German side, despite very recent wars with Turkey, and threatened Serbia. This obliged Hamilton to commit two divisions to Salonika in northern Greece, the foundation of another wasteful front. Amid a virulent campaign in the London and Australian press, based on some understandably hostile reporting of the Gallipoli muddle by war correspondents, Hamilton was dismissed

and replaced by Lieutenant-General Sir Charles Monro
from the Western Front, in October 1915. Keyes went to
London to press for another naval assault, while Monro
argued for a complete withdrawal. Kitchener, initially
sympathetic to Keyes, went out to Gallipoli in November
to see for himself. At the end of the month, a prolonged
blizzard, the worst in living memory, caused ten per cent
casualties on the Allied side. Monro prevailed, despite
his forecast of casualties of up to forty per cent in a
withdrawal. Kitchener made one of those eerie oracular
pronouncements for which he was famous: there would
be no losses at all in the retreat. Faced with French and
Russian pleas for the Salonika front, the British Cabinet
decided on the evacuation of Gallipoli on 7 December
1915. The retreat from Suvla and Anzac Cove was
executed without loss on December 20, to the astonishment and frustrated rage of Limon von Sanders; he
decided on an all-out attack on the last redoubt of the
invaders at Cape Helles, where 35,000 men of four
divisions remained dug in. The British Cabinet decided
to pull them out on December 27, despite the obvious
risk in the face of a forewarned and formidable enemy
who could already taste victory. The French withdrew
unscathed on New Year's Day 1916, and the gap in the
line was so obvious that the singularly unfortunate men
of the British 29th Division, fully aware that it would be
their turn soon, moved round the coast by ship and made
another landing, in a final gesture of quiet heroism and
unquenchable morale, to fill the hole. On January 7, the
Turks duly launched their last attack. Despite its ferocity,
the remaining British troops managed such an intense
hail of fire that not one Turk reached their line. Things
might have been different had Mustafa Kemal been in
charge, but he had been forced to take sick leave a month
earlier, worn down by his unremitting efforts. Against all

the odds and with brilliant ingenuity, the last contingent got away on the night of the 8th to 9th – without loss. Thus in the end nothing so became the disastrous Gallipoli adventure as the leaving it. Kitchener had been right, but his star, once hitched to the ill-chosen and worse managed bandwagon of the Dardanelles campaign, had begun to wane; to some considerable extent, his reputation was saved by his sudden death aboard HMS *Hampshire* six months later, when the heavy cruiser hit a mine off the Orkneys while taking him to Russia for talks.

In 259 days of fighting on land, a total of half a million men took part on each side, each of which suffered fifty per cent casualties. In August 1916 the British appointed a Royal Commission to investigate the disaster, and at the end of 1917 it concluded that the whole affair had been a ghastly mistake. A few years after the war, however, general opinion swung round to the view that it had been a sound strategy botched by bad execution, poor leadership, indecision and ignorance. In some ways, the remarkable retreat foreshadowed Dunkirk; and at least the largest amphibious operation until the Second World War helped to ensure that the largest of all, D-Day in 1944, was a success: the bitter lessons of Gallipoli were put to good use by the next generation, which had little else to go on. Keyes fought for a new naval operation until the end; his reputation hugely enhanced by his work with the Dover Patrol, he persuaded Admiral Lord Wemyss, base commander at Mudros during the campaign and First Sea Lord in 1918, to support him but they were forestalled by the Armistice.

The triumph presented to the Turks at Gallipoli released twenty divisions to menace Russia and Egypt. One million Allied troops were involved in the subsequent campaigns in Salonika and the Middle East, from Egypt to Mesopotamia, until General Allenby defeated Field

Marshal Limon von Sanders. Russia remained cut off and proved unable to sustain the war against the Germans from her own dwindling resources. The Russian Revolution of 1917 was probably inevitable in any event: the defeat by the Japanese in 1905 came close to causing one, and the struggle against Germany was much more enervating for the antediluvian Tsarist regime which ultimately failed to stem the tide with reform. But there can be no doubt that the First World War precipitated the Revolution, or that the defeat of Russia which created the Marxist 'revolutionary situation' became inevitable with the arrival of the *Goeben* in the Dardanelles and was brought to its final fruition by Lenin, sent to Russia by the Germans in his sealed train like a bacillus, as Churchill unforgettably put it. A steady flow of Russian grain would have reduced Britain's dependence on North America for food and her reliance on the North Atlantic shipping route, which the deadly German submarine campaign came alarmingly close to cutting. Shiploads of munitions in the other direction would at the very least have enabled the Russians to take more pressure off the Western Front than they did, while significant British and French forces would not have been diverted to the Near and Middle East. One is irresistibly drawn back to the bald observation of Germany's most formidable general of the time, Ludendorff, that the Turkish involvement in the war was worth two years – in a war that endured for four. To that extent, the Dardanelles became the key to a breakthrough once they had been closed, and one must conclude that Churchill was right. Had the counterstroke come off, and been properly followed through, it would have been a turning point. But his mistake, shared with so many others, was not to appreciate the importance of Turkey before the war, an error the Germans avoided and turned to terrible account. The Ottoman Empire was worth more than two dreadnoughts after all, and the redrawing of the political map in the Middle East after its postwar collapse had consequences which have still not by any means worked themselves out to this day.

The results of Souchon's escape with his ships to the Dardanelles can now be seen in their broadest as well as narrowest sense: having got through against all odds, he forced Russia to declare war on Turkey by the simplest means at his disposal – the attack on the Russian Black Sea coast under Turkish colours. After that the *Goeben* and the *Breslau* carried on with the encapsulated campaign on a landlocked sea that they had begun regardless of its portentous consequences elsewhere, which have been recalled in this chapter. As the Black Sea war continued and died away, the naval assaults on the Dardanelles and the Gallipoli campaign also came and went, leaving the German Mediterranean Division with the mastery of the Black Sea, the Bosporus, the Sea of Marmara and the Dardanelles as a fleet in being. For the sailors there was, however, another enemy with whom there had been no serious naval exchange throughout the war in the eastern Mediterranean – the British and French ships which had been sent to close the Dardanelles stable door behind Souchon and had been there ever since in one formation or another. If the Mediterranean Division was ever to be deployed again in action afloat, it would have to return to the sea whence it and its official title alike had come. It remains to relate what happened when the German ships at last reappeared at the western end of the Straits they had so dashingly blocked by reaching them unscathed. This time triumph did not await them.

12

The Last Foray of the Mediterranean Division

GOBLO . . . GOBLO . . . was the signal which the mainly British naval blockading forces off the Dardanelles had been longing to hear for nearly three and a half years. Inevitably it took them completely by surprise when it came, at 5.20 A.M. GMT on Sunday, 20 January 1918, forty-one months and ten days after the German ships had vanished from the Mediterranean into the Straits. The view halloo, which stood for '*Goeben* and *Breslau* out', was sounded, not by a mighty battlecruiser, but by HMS *Lizard*, a modest destroyer of 780 tons with two 4-inch guns and a pair of 21-inch torpedo tubes, commanded by Lieutenant N. A. G. Ohlenschlager, RN. On sighting a four-funnelled cruiser off the north-eastern tip of the island of Imbros (now Gokçeada), *Lizard* promptly issued the usual visual challenge – until her lookouts saw the unmistakable bulk of the *Goeben* a mile behind the *Breslau*. Despite prompt enemy jamming, the *Lizard* put out the alert by wireless at full power, simultaneously using her searchlight to warn the *Raglan* and the *M28*, the two monitors (special bombardment-ships) moored in Kusu Bay, Imbros. Undeterred by the fact that she was, for the moment, the only British ship at sea and in contact with the enemy, *Lizard* turned towards the *Breslau* and opened fire. The light cruiser had already begun shelling the monitors.

The Battle of Imbros, which profited neither participant while occasioning sad losses to both, was the final sally of the Mediterranean Division and something of a desperate expedient by the Germans in the circumstances. Despite increasing shortages at home thanks to the British blockade of the North Sea, the Germans were still holding their own in the great stalemate on the Western Front; in the middle of December 1917 the 'real enemy', Russia, had conceded defeat and signed an armistice. But their Turkish allies, despite the best efforts of German generalship, were losing ground in the Middle East to Allenby, who captured Jerusalem on December 9. Constantinople in particular was desperately short of food and tension in the city had risen over allegations of widespread war-profiteering: the bread ration fell to just over six ounces per person per day. The food crisis was countered by official inquiries leading to exemplary punishment of black-marketeers, the release of men from the army to work in the fields was promised for spring and the Black Sea was reopened to trade after the Russian armistice.

After three remarkable years in Turkish waters, Admiral Souchon was recalled to Germany to take command of the Fourth Squadron of the High Seas Fleet. Unlike any other German admiral, he could look back on an undefeated contribution of immense strategic significance to his country, which began with the impulsion of Turkey into the war and continued with the containment of Russian naval power in the Black Sea. On 4 September 1917 he was replaced by Vice-Admiral Hubert von Rebeur-Paschwitz.

Vastly encouraged by the defeat of Russia, and the consequent ready availability of coal from the Black Sea coastal ports, the new C-in-C was determined not to allow the Mediterranean Division and the Turkish fleet to lapse into complacent idleness. Turkey and Germany were fighting for their lives in East and West, and although there was no longer an enemy at the gates of the Bosporus, there was another off the Dardanelles with whom the Turco-German naval forces had never fought a battle. In November 1917 Turkish General Headquarters asked Paschwitz if he could use his handful of German submarines against troopships about to move two divisions from Salonika to reinforce Allenby in Palestine. Instead he offered a surface raid on the Greek port, about 120 miles from the Straits. This ought to draw more enemy ships to the eastern Mediterranean and give his submarines more targets. When Jerusalem fell, Paschwitz concluded that a sea-action could help to restore morale. Enver Pasha favoured the idea, but not without misgivings about the risk to the two German ships, now officially and formally promised to Turkey in perpetuity. The Admiralty in Berlin was unreservedly in favour, and preparations were put in motion in conditions of maximum security. Constantinople was still teeming with spies, so much so that Paschwitz did not inform local army headquarters.

Stealthily and at night the gaps in the defensive minefields in the Straits were trebled in width, to be lit up on the night before the sortie by newly positioned searchlights. German air patrols searched for minefields sown by the British off the mouth of the Straits and an exit route was plotted. By January 18, all ships were fully coaled and on the following day the artillery commanders in the forts at the mouth of the Dardanelles were warned to be ready to provide covering fire for the ships when they returned. For the benefit of the spies, Paschwitz let it be known that there were to be manoeuvres on the Sea of Marmara involving the *Yavuz/Goeben, Midilli/Breslau*, four of the best Turkish destroyers and the German submarine *UC23*.

The real operational order gave as its objective the destruction of British observation forces off the Dardanelles. The first target was to be the single destroyer which was always on close patrol, to prevent it giving the alarm. The composition and disposition of the blockading force was well known from regular air patrols over its anchorages among the islands of Imbros, Lemnos and Tenedos. It included two British pre-dreadnought battle-ships, the *Lord Nelson* and, very appropriately given the nearness of Troy, the *Agamemnon*. There were also a French heavy cruiser and a British light one, both of decidedly venerable age, a small flotilla of destroyers and miscellaneous smaller craft, as well as the two monitors. These ungainly vessels, also known as 'blister-ships' from the outer skin their hulls carried as protection against torpedoes, were in effect floating gun platforms, lightly armoured and very slow-moving with a marked tendency to roll, but also exceptionally broad in the beam for stability when firing. The larger of the two, the *Raglan*, 6,150 tons, had one tall turret with a pair of 14-inch guns and subsidiary armament including 6-inch guns; the 540-ton *M28* had just one 9.2-inch gun and some secondary armament. Their main purpose was to bombard enemy shores at long range; their main use in the eastern Mediterranean had been to provide sailors with platforms to swim from – the top of the 'blister' was flat and virtually horizontal, and about level with the surface of the sea, offering a convenient 'pool-side' for men in need of a refreshing dip. The type got its name from a similarly shaped precursor of the battleship which was used on the Northern side in the American Civil War. The last German aerial reconnaissance on January 8 had revealed no change of any significance, with the two battleships in Mudros Bay, Lemnos, and the monitors in Kusu Bay, at the north-eastern corner of Imbros. Paschwitz had scaled down his plan. There was to be no attempt to get to Salonika, because that could easily lead to the destruction of his force. Instead the ships would go out and shoot up whatever they could find of the enemy among the islands off the Straits and return to base before the battleships could get up steam and come out of Mudros, a deep bay on the wrong (southern) side of Lemnos. It was to be a demonstration in the form of a hit-and-run raid, and under its cover *UC23* was to sow mines off Mudros and lie in wait for a target.

The German ships with their Turkish escorts crept down the Narrows under cover of dark and fully blacked out. The searchlights which were used to scan the waters each night focused on the new gaps in the Turkish minefields to let them through safely. As they passed slowly out of the Narrows, a dispatch boat was sent ashore to Chanak on the Asian side, according to plan, to collect the latest intelligence before the breakout. There was nothing of interest so Paschwitz pressed on. But he had altered some details of his plan in the light of a poisoned gift presented to him with the best of intentions by Liman von Sanders. The Fifth Army commander had heard of Paschwitz's operation at the last minute and remembered a small intelligence coup brought off on 20 December 1917, just a month earlier. A British armed steamer had run aground on that day at a point in the Gulf of Saros, on the north-western side of the Gallipoli peninsula. The troops who boarded her found among the ship's papers a chart of the area off the Dardanelles which had a series of markings pencilled over the coastal waters. Assuming the lines represented minefields, military intelligence passed it to the navy on the general's orders. Paschwitz concurred with this interpretation of the unfamiliar British Admiralty chart and altered the course he had plotted for his entry into the Mediterranean – ignoring the rather different markings made on a German chart of the area as the result of air reconnaissance. Taken together the two charts suggested there was no gap at all; but there was no time for another check from the air, and a naval minesweeping effort would give the game away. The admiral therefore suppressed his doubts and decided to go ahead.

Thus it was that the *Goeben*, on emerging from the Dardanelles a few minutes after the *Breslau*, shook to the explosion of a mine at 5.10 A.M. GMT. The battlecruiser stopped for twelve minutes while the damage was examined and found to be minor. A bunker containing 65 tonnes of coal, protectively positioned on the port side below the waterline and on the outside of the armoured skirt built into the hull against torpedoes, took the shock of the blast and filled with water. Leaks in the neighbouring compartments were staunched quickly by the damage-control teams as Paschwitz resolutely decided to carry on. The *Breslau* meanwhile had gone out and turned north-west to attack the enemy ships in the nearest anchorage of Kusu Bay, which turned out to be the two monitors. The *Goeben* was within a mile or so of catching up at 5.30, when both German ships, their destroyer escorts still in the Dardanelles, opened fire on the eastern shore of Imbros. Reacting with commendable speed, the *Raglan* started to return the fire with her 6-inch gun after only one salvo from *Breslau*, whose shot, however, soon began to strike home. The larger of the two British monitors got off just seven rounds from the gun before its crew were killed to a man. Two of the *Breslau*'s 5.9-inch shells got into the engine-room, knocking out all power and electric communications. As frantic efforts were being made to load the pair of great 14-inch guns in the turret, a German shell penetrated the structure and set off the powder bags in their rack beneath the guns. Before the Battle of Jutland in 1916 this alone would have been a complete disaster because of 'flash', the Achilles' heel of the contemporary warship, which accounted for the loss of several British vessels in the greatest sea-battle of the war. After that a device called a 'fearnought sleeve' was installed in ships to prevent flash in a turret from reaching the magazine. But now the *Goeben* was also firing her 11-inch shells at the *Raglan*, scoring several crippling hits including one which penetrated a small magazine directly and blew it up. The monitor began to go down by the bow, which at least had the effect of extinguishing the resulting fire, preventing further explosions in the main magazines. She eventually settled on an even keel with the water lapping round her bridge.

The *Breslau* switched her fire to the *M28*; one salvo of her extremely accurate shooting was enough: the smaller monitor's main magazine blew up and she too went down, but not before getting off a few rounds of 9.2-inch. Meanwhile the *Lizard*, having got no reply to her challenge and having put out her warning several times, turned towards the enemy ships and sought to place herself between them and the Dardanelles, like a cat trying to cut off a tiger. Her shells fell hopelessly short, while those of the *Breslau* which had now turned upon her were soon straddling the little destroyer. The *Lizard* began to zig-zag, changing her course every time the German guns flashed; this saved her because more than once German shot hit the water at the point where she would have been but for her violent evasive action. But the destroyer was completely prevented from getting within torpedo range; the *Breslau* engaged her at 11,000 yards, also preventing *Lizard* from laying an effective smokescreen, although she bravely made the attempt.

The first British ship to come to her aid was also the last – her sister-ship HMS *Tigress*, which had been with her on night patrol but had parted company temporarily before dawn. No other vessel of the thirty-five in the

Aegean Squadron reached the scene. *Tigress* (Lieutenant-Commander J. B. Newill, RN) returned at full speed from the west and came under fire from the *Breslau* at 6.20 A.M., about half an hour after she picked up the *Lizard*'s alert. The only support for the pair of destroyers came from C Squadron of the Royal Naval Air Service, based on Imbros and led by Flight Commander Edward Feeny, RN. He heard the shooting at sea at 5.30 and took his Scout biplanes into the air ten minutes later on hearing the GOBLO alert. One aircraft had wireless and followed the German ships' movements, but their constant jamming stopped the reports getting through. The other aircraft attempted to strafe and bomb the Germans, who were not significantly damaged but were forced to zig-zag. *Tigress* followed them as they steamed southwards along the eastern coast of Imbros, looking for new targets. *Lizard* joined her after briefly visiting Kusu Bay to ensure that rescue craft were on their way to the two wrecked monitors. Of the 310 men aboard them, 132 were saved. The destroyers lost sight of their quarry when the German ships rounded Cape Kephalo at the south-eastern tip of Imbros and turned south-westwards; when they came round the cape, the *Breslau* resumed firing at them, abandoning her shelling of the island, where several steamers and installations were hit. The light cruiser was at this stage over half a mile behind the *Goeben*, and they were on their way to shell Mudros.

At 7.31 A.M. GMT disaster struck the *Breslau*. A mine exploded under the starboard side of her stern, putting her steering gear out of action, a few minutes after she had reopened fire on the British destroyers. On the orders of Paschwitz she had swung out to port with the intention of taking up station ahead of the *Goeben* and sailed straight into a dense minefield. Machine-gun teams on both ships kept up their fire at the British aircraft as the

Goeben turned to help her stricken escort. At 7.55 another mine exploded under *Goeben*'s own stern, and five minutes later two more went off beneath the port side of *Breslau*'s stern, almost simultaneously; as she began to list sharply to port, no longer moving through the water, another mine holed her near the port bow. At 8.05 a fifth went off directly below her conning tower. With the stern already awash, Captain von Hippel ordered the crew of more than 500 men to abandon ship. About half of them were able to do so, including the captain, who led a last salute of three cheers from the water as SMS *Breslau* went under. In a water temperature of only 8°C he got them to join him in singing patriotic songs in the middle of the minefield for half an hour.

The two shadowing British ships meanwhile had faced about to beat off the four Turkish destroyers which had come out of the Straits in support of the Germans. The Turks, having taken several hits on one of their vessels, turned tail and re-entered the Dardanelles, taking no further part in the action, despite the fact that the British destroyers were shooting at them from the middle of one of their own minefields. Only now were the British able to turn their attention to the *Breslau* survivors in the chill, mine-strewn water, of whom many had already died of exposure. They were able to save about thirty per cent of the crew, some 140 men and a dozen officers, including the captain and Sub-Lieutenant Eberhard Souchon, the twenty-two-year-old nephew of the admiral. They were soon to be visited by the unharmed captain of the *Raglan*, Commander Viscount Broome, RN, a nephew of Lord Kitchener.

The *Goeben*'s own attempt to help her crippled escort had been interrupted by the detonation of another mine close to amidships on the port side, which caused her to list to port. Paschwitz and Captain Stoelzel, in command for just sixteen days, now decided to retire the ship, which steamed back to the Dardanelles at 10 knots, keeping up her fire against the British aircraft now ceaselessly harrying her, though with little effect on either side. The second mine explosion at 7.55 A.M. was offset by a third as the battlecruiser was entering the Straits at 8.48. It blew a hole almost exactly opposite the previous one; the partial flooding on the starboard side which followed served to right the ship. The effect of the mines was considerably reduced by the coal in the affected compartments; reinforced by beams, the watertight doors held and prevented flooding of neighbouring sections, but the pumps had to be put to full use. The *Goeben* was able to zig-zag at 14 knots on the last stage of her withdrawal, passing into the defensive minefields at 9.20, still under air attack.

But the great ship's troubles were far from over. No sooner had it been established that the mine damage had been contained as she steamed northwards up the Straits than the final and potentially catastrophic blow fell. As she manoeuvred close to the Asiatic shore off Nagara and Chanak, to circumnavigate a minefield, the *Goeben* grounded herself firmly on a sandbank. Throwing her mighty engines into reverse had no effect: she was stuck fast. As newly arrived German aircraft fought dogfights with the attacking British overhead, Stoelzel ordered the flooding of the rearmost compartments and the crew frantically shifted coal and ammunition towards the stern while others threw what they could over the sides. The *Goeben* was now in the most desperate plight of her career, helpless, her side-nets out and Turkish destroyers forming a screen against submarines, listing far enough to port to make the use of her main armament impossible. She was near enough to the entrance of the Straits to be within range of the biggest British naval guns of the

Aegean Squadron, a sitting target for air attack or a bold stroke by a submarine at night. If British aircraft were to be used as spotters for indirect fire from the sea, the ship would stand no chance. Captain Stoelzel therefore ordered the ship stripped of supplies and had all secret documents, cash and even the contents of the sick-bay taken ashore and most of the crew left her for the night. A mist provided some relief in the afternoon.

The British assumed the German ship had beached herself to prevent sinking from the effects of the mine explosions they had observed. It was not the only mistake they made. In command of the Aegean Squadron, now its official title, was another of Britain's apparently inexhaustible supply of ineffectual admirals. Rear-Admiral Arthur Hayes-Sadler had hoisted his flag only eight days before the German sortie. Like one of his predecessors, Admiral Sackville Carden (see chapter 11), he found the stress of command a strain on his nerves. Needing to visit Salonika to confer with the British Army headquarters there and finding his personal yacht was not available, he set off in the *Lord Nelson* on January 16 and was still away on the 20th. The whole point of keeping two pre-dreadnoughts on station was that only together was their main armament of four 12-inch guns apiece capable of facing the *Goeben*. As it was, the British guard force was perilously dispersed in any case and labouring under the confusion of potentially irreconcilable orders bequeathed by the previous flag officer in command, Admiral Fremantle (Troubridge's prosecutor). Although a rather more competent commander, if no genius, Fremantle had patently failed to absorb one of the great lessons of the case – the importance of clear orders. He required captains sighting the Germans not to attack regardless but to lead them on to a place where the enemy 'could be brought to action by superior force'.

On the other hand, he drafted a signal to be put out if the Germans appeared which baldly ordered: 'Take all necessary action to engage the enemy.' The two lonely destroyers which charged to the attack were, by obeying the second command, clearly in breach of the first! As it happened, the absence of the *Lord Nelson* was not known to Paschwitz, as we have seen; and in the event there would have been no time for the two battleships to be deployed effectively. Nonetheless by his stupidity in separating the pair, Hayes-Sadler had made it impossible to deploy a force superior to the *Goeben* for several days on end. Why he could not have taken a more modest conveyance is not clear.

Vice-Admiral Arthur Gough-Calthorpe, then British C-in-C in the Mediterranean, was furious and demanded an explanation. Hayes-Sadler replied by arguing that the ship's absence made no material difference on the day and added that if the Germans had come out because they knew she was away, it was most fortunate because the British minefields had not been swept, a fact which led to the loss of the *Breslau* and the damage to the *Goeben*. Another stable door was firmly closed when Calthorpe ordered the battleships to stay together at all times in future. On the morning of the 20th, Captain Philip Dumas, Senior Naval Officer at Mudros, in the absence of his admiral ordered all ships in port to raise steam on receipt of the GOBLO signal. They came out of the swept channel through the minefields only at 9.30 A.M. GMT, when they heard from the scene of the encounter that it was all over, so they put about and returned whence they had come. The British Army Aegean Islands command held an inquiry into why look-outs on the islands had not reported the emergence of the German ships earlier than they did, but nothing came of it.

Back in the Dardanelles, the struggle to refloat the *Goeben* was resumed at first light on January 21. A good third of her bottom, as far astern as the forward bridge, lay on the sandbank. The Turks brought up the two largest anchors they could find so that an attempt could be made to pull her off under her own power, but the turbines failed to move her even at full revolutions. When Admiral Usedom, the German in command of the Dardanelles defences, gave his opinion that indirect fire by the British was unlikely to be effective, the crew was brought back aboard, to unship everything else that was movable. As the air attacks resumed in the afternoon the elderly battleship *Torgud Reis* attempted to pull her free, also to no avail. The work of lightening ship continued throughout the next day. On the 23rd, the *Torgud Reis* tried again, but succeeded only in shifting the battlecruiser by seven and a half degrees without freeing her. One British bomb hit the after-funnel, causing little damage, on the 22nd, and on the 23rd another struck the edge of the port side near the stern, again with mimimal effect. The *Goeben*'s lighter guns brought down one aircraft. The largest bombs available to the attackers weighed 230 pounds and were hardly likely to damage a capital ship except by a freak hit, even if the rudimentary bomb-aiming procedure of the time managed to make any kind of hit possible in the face of hostile aircraft and gunfire from below; and anti-aircraft fire was a no more developed science, or not in the Dardanelles at least. One British seaplane had been lost in the dogfights of the 20th, and the air-raids were frequently interrupted by the winter weather. But plots made at the time of the fall of bombs show large quantities of near-misses among the hundreds dropped in more than 250 air sorties.

Work was now continuing on and alongside the *Goeben* round the clock. So did the air-raids; Royal Flying Corps aircraft from Salonika were brought in and others from the pioneer seaplane-carrier *Ark Royal* dropped torpedoes as the artillery of the shore defences poured in more and more anti-aircraft fire from eight batteries, which added to the general pandemonium of detonations, explosions and columns of water without scoring any hits. Two other seaplane-carriers brought reinforcements of aircraft and bombs while feverish efforts were made to adapt depth-charges and even armour-piercing naval 9.2-inch shells for dropping from the air. On the evening of January 24 the small monitor *M17* took up position on the western side of the Gallipoli peninsula at a distance of 18,500 yards from the *Goeben* and attempted to lob shells on her with the aid of a spotter aircraft, across the intervening land. Excitingly, the plane reported the first round of 9.2-inch as falling 200 yards over and 150 left of the target. But after the second shot, guns ashore began to fire back. In the fading light, which made spotting from the air difficult, the attempt was given up after ten rounds, which scored no hits whereas the shore artillery was already straddling the monitor. The *M17* withdrew.

On January 25, the Germans and the Turks, spared the nuisance of air attack thanks to a powerful north wind, made preparations in great detail for a supreme effort to free the stranded warship. The plan was to attach several ships to the *Goeben* by cable for a synchronized tow while other vessels lined up alongside her, their sterns facing the sandbank, for a simultaneous erosion of the sand by running their propellers while firmly anchored in position. A dredger was first used to remove sand from either side, as close to the hull as it could reach. The initial attempt on the morning of the 26th failed. In the afternoon the *Torgud Reis* was brought alongside to starboard and made fast to the *Goeben* by two towlines. When she ran her engines at full speed, churning up the water and thereby loosening the sand, the battlecruiser at last began to shift. At 4.47 P.M. GMT, the *Goeben* was free. She sailed slowly away under cover of dark and dropped anchor off Constantinople the next morning. She never fired another shot in anger.

It was only at first light on January 28 that a British air reconnaissance flight established that she had got away. The submarine *E14* had set off from Mudros the previous afternoon intent on a dawn attack, but only after Hayes-Sadler had dithered for several days about letting the three submarines eventually available to him take the risk. The boat penetrated to Nagara Point, where the *Goeben* had been held fast for almost an entire week, but of course found nothing. She was sunk by gunfire from the shore and patrolling destroyers on her way back, but nine of her crew survived and were taken prisoner.

The *Goeben*'s second escape from the Royal Navy naturally caused another round of chagrin and embarrassment in London. It also put an inglorious end to the career afloat of a third British admiral: Hayes-Sadler was soon relieved of his post in the Aegean. The new First Sea Lord, Admiral Sir Rosslyn (later Lord) Wemyss, was uncharacteristically blunt:

The *Goeben* getting away is perfectly damnable and has considerably upset me, since we at the Admiralty were under the happy delusion that there were sufficient brains and sufficient means out there to prevent it: of the latter there were; of the former apparently not.

The Battle of Imbros and its aftermath did not affect the strategic or tactical situation in the eastern Mediterranean. The raid itself and the salvation of the *Goeben* from what must for a while have seemed certain destruction may have temporarily lifted German and Turkish morale and certainly lowered that of the British. They lost about 200 men, two monitors, one submarine, two aircraft and a steamer, while the Germans and Turks lost about 400 men and the proud *Breslau*, the dashing junior partner in the adventures of the *Goeben*, while one destroyer was crippled. The *Goeben* herself, though damaged, was still afloat as the last German warship in foreign waters, and air patrols could not establish how much she had been harmed by the mines. She and the Turkish Navy therefore demonstrably remained a 'fleet in being' and had to be insured against by the continued presence of a considerable Anglo-French naval force for the rest of the war. It was to be many years before the *Goeben* was seen in the Mediterranean again, but she still had one more task to perform before the Great War ended.

The period from the end of January to the end of April 1918 passed peaceably enough for the battlecruiser, although the pumps had to work several hours a day to keep her afloat. The holes in her hull were dealt with by damage-limitation rather than repair; the war was going badly for Turkey and her guns might be needed at any time, so she could not be put out of action for repairs. On May 1, however, she returned to the scene of her private war with the now defeated Russians and crossed the Black Sea to Sevastopol, which she reached on the evening of the 2nd. German troops had advanced across the Crimea and taken the city and Field Marshal Eichhorn wanted the *Goeben* to keep watch on the Russian naval base she had shelled in October 1914. The Russian Admiral Sablin, in breach of the Treaty of Brest-Litovsk which ended the war between Germany and Russia, had led two battleships, ten destroyers and a similar number of steamers out of the port to Novorossiysk on May 1. The German battlecruiser was there to discourage any further initiatives. Still in port were four battleships and various smaller ships as well as the inverted hulk of

the tragic dreadnought *Imperatriza Maria*. The Kaiser's
ensign was hoisted on the rest of the Black Sea Fleet as
German guards were put aboard each ship. For the first
time in four and a half years, on June 6, the *Goeben* went
into dry dock for a week. Her bottom was scraped and
even repainted, but nothing was done about the three
gaping holes left by the mines off Imbros. Neither the
time nor the labour was available. On June 19, Admiral
Sablin brought back most of the ships he had taken away
and surrendered under the *Goeben*'s guns. On the 27th,
because not all the ships which had fled were back, von
Rebeur-Paschwitz went to Novorossiysk, only to find that
the rest had scuttled themelves and the crews dispersed.
On July 1, the *Goeben* was back in Sevastopol and on the
6th she went to Odessa to collect Eichhorn. On the 11th
she left Sevastopol for the last time, arriving back in
Constantinople the next day. Early in August 1918 serious
repairs to her hull were at last begun, and by about the
middle of October the foremost of the three holes was
finally closed.

By then the world knew that peace was only a matter
of days away. Bulgaria had just ended hostilities with the
British and French (thereby severing the overland route
from Turkey to Germany), the Central Powers were
negotiating for an armistice and on November 1 Britain
and France signed a separate armistice with Turkey. The
next day the long pretence about the ownership of the
Goeben/*Yavuz* became a reality when Paschwitz formally
handed over the ship to his second-in-command in the
Turkish Navy, Rear-Admiral Arif Pasha. The Turks saw
to it that the German sailors were allowed to go home
instead of being handed over as prisoners of war, as the
victorious Allies had demanded. The Germans were given
the chance to sail away on the steamer *Corcovado* to

Odessa, from where they managed to find their way home by train with many delays.

Their once proud and never defeated ship was towed away from Constantinople and was left to settle on the shallow bottom of a little bay some miles off. The Turks refused to let the Royal Navy take her away and she was allowed to rot quietly until 1927. It was only in that year that a resurgent Turkey called in salvage experts from a French company based at St Nazaire to start the repairs that were by then nine years overdue. The work took three years but the hull was made good at last, and in 1930 the *Yavuz* re-emerged as the flagship of the Turkish Navy. As such she once again became a frequent visitor to the Mediterreanean and made a great impression, despite her age, when she visited the British naval base in Malta in 1936. Two years later she was chosen to carry the mortal remains of Turkey's national hero, Mustafa Kemal Atatürk, victor of Gallipoli and father of the regenerated Turkish state, to their last resting place. Only in 1950 was the old warship finally removed from the active list, and four years later from the fleet reserve. After that she became a floating museum, and in 1971 the decision was taken to sell her for scrap. It was in 1973, however, that she actually struck her flag for the last time so that dismantling could begin. This was eventually completed in 1976. With that the last survivor of the Kaiser's navy finally disappeared and the ship which Turkey had gained for the loss of an empire was seen no more. But the profound political upheavals for which her attainment of the Dardanelles on 10 August 1914 was the catalyst continue to this day. The *Goeben* is gone; her legacy is with us still.

Epilogue

Thereafter the red edges of war spread over another half of the world. Turkey's neighbours, Bulgaria, Rumania, Italy and Greece were eventually drawn in. Thereafter, with her exit to the Mediterranean closed, Russia was left dependent on Archangel, icebound half the year, and on Vladivostok, 8,000 miles from the battlefront. With the Black Sea closed, her exports dropped by ninety-eight per cent and her imports by ninety-five per cent. The cutting-off of Russia with all its consequences, the vain and sanguinary tragedy of Gallipoli, the diversion of Allied strength in the campaigns of Mesopotamia, Suez and Palestine, the ultimate break-up of the Ottoman Empire, the subsequent history of the Middle East, followed from the voyage of the *Goeben*.

Barbara Tuchman,
August 1914

A ship is an inanimate if intricate object and cannot strictly speaking be held capable of changing anything. The wise remark of Sir Basil Liddell Hart, quoted at the beginning of this book, is not to be gainsaid: a warship is a weapon and, no matter how powerful, no more than a weapon. But it is not necessary to sink into sentimentality or revel in romanticism to accept that there is more to a warship than the guns, the engines and the armour. Sailors have invested their ships with personality since time immemorial; and English, the supreme language of the sea, abandons its customary indifference to grammatical gender to endow a ship with femininity. Whether this created or was created by the concept of 'the sailor wedded to his ship' is a matter for psychological as well as linguistic speculation. So it was not the *Goeben* as such, but the *Goeben* in the hands of her crew, her captain and her admiral which, on the orders of Germany in arms, became the instrument of profound changes which have still not fully worked themselves out more than seventy years after her arrival at the entrance to the Dardanelles on 10 August 1914. Thus used, she was unquestionably and most resoundingly a weapon which was expended profitably, though to whose ultimate or abiding benefit is a matter for debate. There may in the end be no beneficiary at all but only losers. We may, however, be sure that if the *Goeben* had not been a battlecruiser, she would not have been able to do what she did. A destroyer or a fast light cruiser like the *Breslau* would have got away from the French and the British with much greater ease but would hardly have made such an impression on the Turks. If the vessel sighted so frustratingly by *Indomitable* and *Indefatigable* had been Germany's mightiest battleship, she would not have had the speed to get away before the British were free to open fire. Nor would she have been able to run rings round the Russian Black Sea Fleet. In fact no navy would have deployed a single battleship in such a manner: they were made to operate in squadrons. The *Goeben* has a claim to be the most successful ship of a type with a generally equivocal history, notably in British experience (Jutland in the First World War and the loss of the *Hood* in the Second spring to mind). German ships in this category were generally superior to their British counterparts in both speed and armour. The *Goeben* was used as a cruiser, albeit a huge one, and was not called upon to pass herself off as a battleship as was sometimes the case in the Royal Navy with unhappy results. If Admiral Souchon had had a British battlecruiser of the time under his command, he would not have got away either.

The assessment by General Ludendorff, the driving force of the Kaiser's army, that Turkey's entry into the war on Germany's side, made possible by the timeous arrival of the *Goeben*, was worth two whole years to the outnumbered Germans and their allies in a war which lasted little more than four, has already been noted. So has the effect on Russia's ability to export grain, the mainstay of her foreign trade, and to import badly needed munitions to sustain her faltering war effort. The denial of Russian grain forced the British to place greater reliance on North America and made them that much more vulnerable to the German submarine campaign, which came at least as close in the First World War to bringing Britain to her knees as its much more widely publicized successor in the Second. At the same time, two more years of war made Germany's defeat in 1918 all the worse when it came. The gift of time the *Goeben* brought was both poisoned and double-edged.

It was the Russians who, after feeling the first chill from the closure of the Dardanelles, prompted Lord Kitchener to swing his decisive influence behind the ultimately disastrous Gallipoli expedition which was intended to reopen them. The preceding failure of the Royal Navy to force the Straits, which was the immediate cause of the decision to land troops, thus doubled and redoubled the initial error on the part of the Admiralty and the Foreign Office in discounting Turkey and failing to anticipate German designs on her. It therefore seems unfair that Churchill became the scapegoat for the Gallipoli disaster even though his strategy was as right as its execution was wrong. He was badly served by most of the admirals involved; but as First Lord of the Admiralty he could hardly escape the consequences of their weakness. The inexplicable failure to use the vast and unique experience of Admiral Limpus is just one of a series of mysterious pulled punches in the Gallipoli tragedy. Churchill promptly went to the Western Front to fight, but was recalled to the government by Lloyd George. As Minister of Munitions he threw his unquenchable energy into the production of the land weapon of the future, the tank. The *Goeben* cast a shadow upon his career but did not extinguish it, a fact which subsequent events make self-evident.

In Russia the war had paralysed the government of Tsar Nicholas II by March 1917. The fog of war, generalized inefficiency and the shortage of manpower on the land were some of the main reasons behind widespread hunger across the vast and tottering empire. This led to strikes and riots and then outbreaks of military mutiny when troops refused to fire on demonstrators. On March 15 the earth of Mother Russia trembled when her ineffectual 'Little Father' abdicated. A provisional government of politicians from the new-fangled Duma (parliament) took over, its powers inhibited from the outset by the mushrooming organization and strength of the Soviet of Workers' and Soldiers' deputies in the recently restyled Petrograd, previously St Petersburg. There need be no doubt that the closure of the Dardanelles occasioned by the *Goeben* played a major role in creating the 'revolutionary situation' recognized by the Marxists. But for the stranglehold this conferred on Russia's Turkish and German enemies, she would surely have emerged on the winning side of a war which her allies finally managed to win without her, thanks to the belated entry on their side of the United States. On Ludendorff's subsequent reckoning, that earlier victory could have come in 1916. This is surely one of the greatest 'ifs' in all history: what if the Tsar had been able to claim a share in a Triple Entente victory over the Central Powers (and what if the

United States had not entered the war at all)? We may be sure that the world would have looked rather different today. It would be reckless to suggest that there would have been no Russian Revolution but for the *Goeben*; yet it seems reasonable to argue that, but for her, it would not have come as early as it did and might have taken a different form. But, thanks to Admiral Souchon and the Turks, Germany was still very much in the war in April 1917 when the Kaiser's government made its crowning contribution to the Revolution: the dispatch of Vladimir Ilyich Lenin across the territory it controlled to his prostrate homeland. Thereupon the precarious balance of power within Russia swung decisively away from the Mensheviks towards the Soviets and the Bolsheviks, who won control of the key revolutionary councils in Petrograd and Moscow in September 1917. The classic coup, masterminded by Trotsky, which set the pattern for the subsequent development of the modern Soviet Union, duly ensued on 25 October 1917 in the old Russian calendar (now commemorated on November 7). Within a matter of weeks Lenin, in order to gain time for the Revolution, signed a humiliating, separate peace with Germany at Brest-Litovsk. The civil war which soon broke out in Russia drew in most of the powers of both sides in the World War, but the identity of the ultimate victors is too well-known for us to need to pursue the story of post-revolutionary Russia any further here. We may note, however, the equivocal role of the Soviet Union in helping postwar Germany to rearm and retrain in secret and in later concluding a treaty with Hitler (if only, once again, to gain time). This did not save Russia from having to bear the brunt of the suffering it helped to make necessary before Nazism could be destroyed and German expansionism finally halted. If only Admiral Troubridge had followed his instinct and attacked the *Goeben* as Commodore Harwood set about the *Graf Spee* . . . But in fairness to the unlucky admiral we should remember that the Turco-German treaty was concluded before Souchon turned east, that the Germans were already effectively in control of the Turkish Army and that Enver Pasha would almost certainly have found a way of precipitating Turkey into the war. Without the prompt and unexpected arrival of the *Goeben*, however, that crucial development would have been much longer in coming, given the poor condition of the Turkish forces. It might have been delayed long enough for it not to have had such an impact on Russia. We have seen how the formidable General Liman von Sanders succumbed to despair and sought to give up a task which seemed impossible to him even after Souchon's arrival. It thus fell to the German Navy and the *Goeben* to change the course of history – the only occasion when Germany's junior service succeeded in altering the balance of power in the world for ever.

Nonetheless, Enver had picked the wrong side. The best efforts of the German Army officer-corps notwithstanding, the British and their allies in the Near and Middle East slowly and bloodily gained the upper hand until Turkey capitulated on 31 October 1918. The decisive stroke was General Allenby's smashing victory in September at Megiddo in Palestine over a Turkish force led by Liman von Sanders. But it had taken four years to get the upper hand over the Turks in a costly diversion of strength from the Western Front. The peace terms imposed on Turkey in the Treaty of Sèvres in 1920 entailed the dismemberment of the Ottoman Empire. The Greeks were allowed to occupy the area round Smyrna (Izmir) on the western coast of Anatolia in the same year.

It was the very harshness of the terms imposed on the Turks which eventually made Sèvres as counter productive as the Treaty of Versailles proved to be in Germany's case. The Greeks sought to expand their toehold eastwards and for two years the Turks fought bitterly for the recovery of the west of their country. With Constantinople (renamed Istanbul) under Greek control, a new capital was established an Ankara where it remains to this day. Nationalist sentiment focused upon Mustafa Kemal, the one Turkish general with an unblemished record in the World War. At first the Greeks carried all before them, but early in 1921 the tide began to turn when Colonel Ismet, Kemal's most gifted colleague and eventual successor, defeated the occupiers at the two battles of Inönü in January and March. The decisive victory was won by Kemal himself in twenty-two days of slaughter during the Battle of the River Sakarya in western Anatolia in August. But it took another twelve months for the resurgent Turks to recapture Smyrna. When they did so in August 1922 they massacred the Greek half of the port city's population in a bloodletting unmatched since the terrible days of the Armenian genocide. This brought the Turkish Army into direct confrontation with the last major occupying force still in place on national soil – the British Army dug in on the Asian shore of the Dardanelles at Çannakale (Chanak).

In the meantime the Turkish nationalists had signed a border treaty with the Russians in March 1921 (the Soviet signatory was Stalin). Kemal's representatives also in the same year concluded separate pacts with the French and the Italians leading to the withdrawal of their forces from the Turkish mainland. The British, faced with the prospect of war with Turkey, realized in time which way the wind was blowing and Lloyd George, still Prime

Minister, decided to bow out of Turkish politics as gracefully as he could. Eventually Sèvres was rewritten by the Treaty of Lausanne in 1923, which helped to pave the way for the transformation by Kemal of the Ottoman Empire into the modern Turkish republic in 1924. But the empire beyond Turkey's borders had already been dismantled, largely under the auspices of the new League of Nations which gave the French mandates to administer Syria and Lebanon, and the British Iraq, Palestine and Transjordan. Saudi Arabia and Yemen were granted limited independence but in the process were detached for ever from Turkish suzerainty. Nominal Turkish sovereignty over Egypt and Sudan, long since within the British sphere of influence, was officially terminated. In 1924 Kemal and his supporters created the constitutional republic which abolished Islamic law, the old Turkish alphabet, the subjection of women and the claim to leadership of the world's Muslims. Until his death in 1938, Mustafa Kemal, surnamed Atatürk (father of the Turks), set about the ruthless modernization of his country. In the meantime the British mandate over Palestine paved the way for the creation of the state of Israel in accordance with the 1917 Balfour Declaration asserting the right of the Jews to a nation-state on Palestinian soil. The Arabs of the region were already in revolt against this idea in the period 1935–9, but the aftermath of the Second World War saw it brought to fruition by 1948. It hardly seems necessary to add that this problem remains an issue in our own time which could still provoke unimaginable consequences.

Overall, the defeat of Turkey in 1918 led to the breakup of the Ottoman Empire and thus, directly or indirectly, to the independence of its components. This took place just as the importance of the oil deposits in the Middle East began to be exploited by the Western imperial powers in their last years of domination. There is no resisting the contention that the Ottoman domain existed largely in name only, even before the events of 1914; but at the same time the powers which had moved in to exert *de facto* control over its western parts in the nineteenth century, from Morocco to the Balkans, were committed to its survival, if only as a concept, until Turkey's intervention in the First World War and its ensuing defeat forced a division of the spoils which had been deferred for so long. Thus the advent of the *Goeben* eventually forced a cure upon the 'sick man of Europe'; but the amputations which came with it and the continuing wrangles over his abandoned estate have already had consequences which we would have done better without. As we nervously follow events in the Middle East today, we cannot exclude the possibility that the worst has yet to come.

A Note on Sources

The principal sources from which this book is derived are the files of the West German Federal Military Archive in Freiburg-im-Breisgau and of the Public Record Office in Kew, Richmond, Surrey. The German records are all in the *Reichsmarine* collection and the British papers I used are mostly in the ADM 137 series of naval intelligence documents. I also consulted the following books.

La Guerre Navale, fautes et responsabilités by Admiral Amadée Bienaimé (Tallandier, Paris, 1920) is the rare and indignant account of the chief French investigator of the conduct of the First World War in the Mediterranean. He wrote this book when it became clear to him that the National Assembly was not going to publish the material from which it is drawn and much of which he discovered himself. Once due allowance is made for untidy presentation and the indignation factor it becomes a most valuable source.

Histoire Maritime de la Première Guerre Mondiale by Paul Chack and Jean-Jacques Antier (Editions France-Empire, Paris) is a useful modern account of the war at sea from the French point of view. In this context *Tome II: Méditerranée (1914–1915)*, published in 1970, is directly relevant.

Der Krieg zur See 1914–18 is the vast official German history published under the auspices of the *Reichsmarine-Archiv*. Section five, *Der Krieg in den türkischen Gewässern*, edited by Vice-Admiral Eberhard von Mantey, covers the war in the eastern Mediterranean and the

Black Sea; volume I of this section, *Die Mittelmeer-Division* (Mittler, Berlin, 1928) covers the actions of the Mediterranean Division and was edited by Rear-Admiral Hermann Lorey.

Auf See Unbesiegt ('Undefeated at sea'), also edited by Admiral von Mantey and published for the *Reichsmarine-Archiv* by Weller, Berlin, 1927, contains a rare account of his campaign by Admiral Souchon, whose memoirs were never published. There is a French translation in *Les Marins allemands au Combat* by Capitaine R. Jouan (Payot, Paris, 1930).

Souchon der Goeben-Admiral (greift in die Weltgeschichte ein) – 'intervenes in world history' – is the curiously titled, openly favourable but accurate biography of Souchon by a lifelong Finnish admirer, Matti E. Mäkelä (Vieweg, Brunswick, 1936). Forty-three years later, Mäkelä followed this up with *Auf den Spuren der Goeben* ('On the trail of the *Goeben*'), a brief and episodic account with excellent photographs and charts (Bernard und Graefe, Munich, 1979).

Das Teufelschiff und seine kleine Schwester by Georg Kopp ('The devil-ship and her little sister'), translated by Arthur Chambers under the title, *Two Lone Ships, Goeben and Breslau* (Hutchinson, London, 1931), is the only account of book length by a participant. It is excellent on atmosphere and anecdote but treacherous on facts beyond the horizon of the two ships on which he served.

Die Fahrten der Goeben und der Breslau by Emil Ludwig (S. Fischer, Berlin, 1916) is a journalist's wartime propaganda account, too early to be factually useful but making clear the value to Germany of Souchon's initiative.

The Flight of the Goeben and the Breslau by Admiral Sir A. Berkeley Milne (Eveleigh Nash, London, 1921) is the bitter and ineffectual apologia of the British C-in-C in the Mediterranean at the time Souchon got away. It is useless to the historian except as a source of clues to Milne's character.

Policy and Operations in the Mediterranean 1912–14 edited by E. W. R. Lumby (Navy Records Society, London, 1970) is a priceless and indispensable collation of texts, signals, documents and charts. It also contains the minutes of the court of inquiry which led to Admiral Troubridge's trial, and above all a full record of the court-martial itself. As the relevant court records were not yet available to the public at the time of writing, the book was a crucial source.

The Escape of the Goeben by Redmond McLaughlin (Seeley Service, London, 1974) is the most recent account. Crisply, excitingly and accurately written by a consultant surgeon with a taste for military history, it does not draw upon primary German sources or cover the French involvement.

History of the Great War – Naval Operations, volume I, by Sir Julian Corbett (Longmans, London, 1920) is the relevant volume of the British official history. Considering how soon it was written and that the author did not see all the pertinent documents, it is a solid achievement if now outdated.

From the Dreadnought to Scapa Flow (five volumes, Oxford University Press, 1961–70) by Arthur J. Marder remains the definitive history of the Royal Navy of the period and contains material not available elsewhere. The general reader who has hitherto looked in vain for a one-volume British account covering roughly the same ground can now turn to *The Great War at Sea 1914–1918* by Richard Hough (OUP, 1983), an admirably clear and readable history.

History of the First World War by B. H. Liddell Hart (Cassell, London, 1970) is still a bible for those seeking to grasp the strategic framework of the conflict at sea as well as on land.

The World Crisis, volume I, 1911–1914, by Winston S. Churchill (1923) is a wonderfully gripping narration of the relevant period by one of its most important figures. Its value to the historian is summed up in the quotations from Marder in the text above (chapters 4 and 9).

August 1914 by Barbara Tuchman (Macmillan, London, 1980) is a masterly description of the opening weeks of the war and how these set the pattern for the ensuing four years of struggle. It includes an account of the *Goeben* affair in chapter 10 and in a few memorable lines spells out the significance of Souchon's escape for the course of the war (see Epilogue above).

Modern Turkey by Geoffrey Lewis (Ernest Benn, London, 1974) lucidly explains the complexities of Turkish politics over the past century and the personalities involved.

Gallipoli by Alan Moorehead (illustrated edition), published by Macmillan, London, 1975, is a moving and thorough account by an outstanding Australian descriptive writer of a campaign which has a special place in his country's history.

The principal reference books to which I had frequent recourse include: *The Times Atlas of the World* (comprehensive edition) – Times Books, London, 1980 – whose spellings of place-names I followed when in doubt; *The Times Atlas of World History* (Times Books, London, 1981); *Jane's Fighting Ships 1914* (uncensored fourth edition) – London, 1914 – whose spellings of the names of Russian and Turkish ships (Turkish script was not Latinized until after the First World War) I have followed; *German Warships of World War I* by J. C. Taylor (Ian Allan, London, 1969); *The Oxford Companion to Ships and the Sea* edited by Peter Kemp (OUP 1976; Granada paperback, 1979).

Index

True war – now available in paperback from Grafton Books

Alexander Baron
From the City, From the Plough   £1.95 ☐

C S Forester
Hunting the Bismarck   £1.50 ☐

Ka-Tzetnik
House of Dolls   £2.50 ☐

Olga Lengyel
Five Chimneys   £1.95 ☐

Dr Miklos Nyiszli
Auschwitz   £2.50 ☐

Alexander McKee
Dresden 1945 (illustrated)   £2.50 ☐

Bruce Myles
Night Witches (illustrated)   £1.95 ☐

F Spencer-Chapman
The Jungle is Neutral [illustrated]   £1.95 ☐

Bryan Perrett
Lightning War: A History of Blitzkrieg (illustrated)   £2.95 ☐

Leonce Péillard
Sink the Tirpitz!   £1.95 ☐

Richard Pape
Boldness Be My Friend (illustrated)   £2.50 ☐

Baron Burkhard von Mullenheim-Rechberg
Battleship Bismarck (illustrated)   £3.50 ☐

Livia E Bitton Jackson
Elli: Coming of Age in the Holocaust   £2.50 ☐

Charles Whiting
Siegfried: The Nazis' Last Stand (illustrated)   £2.50 ☐

To order direct from the publisher just tick the titles you want
and fill in the order form.   **GF2181**

All these books are available at your local bookshop or newsagent, or can be ordered direct from the publisher..

To order direct from the publisher just tick the titles you want and fill in the form below.

Name _____

Address _____

_____

Send to:
Panther Cash Sales
PO Box 11, Falmouth, Cornwall TR10 9EN.

Please enclose remittance to the value of the cover price plus:

UK 45p for the first book, 20p for the second book plus 14p per copy for each additional book ordered to a maximum charge of £1.63.

BFPO and Eire 45p for the first book, 20p for the second book plus 14p per copy for the next 7 books, thereafter 8p per book.

Overseas 75p for the first book and 21p for each additional book.

Panther Books reserve the right to show new retail prices on covers, which may differ from those previously advertised in the text or elsewhere.